# THE POLITICAL THOUGHT OF AMERICA'S FOUNDING FEMINISTS

# The Political Thought of America's Founding Feminists

Lisa Pace Vetter

NEW YORK UNIVERSITY PRESS

New York

NEW YORK UNIVERSITY PRESS
New York
www.nyupress.org

© 2017 by New York University
All rights reserved

References to Internet websites (URLs) were accurate at the time of writing. Neither the author nor New York University Press is responsible for URLs that may have expired or changed since the manuscript was prepared.

ISBN: 978-1-4798-5334-2 (hardback)
ISBN: 978-1-4798-9325-6 (paperback)

For Library of Congress Cataloging-in-Publication data, please contact the Library of Congress.

New York University Press books are printed on acid-free paper, and their binding materials are chosen for strength and durability. We strive to use environmentally responsible suppliers and materials to the greatest extent possible in publishing our books.

Manufactured in the United States of America

10 9 8 7 6 5 4 3 2 1

Also available as an ebook

# CONTENTS

# ACKNOWLEDGMENTS

When I began this book project, I joked that it would take me ten years to write it. Turns out, I was correct. Not surprisingly, I have incurred many debts over that long stretch of time. First and foremost, I thank my husband Joseph Vetter for his unflagging enthusiasm about this project and his unwavering support through some trying times. I am deeply grateful to my University of Maryland, Baltimore County, colleagues Devin Hagerty and Carole McCann for reading the entire manuscript and providing much-needed encouragement. Additional colleagues, including Jeffrey Davis, Carolyn Forestiere, Arthur Johnson, and Thomas Schaller offered helpful advice and support at various stages of the project. Michael Nance graciously invited me to incorporate my research into the UMBC Humanities Seminar we co-taught in Spring 2016. Gracie Bradford provided invaluable teaching and research assistance when I needed it the most. I am deeply thankful to Patricia LaNoue for welcoming me back into the UMBC fold and to Steven McAlpine and Carrie Sauter for being such great colleagues. I thank Mary Dietz for her perseverance in guiding my article on Harriet Martineau to publication in *Political Theory* and Eileen Hunt Botting for providing me with opportunities to present and publish parts of this project.

I received several awards that allowed me to perform archival research and devote myself full time to writing at crucial stages of the project: a UMBC Dresher Center Summer Faculty Research Fellowship; a UMBC Summer Faculty Fellowship; a UMBC Travel Grant; a Caroline D. Bain Scholar-in-Residence Fellowship, Sophia Smith Collection, Smith College; and a National Endowment for the Humanities Summer Research Stipend. Sincere thanks to Jessica Berman, director, Dresher Center for the Humanities, UMBC, and Scott Casper, dean, College of Arts, Humanities, and Social Sciences, UMBC, for their support. For their invaluable assistance, I thank Margaret Jessup, assistant curator of the Sophia Smith Collection, Smith College; Christopher Densmore, curator of Friends Historical Library, Swarthmore College; and the research staff at the Boston Public Library and the Nantucket Historical Society.

It has been a true pleasure to work with Ilene Kalish, executive editor, and Caelyn Cobb, assistant editor, at NYU Press. I appreciate their encouragement and enthusiasm for the project. The comments provided by two anonymous reviewers were very helpful as I revised the final version of the manuscript.

It takes a village to write a book—or at least it did mine. I thank my parents, Madge Pace and Cecil Pace, for always having faith in me and my in-laws David Vetter, Carole Vetter, and Neil Van Valkenburgh, for their generosity. The comradery of the Bethesda Edge(moor) Cycling Club ladies group, led by Sue Hendrickson, has often buoyed my spirits, and I am grateful to Kevin Beverly for introducing me. And our recently adopted dog Paulie has provided welcome distraction, refusing to believe that writing a book is more important than a game of fetch.

An earlier version of chapter 2 was published as "Harriet Martineau on the Theory and Practice of Democracy in America," *Political Theory* 36, no. 3 (June 2008): 424–455. Reprinted by permission of the author and the publisher.

An earlier version of chapter 5 was published as "'The Most Belligerent Non-Resistant': Lucretia Mott on Women's Rights," *Political Theory* 43, no. 5 (October 2015): 600–630. Reprinted by permission of the author and the publisher.

# ABBREVIATIONS

Citations to Adam Smith's works are to the Glasgow edition published in hardcover by Oxford University Press and paperback by the Liberty Fund. Passages are referenced using the Glasgow edition's standard system of paragraph numbering and take the following abbreviations. Original spelling, capitalization, and punctuation have been maintained from the texts.

*LRBL*: Bryce, J. C., ed. *Lectures on Rhetoric and Belles Lettres*. Indianapolis: Liberty Fund, 1985.

*TMS*: Raphael, D. D., and A. L. Macfie, eds. *The Theory of Moral Sentiments*. Indianapolis: Liberty Fund, 1982.

*WN*: Campbell, R. H., A. S. Skinner, and W. B. Todd, eds. *An Inquiry into the Nature and Causes of the Wealth of Nations*. Indianapolis: Liberty Fund, 1981.

The works of the early women's rights advocates and abolitionists that are cited in this book have been taken from collected editions, many of which include transcriptions that maintain the spelling and punctuation of the original documents. I have reproduced these passages as they appear in the collected editions and follow their editorial practices.

# Introduction

## *Political Theory and the Founding of American Feminism*

In his second inaugural address, President Barack Obama made history with the following declaration:

> Our journey is not complete until our gay brothers and sisters are treated like anyone else under the law, for if we are truly created equal, then surely the love we commit to one another must be equal as well.[1]

Obama was the first sitting president to mention—let alone endorse—gay marriage in such a historic context, a fact widely noted in contemporary accounts of the address. Yet in the same speech, Obama did another remarkable thing by connecting Stonewall, the bar that became the center of 1969 protests for gay rights in New York's Greenwich Village, to Seneca Falls, New York; Selma, Alabama; and the National Mall, site of the 1963 March on Washington—landmarks where generations of Americans were "guided" by the "star" that is the belief that "all men are created equal."[2] This would not be the first time Obama would portray these pivotal events as a constellation of reforms to advance equal rights for marginalized populations, including women, African Americans, and homosexuals, which in his view were necessary to make America "a more perfect Union."

Adding to the distinctive nature of Obama's view of history is that it connects disparate actors who contributed to American history in various ways—many of whom are relatively unknown or have languished in obscurity. Again alluding to the deep bond between women's rights, civil rights, and gay rights in the second inaugural speech, Obama states that "our journey is not complete until our wives, our mothers and daughters can earn a living equal to their efforts."[3] And at the fiftieth anniversary of the Selma to Montgomery Marches Obama connects Sojourner Truth and the civil rights activist Fannie Lou Hamer, whose pivotal contributions had been overlooked in the conventional male-dominated narrative of the movement, with the well-known suffragist Susan B. Anthony, "who shook the system until the law reflected [the] truth" that these women "could do as much as any man and then some." In the same speech Obama would connect Lewis and Clark with the hitherto neglected Sacajawea and "gay Americans whose blood ran in the streets of San Francisco and New York" with civil rights activists whose "blood ran down" the Edmund Pettus Bridge.[4]

Obama would also devise an understanding of American exceptionalism that is fundamentally rooted in constant political transformation, "For we were born of change." We should not rest on our laurels, but rather we should revere America's ability to subject itself to intensive self-scrutiny for the sake of improvement and its continuing awareness of its own imperfections and limitations:

> What greater expression of faith in the American experiment than this, what greater form of patriotism is there than the belief that America is not yet finished, that we are strong enough to be self-critical, that each successive generation can look upon our imperfections and decide that it is in our power to remake this nation to more closely align with our highest ideals? That's why Selma is not some outlier in the American experience.[5]

Given the variety of events that have shaped America—and the diversity of the people who have shaped those events—for Obama, dissent is woven into the American project itself, which is a continually evolving process:

> Being true to our founding documents does not require us to agree on every contour of life. It does not mean we all define liberty in exactly the same way or follow the same precise path to happiness. Progress does not compel us to settle centuries-long debates about the role of government for all time, but it does require us to act in our time.[6]

I begin this book with these passages not because I plan to analyze the intricacies of the Obama presidency, examine his rhetorical strategies, or defend or attack his political ideology. Rather, his remarks indicate the broader theme of the work I present here. Obama's view of America envisions a series of upheavals that advanced the rights and freedoms of marginalized populations initially left out of the founding narrative. For many members of these groups, the American project was a process whose fundamental principles were subject to constant scrutiny and adjustment with a view to becoming "a more perfect Union."[7] As these previously neglected Americans have been increasingly recognized, so, too, have their unsung advocates and chroniclers emerged from obscurity and helped reshape the narrative of America.

The Jacksonian era was certainly one of those tumultuous periods in which the strain of marginalized populations, especially women and enslaved persons, grew in severity to such an extent as to raise fundamental questions about their enfranchisement.[8] Foundational American principles such as constitutional intent, federalism, citizenship and representation, and equality and freedom came under close scrutiny, and the results have fundamentally reshaped the country. Much of what we understand of this time of upheaval has come from historians, scholars of literature, and others who have thoroughly examined the works of those whose efforts drove the development of abolitionism and the early women's rights movement. In the process, the invaluable contributions of many early women's rights advocates and abolitionists have come to light and have been increasingly integrated into the historical and literary narratives of the evolution of America.

In comparison, from the perspective of political theory, our understanding of two of the most serious challenges faced by the nation, slavery and the oppression of women, is still relatively limited. Many early women's rights advocates and abolitionists still languish in obscurity largely because of the restrictions that persist in American political thought on the sources of information considered theoretically significant and legitimate objects of study. Many abolitionists and early women's rights advocates were not professional philosophers and wrote no theoretical treatises. Although American political thought must by necessity include non-traditional theorists and unconventional modes of theorizing to accommodate pivotal figures such as the Founders and Abraham Lincoln, it does not extend the same recognition to many abolitionists and early women's rights advocates. As a result, the contributions of the very people whose efforts directly shaped the arguments over essential questions about the American project have remained unexamined.

In fact, the wealth of letters, speeches, pamphlets, and newspaper articles left behind by these figures contain important theoretical lessons. In particular, the works of seven influential early women's rights advocates and abolitionists in the Jacksonian era, who have largely escaped the purview of American political thought—Frances Wright (1795–1852), Harriet Martineau (1802–1876), Lucretia Mott (1793–1880), Angelina Grimké (1805–1879), Sarah Grimké (1792–1873), Elizabeth Cady Stanton (1815–1902), and Sojourner Truth (ca. 1797–1883)—offer significant theoretical insights into two of the most important developments in American history. Through close and careful analysis of their contributions, I bring their theoretical underpinnings to light. When necessary, I use political theorists who have already been recognized as worthy of examination as frames of reference to reveal that, not only were these advocates engaging in many of the same theoretical debates and on many different levels, but, equally important, they were also broadening and innovating on traditional mainstream theoretical concepts to better accommodate women and the disenfranchised. Although a few of these advocates have been characterized primarily as religious thinkers whose spiritual commitments overrode their political concerns, I show the relevance of their contributions by highlighting the political significance of their efforts.

Closer inspection reveals that the work of these women anticipates subsequent, more commonly known developments in abolitionism and early women's rights. Their pivotal role as precursors to other thinkers and advocates has been so severely underestimated precisely as a result of their neglect. They help frame the work of other nineteenth-century reformers such as Catherine Beecher (1800–1878), Susan B. Anthony (1820–1906), Lucy Stone (1818–1893), Ernestine Rose (1810–1892), and Margaret Fuller (1810–1850). Popular writers who left indelible marks on the American conscience such as Lydia Maria Child (1802–1880) and Harriet Beecher Stowe (1811–1896) are also deeply indebted to the insights provided by these women. The passionate appeals to the American Founding and the Declaration of Independence with which Abraham Lincoln and Frederick Douglass are credited echo the appeals made by the women I discuss in this book, who continually refer to that bygone era while adapting its theoretical meaning to better accommodate the shifting needs of the American people. The same is true for the principles of self-ownership and self-rule articulated by Lincoln and Douglass for which they are renowned.[9] The emphasis by these women on independent thought and action as the basis of true equality and freedom rests on similar theories of the self. The account of American civil society for which Alexis de Tocqueville is rightly celebrated should be seen as one among many elaborations offered by these women and others who, through keen observation of the state of democracy in America, sought fundamental change not just politically but morally, culturally, socially, and religiously as well. The female travelers to the young nation whose works I explore were clearly and profoundly distraught by its failure to live up to its own founding principles when it came to slavery and the oppression of women, and they focused their efforts on appealing to the best selves of the American people.[10] By developing greater appreciation for the deep lineages and the variety of iterations of these important theories and ideas, we also better understand the theoretical upheavals of the Jacksonian era and the American project generally. We can begin to see the ways in which abolitionism and the early women's rights movement properly understood in all their diversity are central to the development of American political thought.

More broadly, the efforts of these women lay the groundwork for "important twentieth-century constitutional doctrines, including universal suffrage, equal representation, and one person, one vote."[11] Together they articulated "a vision of gender justice" that underpins feminist legal claims as well as racial justice. They developed a new view of citizenship that was based on a revised understanding of "We the People," one that insisted on "voting as a fundamental right," "one person, one vote," and the "national enforcement of rights" that required an expansion of federal power.[12] Their participation in civic institutions expanded notions of freedom of speech, expression, and assembly, the right to petition government, and civil disobedience.[13] Their efforts, along with others, "helped elevate new conceptions of equal opportunity and antidiscrimination as principles of equality that prohibited arbitrary gender restrictions and male prerogatives."[14]

The work of these women also represents a "constituent moment" in American history in which "the underauthorized" or marginalized individuals and groups, including the early women's rights and abolitionist advocates I analyze, "seize the mantle of authorization, changing the inherited rules of authorization in the process," and thereby "invent a new political space."[15] On this view, "enthusiastic" speech or action, such as religious, poetic, or literary speech that animates everyday life in civil society but is deemed illegitimate in the political realm—much of which is articulated by women reformers such as those I examine—takes on "transformative potential."[16] In their enthusiastic speech and in deed, the early women's rights and abolitionist advocates in this book sought to create a transformative understanding of democratic citizenship.

### Situating *The Political Thought of America's Founding Feminists* among Early Women's Rights and Abolitionist Narratives

Despite the overall lack of consideration given to abolitionists and early women's rights advocates in American political thought, recent scholarly trends spanning several disciplines have helped pave the way for the kind of detailed theoretical analysis I undertake. By showing how my work is indebted to, and yet departs from, other studies, I explain the structure of the argument and demonstrate the relevance and originality of my contribution.

For insights into political theory in the Jacksonian era, a major source continues to be Alexis de Tocqueville's expansive treatise *Democracy in America*, not only because interpreters find his observations compelling but also because there were relatively few comparable treatises of its kind produced in this period and relatively few thinkers who devoted themselves to this type of theoretical work in America.[17] In response to this challenge, American political thought has broadened its purview to include thinkers who were not formal theorists and sources that go beyond conventional modes of theorizing. Major figures such as Jefferson, Madison, and Lincoln, for example, were pragmatic politicians and public figures, not professional philosophers or intellectuals. They left behind no extended treatises, yet their writings and speeches clearly offer rich theoretical contributions about the fundamental questions that shape political life and are therefore recognized as legitimate sources of political theory.[18] The development of American political thought has also been traced in works of American literature that similarly fall beyond conventional political theory genres by authors such as Walt Whitman, Henry David Thoreau, Herman Melville, Nathaniel Hawthorne, and others.[19] And by acknowledging the political and theoretical contributions of religious writings, speeches, and other forms of communication, American political thought has expanded its traditional focus on secular sources.[20]

A few abolitionists and early women's rights advocates have been the focus of extended study in political theory, including Frederick Douglass and, notably, Elizabeth Cady Stanton.[21] The contributions of Frances Wright, Sarah Grimké, and Margaret Fuller have been situated within larger theoretical movements such as utopian socialism, utilitarianism, Anglo-American radical sectarianism, and Romanticism.[22] One of the most influential figures on the early women's rights movement, Mary Wollstonecraft, has been firmly established as an important political theorist in her own right, through examinations of her liberalism, radicalism, Aristotelianism, and civic republicanism.[23] Wollstonecraft's considerable influence in both the United States and Europe has been explored in detail as well.[24]

Historical examinations of the early women's rights movement have been instrumental in opening new opportunities for analysis. Stanton and Anthony's monumental work, the *History of Woman Suffrage* (1881–1922) traces the origin of the early women's rights movement and Stanton's own emergence as a leader. Widely accepted as the definitive account of the movement, the *History* has shaped the conventional narrative and provides the framework for a number of influential studies.[25] While greater attention to the early stages of feminism and the suffrage movement is laudable, it has also led to unintended consequences. As the prominence of Stanton and other advocates was elevated, others were marginalized, mischaracterized, underestimated, or overlooked altogether, especially African American women, white and African American men, and advocates who pre-dated Stanton, such as Wright, Mott, and the Grimkés.

To address these concerns, the conventional narrative has been challenged by a number of path-breaking works that broaden our understanding of the movement by including a far more diverse set of actors and influences.[26] Detailed historical biographies of the Grimké sisters and Mott, as well as Stanton herself, have recast their roles in the early women's rights movement by calling attention to the multiple influences on their ideas and the complexity of their views.[27] Now we see a transnational movement that begins not necessarily with Stanton in 1848 but perhaps even far earlier, with the French Revolution and the publication of Wollstonecraft's pioneering treatise, *A Vindication of the Rights of Woman* (1792).[28] The primary focus on the contributions of elite white American women in the narrative has been broadened by recent analyses that reveal interracial networks of men and women who worked together to end slavery and secure greater rights for women.[29] Black and white men served as influential collaborators in the early women's rights and abolitionist movements, including Frederick Douglass (1818–1895), David Walker (ca. 1796–1830), Robert Purvis (1810–1898), James Forten (1766–1842), Wendell Phillips (1811–1884), Gerrit Smith (1797–1874), and William Lloyd Garrison (1805–1879). Black women such as Maria Stewart (1803–1879), Harriet Forten (1810–1875), Sarah Louisa Forten (1814–1883), Harriet Tubman (1822–1913), Harriet Jacobs (1813–1897), and Frances Ellen Watkins Harper (1825–1911) played pivotal roles in the abolitionist movement and advanced the status of women as well.[30]

Tracing an early women's rights movement that pre-dates Stanton has also led to the reexamination of its relation with abolitionism. In the conventional narrative of the *History*, the women's rights movement begins in the 1840s, after the emergence of the leading abolitionist Garrison. Thus the prevailing view has been that the early women's rights movement derived from American abolitionism.[31] It is true that in 1829 Garrison explicitly invited American women who were already participating in various benevolent societies to join forces with him and end slavery. After controversy surrounding women's newfound political role led to the 1840 split in the American Anti-Slavery Society, female supporters remained aligned with Garrison and over the next two decades held several women's rights conventions throughout the country, including the pivotal 1848 gathering at Seneca Falls.[32]

If the origins of the early women's rights movement is traced back to the 1820s and 1830s, however, we see a more complementary relation between the two causes.[33] The inclusion of women in the abolitionist movement would challenge fundamental assumptions about American citizenship and women's political participation.[34] The female antislavery societies and petitioning campaigns that formed during this period would raise important questions about women's political role as well as the relation between governmental and non-governmental power.[35] The connection forged by Garrison between natural rights and equal rights for slaves created a "liberalism of rights" that women reformers found sufficiently compelling to advocate for themselves.[36] Not only did abolitionism play an important role in the formation of the early movement, but a number of political, social, and religious factors were deeply influential as well.[37] Early women's rights advocates were instructed in a variety of philosophical and ideological teachings and adapted these lessons for their own purposes.[38]

Not only have the origins of the women's rights movement been subject to more intensive scrutiny, the nature of Garrison's influence itself has also been reexamined. Many of the early women's rights advocates who precede Stanton have been categorized simply as Garrisonians, which understates the theoretical diversity among them. Whereas Garrison adhered to an anarchic "no-governmentalism," others with ties to Garrison such as Frederick Douglass and Gerrit Smith supported the Liberty Party and with it the possibility of political reform through direct involvement. Closer examination reveals that another group of abolitionists "believed that human governments should be reordered to correspond with God's democratic moral government" and "left a place for localized, voluntary external structures."[39] As I will show, several women's rights advocates typically labeled "no-government" Garrisonians, including Mott and the Grimkés, actually fall into the latter, more politically engaged category. The complexity and diversity of the early women's rights movement underscore the need for additional analysis from the perspective of political theory.

With the reconsideration of the conventional narrative, our historical understanding of the early women's rights movement as a primarily secular phenomenon has also changed. Given the patriarchal nature of established religions, especially Christianity, it had been seen as necessary for early women's rights advocates to move away from religious principles and embrace various forms of secular rationalism.[40] The influence of Stanton's deeply skeptical view of established religion, a lifelong preoccupation that culminates in one of her last major works, *The Woman's Bible*, undoubtedly shaped the conventional narrative of the movement, which predictably grows more secular over time. However, a variety of religious principles permeated the early women's rights movement and served a number of constructive purposes.[41] Progressive Quakerism offered girls access to education that closely approximated the instruction of boys as well as opportunities to speak before religious audiences.[42] Equally important, many progressive Quaker reformers envisioned religion and reason as complementary.[43] Religion was not relegated to the isolated realm of female domesticity but instead occupied a prominent public position. As early women's rights advocates "developed a critical perspective of religious castes, . . . church creeds," and patriarchal hierarchies, religion became politically relevant as well.[44] Thus, rather than posing insurmountable obstacles to reform, religion provided important entry points for early women's rights advocates.

My analysis explores the influence of religion by examining the ways in which the theological convictions of early women's rights reformers, rather than leading to political apathy or apolitical anarchism, were instead extended and reformulated into rich and complex views of political life. The progressive Quakerism that informed several of these advocates was based on a view of human nature and collective action that was deeply egalitarian and voluntarist. The progressive Quaker critique of religious dogmatism serves as the foundation for a view of active citizenship and a kind of participatory democracy. Progressive Quakerism is also the foundation for a theory of American constitutionalism. "Quaker constitutionalism" asserts an eternal or fundamental constitution that is apprehended through "synteresis," an "inner voice" that is spiritual but also guided by the extensive application of human reason. This constitutionalism in turn informs the creation of political institutions as well as social and cultural practices. On this view, social ills arise when the fundamental constitution is misinterpreted or obscured. Reform is made possible by a return to first principles, which requires the combination of human reason and synteresis.[45]

Although historical studies have greatly advanced our understanding of the early women's rights movement and abolitionism, literary criticism has also contributed to our knowledge in significant ways. Particularly helpful are efforts to explore the deployment and evolution of sentimental literature and related concepts of sympathy, sentiment, and empathy in nineteenth-century literature. Sentimental literature, understood generally as a genre that emerged in the late eighteenth and early nineteenth centuries, appeals primarily to emotions and feelings rather than reason. Reform efforts in the nineteenth century sought to establish connections between those who are marginalized and those who are not and increasingly used sentimental literature to accomplish that goal. By encouraging greater understanding of, or appreciation for, the plight of enslaved persons and marginalized women, works of literature sought to motivate those who were in a position of influence to advocate for change.[46] Abolitionist literature, including slave narratives such as Douglass's autobiography and novels such as Stowe's *Uncle Tom's Cabin*, relied heavily on sentimentality to gain support for ending slavery.[47] Women's rights advocates also tapped into the power of sentimentality, often through domestic fiction, to help others identify with the plight of women.

Much of the scholarly discourse surrounding sentimental literature falls into two general categories within what is widely referred to as the "Douglas-Tompkins Debate," named after the two prominent scholars credited with defining its terms, Ann Douglas and Jane Tompkins. Those in Douglas's camp adhere to her critical view of sentimentality as "a fall from tough-minded . . . Calvinism into 'rancid,' individualistic emotionalism, the beginnings of a debased mass consumer culture."[48] These critics argue that sentimental literature often objectified the sufferers of oppression and failed to motivate audiences to channel their emotions into concrete action.[49] Thus, although Angelina Grimké sought to appeal to a general audience, her "rhetoric of sympathy" was geared primarily toward elite white women. As a result, Grimké "creates an authority for herself and other well-to-do white women while erasing the influence of other women."[50] A similar claim can be made about Sarah Grimké's graphic portrayals of cruelty against slaves. Although her work seeks to invoke a "vicarious sharing" of suffering, it ultimately "calls attention to the power imbalance between the person experiencing actual oppression and the sympathetic advocate" because her appeal is focused primarily on "white women who, looking on, should be called to action."[51] Lucretia Mott deploys a "rhetoric of courtship" in which she appears "to accept the dominance of male leaders" and at the same time instills in her audience "a desire to identify with them, to temporarily transcend their differences in status." Thus, although Mott does not "question the hierarchy of gender," she "nonetheless take[s] authority by evoking its influence."[52] Although such criticisms highlight the rhetorical prowess of these advocates, the analyses also undermine the legitimacy and theoretical importance of their appeals.

Adherents of Tompkins's interpretations, by contrast, envision sentimentality in more constructive terms, as "a complex and effective affirmation of women's power, a grass roots antipatriarchal politics."[53] Along similar lines, although typically understood as a kind of compassion or concern, sympathy can also be considered a cognitive process of "imaginative identification" that seeks to eliminate the ignorance caused by bias.[54] As such, sympathy could be a "positive force in politics."[55] A related avenue of study has focused on the moral and philosophical concept of sympathy and its role in nineteenth-century reform. Scottish Enlightenment moral theory is founded on the concept of sympathy that, depending on one's perspective, supplemented or corrected Enlightenment individualism. For Scottish Enlightenment theorists, "emotions . . . assume a central place in moral thought," and "ordinary life comes to be affirmed as profoundly valuable." This affirmation "sustains what is virtually a moral consensus of the modern world on the values of justice and benevolence."[56]

Adam Smith is perhaps the best-known proponent of the moral theory of sympathy and the related concept of the impartial spectator, and his work influenced a number of Scottish Enlightenment thinkers. Recent scholarship has explored the impact of Smith's theory in particular and Scottish Enlightenment thought generally on the American founding.[57] Nineteenth-century American rhetoric was significantly shaped by popularized versions of Smith's works written by George Campbell, Hugh Blair, Richard Whately, and other Scottish Enlightenment proponents of "New Rhetoric." These popularizers sought to combine classical rhetoric with "belletristic interests in 'criticism and literary taste' and epistemological approaches to rhetoric as a 'science' closely related to the study of the 'mental faculties.'"[58]

Given the pervasive influence of Smith and other Scottish Enlightenment thinkers in American culture, it should not be surprising that early women's rights advocates and abolitionists made extensive use of their theories as well. Smith's moral theory of sympathy, for example, and Scottish Enlightenment philosophy more broadly helped shape popular views of Republican motherhood, thereby setting the stage for nineteenth-century reformers.⁵⁹ Indeed, Smith and Scottish Enlightenment thinkers are often included among the hybrid of moral theorists who helped shape abolitionism and the early women's rights movement.⁶⁰ Although the *Lectures on Rhetoric and Belles Lettres* had not yet been published, popularizers of Smith's teachings such as Campbell and Blair managed to impart many of the concepts it would advance through their own work, which in turn influenced the work of many activists.⁶¹ Elements of Smith's *Theory of Moral Sentiments* can be seen in Stowe's tour de force of sentimental abolitionist literature *Uncle Tom's Cabin* via Archibald Alison, another influential popularizer whose work she studied in detail.⁶² Smith's principle of sympathy reappears throughout nineteenth-century novels by Jane Austen, Charles Dickens, George Eliot, and others.⁶³ His theory of the impartial spectator is helpful in understanding antislavery appeals and the emergence of "humanitarianism" in the nineteenth century.⁶⁴ Along with Smith's moral principles and theories of rhetoric, his critique of commerce and the division of labor in the *Wealth of Nations* reemerges in abolitionist and early women's rights rhetoric, as does the tension between the progress of commercial society and the persistence of slavery.⁶⁵

My work expands on these studies of Smith as a moral and political theorist whose concept of sympathy and views on rhetoric help us better understand the challenges to the American project waged by early women's rights advocates and abolitionists. For example, I frame Wright's theoretical contributions partly in terms of Smith's idea of sympathy and his critique of commerce and the division of labor. I also show how Martineau innovates on Smith's concept of sympathy in order to provide an understanding of America's foundational principles that better accommodates the needs of an increasingly diverse society, which includes previously disenfranchised populations such as women and enslaved persons. To help explain Angelina Grimké's moral rhetoric of persuasion and Stanton's moral rhetoric of ridicule, I draw from Smith's important yet relatively neglected *Lectures on Rhetoric and Belles Lettres*.

As the examinations of sympathy and sentimentality overlap in literary studies and political theory, so, too, does the study of rhetoric and communication in the early women's rights movement offer useful insights into the strategies used by women speakers and writers to carve out a public space and, ultimately, to create a political identity for themselves. Although American women made inroads into the male-dominated public realm as lecturers, students and producers of literature, activists in benevolent societies, petitioners, and organizers of reform activities, they still did not enjoy the full benefits of that sphere. Women were not granted rights to free speech, suffrage, private property, divorce, equal education, or extended vocational opportunities that were enjoyed by most men. As part and parcel of the conventional early women's rights narrative, the influence of women typically was relegated to the "private sphere" that was separated from the public political realm of men and framed in terms of a "cult of (true) womanhood" or "discourse of domesticity," which emphasized values such as piety, chastity, and submissiveness.[66] Whatever rhetorical activity women participated in would by implication be relegated to this separate and sequestered sphere as well. Thus the efforts of reformers were characterized as inappropriate encroachments that threatened to upend cherished American tradition and were vilified for failing to conform to its masculinist norms.[67]

However, the theory of separate spheres has been supplanted by interpretations that acknowledge the "complex historical processes that weave" the two worlds together. Along similar lines, the "discourse of domesticity" has proven an inadequate analytical tool because it relies on an "unremarked, confusing elision between sentimentality and domesticity." Because domesticity is "the very home of consumer culture" that constructs a "packaged" version of "emotion" that is ultimately "distasteful," sentimentality, with which it is identified, has been devalued.[68] As sentimentality is devalued, so, too, are the contributions of reformers who rely on sentimental literature to convey their ideas. Indeed, a closer look at the movement before Stanton reveals that the boundary between the public and private realms in nineteenth-century America was far more porous and fluid than normally thought. In fact, women played a variety of roles in public that, while not overtly political, were nonetheless deeply influential in political affairs.[69] Moreover, women often used their personal and individual experiences to fashion a public identity that was geared toward equally public activism.[70] To better accommodate the multifaceted nature of women reformers and the multidimensionality of their contributions, a more nuanced understanding of the public realm is needed.

As a mediator between the political realm of the state, on the one hand, and the private realm of individual self-interest, on the other, Jürgen Habermas's theory of the bourgeois "public sphere" has been helpful in providing a framework through which to study the rich and diverse contributions of early women's rights advocates and abolitionists. In Habermas's public sphere, "citizens behave as a public body when they confer . . . about matters of general interest" as if they were male citizens because they do so "with the guarantee of freedom of assembly and association and the freedom to express and publish their opinions" they do not otherwise enjoy.[71] By definition, Habermas's public sphere includes modes of communication that straddle the political and private realms, such as political or "intellectual" newspapers, and have been expanded to include sentimental literature broadly defined: written by men and women, black and white; including a variety of authors, such as "temperance novelists, black nationalist activists, female sentimentalists, and children's writers"; and incorporating diverse genres, from "novels and poetry to autobiographical writings, utopian fiction, and essays," among others.[72]

Although Habermas's public sphere is helpful in characterizing the unique status of women in nineteenth-century America, it still relies on and perpetuates masculinist norms, such as an abstract ideal of the individual as utterly free to assemble and speak out at will, and a "common moral and legal vision, which was derived from [men's] class position as bourgeois property owners."[73] The public sphere privileges rational and deliberate elements because it relies on rational deliberation as the basis for mutual understanding in a democratic society. Thus, in spite of its apparent openness, the public realm by definition excludes the very people most in need of "publicity" in the nineteenth century, namely, women and enslaved persons.[74] Habermas's theory fails to account for the "transformative potential" of enthusiastic speech or action, such as religious, poetic, or literary speech, which animates everyday life in civil society.[75] As a result, the public sphere is inadequate in bringing together and defining "who comprises the self-legislating people, that 'pure original fountain of all legislative authority'" in America.[76]

As an alternative to the single "public" realm that enforces and perpetuates masculinist bourgeois values, critics have developed a realm of "counterpublics," a system of "parallel discursive arenas where members of subordinated social groups invent and circulate counterdiscourses . . . to formulate oppositional interpretations of their identities, interests, and needs."[77] On this view, abolitionists and early women's rights advocates formed a variety of oppositional counterpublics that struggled against social and political norms.[78] These recent studies have included diverse American thinkers such as Benjamin Rush, Walt Whitman, and Douglass.[79] Others have begun to explore the ways in which reformers such as Child, Stowe, Sarah Grimké, Stanton, and Anthony carved out a space within constitutional debates in which a constitutionalism that abolishes slavery and provides greater rights for women could emerge.[80] My study offers a significant contribution to this line of inquiry. By constituting a counterpublic of their own, the words and deeds of the early women's rights and abolitionist advocates examined here form "constituent moments" in which "the underauthorized—imposters, radicals, self-created entities—seize the mantle of authorization, changing the inherited rules of authorization in the process," and thereby "invent a new political space."[81] These women also serve as "*civic founders* or co-founders of the U.S. constitution" because their efforts also help advance vital constitutional doctrines on suffrage, representation, federal power, freedom of speech, expression, and assembly, the right to petition government, and civil disobedience.[82]

Drawing from all of these trends in scholarly literature, I offer original theoretical insights into the beginnings of the early women's rights and abolitionist movements in America. By beginning my study, not with Stanton, but with the influential reformers who preceded her, I underscore the view that the struggle for women's rights began well before 1848. Several women analyzed here were affiliates of, or sympathizers with, Garrison, but each of their contributions was unique and not simply attributable to Garrisonianism. Their activities blurred the distinction between the public and private realms and were not merely expressions of the "cult of true womanhood" or "discourse of domesticity." Although these women could not legally vote or serve in political office, their efforts proved politically relevant and formed a Habermasian public sphere of activism or, more accurately, a network of counterpublics of ardent reformers. Their views on human nature and human rights, many of which arose primarily from religious convictions, did not merely shape their private lives but also informed their conceptions of political citizenship. The activism of these women laid much of the groundwork for the suffrage movement and subsequent legal and political reforms in the United States that characterize the feminist movement, with which people tend to be more familiar.

## Interpretative Approach

To highlight the important contributions these advocates make to American political thought, I develop an approach that helps address criticisms of political theory in particular and theorizing generally.

A broad overview reveals that the ideas of these early women's rights advocates reflect schools of thought such as Enlightenment rationalism, utopian socialism, utilitarianism, Anglo-American radical sectarianism, and Romanticism.[83] To this should be added the ubiquitous categories of civic republicanism and Lockean liberalism, which denote the tension between community, the common good, and public-spiritedness, on the one hand, and a more limited view of government designed to protect individual rights and liberties, on the other.[84] While helpful in situating the ideas of early women's rights advocates generally, these categories are also imprecise and, in some cases, highly contested.[85] Equally problematic, these categories are ill suited for fully capturing the innovative nature of the contributions of these women because they have been constructed with already existing political theories that were created by—and for—men.[86] Civic republicanism, liberalism, socialism, utilitarianism, sectarianism, and Romanticism were not explicitly concerned with women's rights or abolitionism and were not equipped to provide a real space for feminist theory to emerge. Instead, mainstream theories were "ontologically committed to a reality in which 'man' is the measure of all things" and whose "manner of discourse within political theory has been structured, conceptually and methodologically, to favor or reflect men's modes of intellectual practice."[87] To impose broad categorizations is to force substantive contributions—in this case, the unique contributions of early women's rights advocates—into an "ideological paradigm" of mainstream ideas established by men for men, to "wrongly presume an equality of the speaking subject or a unified space of representation" or to impose "an underlying (overlapping) . . . consensus" when there is none.[88] By seeking "to integrate women into the very categories of political membership from which they had been originally excluded" essentially by "adding women into the mix," we sidestep the important task of fundamentally "rethink[ing] core concepts of 'male-stream' political theory" and "altering the very framework of politics in which the concepts were first developed and the so-called woman question has been posed."[89]

Judicious use of these categories in analyzing the theoretical contributions of women can, however, be defended on feminist grounds. Feminist theorizing must take into account the historical, political, and philosophical context in which it arises to avoid the trap of portraying itself as an ahistorical conversation about eternal questions among professional intellectuals and their successors—a conversation that has traditionally excluded women.[90] "Comparisons between feminist theorists and their canonical male counterparts" continue to be useful because they help "build on knowledge we already have" in the history of political thought "as we discuss the unfamiliar" terrain of feminist political theory. Canonical thinkers function "as familiar means to the end of introducing and incorporating women thinkers with whom they contrast fruitfully."[91]

To provide an analysis that works beyond problematic generalities and classifications, I bring the theoretical underpinnings of these reformers' efforts to light by framing them from the perspective of specific contemporaneous political theorists such as Alexis de Tocqueville, Adam Smith, and Jeremy Bentham, whose significance has been firmly established in political philosophy. Although the same objections to employing male-dominated paradigms of thought can be raised to applying particular male theorists, I try to address these concerns in several ways. My work uses mainstream political theory to frame the contributions of marginalized thinkers, yet it does so without portraying early women's rights theorists as derivative of their male counterparts.[92] Nor is the goal to draw any direct or causal connection or to establish any kind of "trans-historical dialogue" between the ideas of male theorists and those held by early women's rights advocates.[93] I use the theories of Tocqueville, Smith, and Bentham as frames of reference to show how *innovative* early women's rights advocates were, for it is only through detailed analysis and point-by-point comparison that similarities *and* differences appear. By applying the sort of detailed textual exegesis performed by political theorists to highlight the nuances in these works, I hope to demonstrate that political theory has an important role to play in understanding the original contributions of early women's rights and abolitionist advocates, in addition to history, literature, and other disciplines.

There is, of course, considerable precedent in political theory and other disciplines for using thinkers to frame arguments without establishing causality or implying unoriginality.[94] For example, my work builds on recent studies of Smith's political thought that explore his contribution to the American founding and the American project, which significantly broaden the scope of his work beyond economic prescriptions to encompass moral and rhetorical theory and their political implications but do not necessarily prove direct causation.[95] Studies in history, literature, rhetoric, and communications also view Smith as representative of Scottish Enlightenment theory as it was popularized in America without necessarily claiming that Smith is the actual source of American doctrines.[96]

Although the primary focus of the book is not on the political theories of Tocqueville, Smith, or Bentham, I do not wish to use these thinkers merely as props. Rather, I hope to offer some new insights into their ideas, as well. For example, I demonstrate the relevance of Smith's political theory in unexamined areas of nineteenth-century American political thought and by analyzing previously neglected aspects of his work. In particular, I interpret the *Lectures on Rhetoric and Belles Lettres*, a work that is familiar to scholars of literature and rhetoric but relatively unknown to political theorists, as an extension of Smith's moral and political thought.[97] Because these investigations are relatively new, I devote considerable time to elaborating less familiar passages of Smith's works and unexplored aspects of his theory. Along similar lines, less is known about Bentham's account of political corruption in his late work *Constitutional Code* (1830) than about his theory of utilitarianism, and a better understanding helps frame the unique contributions of Wright. Tocqueville's *Democracy in America* has been analyzed extensively by political theorists, but few have noted the variety of sources—many of which were written by women—from which Tocqueville could have drawn to develop his account of women in America, but did not. Tocqueville's account of American slavery also emerges among a variety of competing abolitionist narratives that remain largely unnoticed by political theorists, including Tocqueville himself.[98] Thus my book should be seen as presenting new findings not only on the works of early women's rights and abolitionist advocates but on aspects of Tocqueville's, Smith's, and Bentham's ideas as well. I want to help advance our knowledge of canonical thinkers in ways that scholars in mainstream history of political thought and American political theory should find useful.

My method also addresses a more general critique of the relevance of theorizing itself, namely, the charge that it lacks determinative value, that it plays no direct role in influencing political debates or altering political conditions. There is little evidence indicating that these reformists were aware of the theoretical underpinnings or the intellectual heritage of their ideas. Indeed, it is often difficult to determine the extent to which the advocates directly influenced each other.[99] Equally important, there is no way to determine with certitude the practical effects of these theories on the reform efforts themselves or the precise ways in which ideas were translated into practice. In this sense, it can be argued that abstract ideas are not clearly "determinative" in explaining human behavior. Interpreters have sought to address this problem by characterizing written works of a theoretical cast as either "the product of a complex set of social practices" or by focusing on their use of a particular "political language" associated with the culture in which they are created.[100]

This move away from abstract theory understood as a set of principles whose determinative value is difficult to ascertain and toward a view of theory as constituted by social, cultural, and political practices has led to a much broader critique of the very use of canonical theory to shed light on issues of gender, race, and class. On this view, the works of Tocqueville, Smith, and Bentham cannot be expanded to accommodate the needs of women, African Americans, and other marginalized populations precisely because their theories are founded on, and define themselves by, the exclusion of these very groups, an exclusion that is itself an outgrowth of the social, cultural, and political practices about which they theorized. For instance, to varying degrees, their theories endorse the concept of the "subject as rational agent," which in turn shapes their understandings of core political concepts such as "authority, rights, equality, and freedom." However, critics note, their understandings of sovereignty and rationality are simply "fantasies" because they are founded on a kind of "dangerous masculinity" that "is productive of, and dependent on, the feminine subject as subjected." By implication, these canonical theorists also rely on a kind of "dangerous" racism in which the racial subject is and must be subjected as well. Universalizing by abstraction masks the "exclusionary practices" on which such narratives are based and erases the distinctions between individuals with unique identities and experiences, especially those who are marginalized.[101]

The broader "turn toward the subject" can also work against many of the women thinkers who are the focus of my book. For critics, their shared status as elite white women problematizes their otherwise marginalized position in American society. Virtually all of these women count themselves among "the culturally privileged" who seek to "humanize those subjects who have been excluded" and allow them to be "recognized as candidates for inclusion in the body politic."[102] Even Truth, a freed slave who spoke at women's rights conventions, stands apart from other black women. Much like canonical theorists, their efforts to reach out to other marginalized groups—including poor and working-class white women, African American women, and African American men—rely on the concept of the subject as agent and are premised upon universal truth claims about sovereignty, equality, freedom, and human rights. And yet critics observe that, because these efforts are constituted largely from the perspectives of elite white privilege, they cannot help but recreate and reinforce the same power structures from which they arise. The "compassionate liberalism" that serves as the basis of early women's rights and abolitionist efforts, for instance, is "at best, a kind of sandpaper on the surface of the racist monument" of nineteenth-century American culture "whose structural and economic solidity endures." The universal category of "woman" on which early women's advocates rely, defined as a subject who possesses certain essential characteristics or shares particular experiences, conceals within "a kind of soft supremacy rooted in compassion and coercive identification [that] wants to dissolve all that structure [of racism] through the work of good intentionality, while busily exoticizing and diminishing the inconvenient and the noncompliant."[103]

Important insights have been gained by exposing the problematic assumptions on which canonical theories are based, and they have informed many aspects of my work, as subsequent chapters shall show. However, there are considerable risks involved in this approach that I want to address as well. Critics "seem to have lost sight of the classic and legitimate political concerns of the canonical authors." As a result, critical theory leads us "away from questions of collective action and citizenship, indeed from any robust understanding of the public sphere altogether [and] away from broader questions about structures of power and economic justice." Instead, "social change seems restricted to work on the self or micro-practices of self-transformation."[104] And yet abolitionism and the women's rights movement represent two of the most important examples in which "collective action and citizenship" raise important questions about "structures of power and economic justice" in America. As such, they must be understood in all their complexity, acknowledging the weaknesses of their advocates but also recognizing their strengths.

Although the intention of critical theory is not to "declare canonical theory bankrupt," it is difficult not to conclude that because the canon is so deeply contaminated by sexism, racism, and classism, little, if anything, can be salvaged from it. In the process of exposing the power dynamics underlying the "inherited categories" of canonical theory, critics risk creating a homogenizing narrative of their own in which a new set of abstract ideas—racism, sexism, classism—themselves contribute to the continued marginalization of oppressed peoples by glossing over important distinctions and missing opportunities to shed light on broader questions regarding political action.[105] To portray theorizing as simply the product of a complex set of social practices is to offer a materialistic understanding of human affairs that cannot adequately account for the originality and novelty of ideas that transcend a particular time and place and lead to reform. Similarly, if theorizing is seen as merely employing the particular political language associated with the culture in which it is created, such a descriptive account of constituted subjects fails to explain why a particular political language was used or to what specific effects.

To address these concerns, I offer an alternative conception of what it means for abstract theories to be "determinative" that is not materialistic, reductionist, or merely descriptive. It is true that these early women's rights and abolitionist advocates worked within the confines of the social, political, and cultural norms in which they lived. And yet they also tried to expand and ultimately transform those very same norms to accommodate a changing society. These women served as "civic founders" of an

"American civic constitution," an understanding of the "governing ideals of liberty, equality, and justice" that "did not spring naturally from the text of the original Constitution, were not envisioned by famous framers, and were not set in motion by judges or political leaders." These reformers considered their efforts to be continuations of, not innovations to, the American founding properly understood. And yet they expanded the fundamental principles of the American project to address the needs of the disenfranchised, thereby laying the groundwork for "new constitutional rights and commitments."[106] As these women reassert themselves in the present as they are uncovered and interpreted in books like this one, they help America undergo the intensive self-scrutiny that is essential to its identity. The seven early women's rights advocates I examine can help guide and reshape the ongoing American experiment as it works toward "a more perfect Union." As abstract theories are uncovered and analyzed, in examinations like mine and others, and as they continue to inform generations of people, ideas reveal their truly transformative power.

Thus I seek to "innovate within a tradition" in order to explore "how we may speak through a set of languages handed down to us by disciplinary conventions that may not comfortably accommodate feminist politics" and "remake them for the present" as well as the future. I count myself among those who "work within a canon of texts and textual practices" and who seek to "produce the critical present as distinct from its past(s) by looking to those moments, those texts, those 'historical accidents' [or countercurrents] where difference emerges."[107] By offering an interdisciplinary approach that incorporates a significant amount of scholarship from a variety of perspectives, I hope to contribute to the "feminist conversation" that not only seeks to "disrupt the terms of the canonical one—premised as it is on women's absence"—but also "to constitute a sense of political community" among theorists themselves, "based in part on the practice of forming judgments about the canonical texts."[108]

## Plan of the Book

The book is organized chronologically, based on the publication dates of the works I analyze, to avoid imposing any developmental model on the movement. Given the difficulty in establishing causal connections between reform advocates at this time, such a model would likely be inaccurate or overly homogenizing. Instead, I want to allow the theories of these women to emerge in their own ways. Chapter 1 examines the contributions of Frances Wright, one of the most controversial freethinkers to visit the United States from Scotland and England. Unlike many of her female contemporaries, Wright did leave behind a considerable body of work and extended theoretical reflections. Yet they have eluded close theoretical analysis for several reasons. Like Wollstonecraft, whose philosophical work was long obscured by portrayals that emphasized her radical lifestyle, Wright's scandalous reputation also distracted from the originality of her ideas. Wright has been seen as largely derivative of her male contemporaries, a popularizer of the theories of utilitarian philosopher Jeremy Bentham and utopian socialist Robert Owen, and as a mere devotee of liberal rational Enlightenment thought or Scottish Enlightenment thought, which were established by male thinkers.

While the influence of Bentham on her worldview is undeniable, and her close association with Owen is beyond dispute, Wright's theoretical contribution should not be reduced to a simplified version of Benthamite utilitarianism or Owenite utopianism. These elements of Wright's thought, while significant, constitute a part of a larger and more complex whole. Wright expands and improves upon these theories to develop an insightful and original analysis of the American project and to propose solutions to the problems that plagued it.

Wright makes several major contributions to our theoretical understanding of the early women's rights movement and abolitionism. She serves as an essential transitional figure from early republicanism to one of the earliest forms of socialism that would emerge in mid-nineteenth-century America, a development that has been largely unexplored in American political thought. Wright's romanticized early view of America, and the working agrarian commune she established to enable slaves to purchase their freedom, Nashoba, were extensions of her republicanism. When Nashoba failed, Wright distanced herself from her idealistic republicanism and began to write and speak about American racism, sexism, and economic inequality as systematic forms of oppression that would require radical political and social change. In a series of widely publicized and well-attended lectures delivered in several states, Wright outlined a comprehensive system of reform based on an epistemological method of inquiry to help Americans live up to the fundamental principles of the Founding. Wright's devastating critique of slavery in America also includes elements that would become part of critical race theory. Building on recent scholarship that identifies aspects of critical race theory in Tocqueville's thought, I show that Wright's ideas also include several key arguments of early "criticalists" such as Tocqueville. Wright and Tocqueville recognize racial identities as social constructions and not fixed biological categories. Both offer an early understanding of "interest convergence," according to which efforts to promote racial equality occur only when the goal of racial equality "converges" with an overarching "interest" of the dominant elite. Both account for the backlash that often results when the privileged class resists efforts to roll back the advantages they enjoy. Finally, both trace the emergence of "negative externalities" that result when whites remain oblivious to the material and ethical price they pay in exchange for the perceived benefits they enjoy in a racist society.

Wright's application of principles associated with critical race theory to the plight of American women constitutes another major contribution to what would become critical feminist theory. Although Tocqueville develops a relatively progressive view of racism in America, his account of American women remains attached to the early republican principles of the past. Wright presents an early version of intersectionality by portraying the oppression of women, the enslavement of African Americans, and the injustice of economic inequality as fundamentally intertwined in an institutionalized system of corruption.

Wright's fourth contribution is also found in her later lectures, in which she transforms what appears to be an empirical and materialist doctrine of knowledge and morality into a method of inquiry that forms the basis of a theory and practice of citizenship. Wright models freethinking and citizenship for others to emulate and make their own. Her speeches offer an experiential view of knowledge and morality that anticipate aspects of American pragmatism. By bringing together a pragmatic approach with a commitment to social reform, Wright anticipates additional elements of critical feminist theory, which begins, not with abstract epistemological theories, but rather with the concrete experiences of women.

Chapter 2 focuses on Harriet Martineau, who, like Wright, traveled to America and wrote extensively about her findings on slavery and the oppression of women. Martineau was cited by a number of early women's rights advocates, as was Wright. In spite of the fact that Martineau remained in the United States far longer and met with more prominent political figures than her contemporary, Tocqueville, her work has been largely neglected by political theorists. Martineau's original contributions have been obscured by the frequent characterization of her as a popularizer of mainstream economic and political doctrines developed by better-known men. Thus, in her examination of American society, Martineau is seen merely to echo the Garrisonian arguments against slavery and the oppression of women. Noting the passionate nature of her condemnations, scholars have classified her as one among the many writers who deployed a problematic version of sentimentality, which elicited pity from the audience as well as a degree of condescension toward the suffering. The sheer volume of work she produced as a professional writer has also led some to accuse her of dilettantism. However, close analysis of her lengthy examination of American life, *Society in America* (1837), and her methodological treatise, *How to Observe: Morals and Manners* (1838), reveals that Martineau adapts Smith's theory of sympathy to accommodate greater diversity among observers and observed. Her theory is better able to address the disenfranchisement of women and the oppression of slaves because it allows people to empathize with those who are radically different from themselves. As individuals connect to others in this way, they are in a far stronger position to realize the disparate treatment and injustices others face and to open themselves to the possibility of reform. Martineau's innovative account of sympathy distinguishes her from the Garrisonians as well and further highlights the originality of her work.

Chapter 3 analyzes Angelina Grimké's use of rhetoric in constructing a moral and political theory. Grimké was one of the first women to speak in public to mixed audiences in the United States (the first being Frances Wright). Her *Appeal to the Christian Women of the South* (1836), along with Sarah Grimké's *Epistle to the Clergy of the Southern States* (1836), served as the opening salvo unleashed by the sisters against the "sins of slavery" and contributed to the burgeoning women's rights movement. The virulence with which Angelina's efforts were criticized effectively drove her out of the public realm and into a private life of relative obscurity. The brevity of her career, combined with the deeply emotional and passionate nature of her appeals, has led commentators to emphasize her historical importance in the Garrisonian abolitionist movement and to highlight her rhetorical prowess while minimizing her theoretical relevance within the abolitionist and early women's rights movements. Grimké's work has also been used as an example of the incendiary sentimentalist rhetoric whose excesses have been widely criticized.[109] This chapter focuses on the highly charged public interchange in 1837 between Grimké and the education reformer Catherine Beecher over the abolition of slavery and the rights of women. To explore her unique theoretical contributions, I resituate Grimké's work within Scottish Enlightenment political theory debates about rhetoric and its vital role in moral and political life. Grimké advances a powerful defense against Beecher's critique by offering a sophisticated theory of sympathy that avoids charges of sentimentality by carefully balancing reason and emotion. Grimké's understanding of sympathy and its role in rhetoric bears a number of striking similarities to Smith's moral theory of rhetoric outlined in the *Lectures on Rhetoric and Belles Lettres*. Employing various rhetorical strategies resembling those described by Smith, Grimké is able to convey a moral and political teaching that is crucial to abolitionism and the advancement of women. Yet she also expands Smith's understanding by offering a number of poignant examples in which sympathy may forge closer connections between the enfranchised and the marginalized and thereby contribute to meaningful political change.

Sarah Grimké, author of *Letters on the Equality of the Sexes* (1838) and the focus of chapter 4, has been recognized as "a major feminist thinker" and perhaps even as "the first woman to write a coherent feminist argument in the United States."[110] The exact nature of Grimké's theoretical contribution, however, is less clear. Her work has been classified generally as a product of the liberal Enlightenment because of a reluctance among secular-minded interpreters to acknowledge Grimké's strong religious convictions. There is some evidence for this view in Grimké's later writings, in which she seems to turn away from her religious understanding of women's rights and embrace a secular perspective. However, feminist theory has been criticized for selective interpretation by downplaying the importance of religion because of its role in imposing patriarchal worldviews.[111]

To highlight the political implications of her theory, while not losing sight of its religious underpinnings, I frame Grimké's work within recent research on Quaker constitutionalism exemplified by the contributions of frequently overlooked founding father John Dickinson. Grimké's views on religion and women's rights are deeply consistent with Dickinson's constitutionalism, which also offers an alternative nonpatriarchal understanding of the relation between religious teachings and political life. In this regard, Quaker constitutionalism differs from the secular Whig perspective characteristic of Enlightenment liberalism, on the one hand, and divine rights theories of natural law, on the other. Like Dickinson, Grimké believes that the word of God is accessible directly through individual synteresis, rather than through Scripture or religious doctrine, as traditionally believed. Divine teachings, however, can be understood only through human reason. On this view, an eternal fundamental constitution, apprehended through synteresis and guided by the extensive application of human reason, informs the creation of political institutions as well as social and cultural practices such as those in America. Because reason is fallible, however, the fundamental constitution in general and the American Constitution in particular are often misinterpreted and misunderstood. Reform is made possible only by a return to first principles through collective deliberation and discernment, which in turn rely on the combination of human reason and synteresis.

Grimké's theory is clearly grounded in religious conviction and yet emphasizes the importance of human reason in realizing and achieving equality. Grimké's critique of scriptural teachings about women and slavery itself demonstrates the very process of reform by rationally reconstructing those same teachings. And it is this rational reconstruction of women's equality, not divine teaching per se, that she applies to the legal, social, and cultural prescriptions for women. Thus, like other progressive Quaker reformists of her time, Grimké differentiates herself from the Garrisonian movement by refusing to abandon political life in favor of an anarchist "no-government" solution. In fact, Grimké contributes further to a deeply egalitarian, voluntarist view of political power that is rooted in progressive Quakerism. As Dickinson's understanding of constitutionalism offers a compelling counterpoint to the received narrative of the American founding, so, too, do Grimké's reflections offer an alternative narrative that was crucial to the early women's rights movement.

Chapter 5 examines the works of Lucretia Mott, the widely recognized moral and spiritual leader of the abolitionist and early women's rights movements. She has been characterized variously as a disciple of Garrison, a proliferator of Wollstonecraft's ideas, and a religious promoter of human rights whose earnest efforts were surpassed by the more theoretically sophisticated and politically astute Stanton. These portrayals paradoxically elevate Mott's status while understating the originality of her views. I analyze Mott's speeches and writings in detail to show that her unique theoretical contributions are shaped by a combination of elements: a radically antidogmatic worldview rooted in her progressive religious faith, an unwavering commitment to autonomy for all people, and an egalitarian conception of power. Through her speeches and writings, Mott proposes a dialectical, self-reflective, critical approach that serves as the basis of political citizenship. By exposing the hidden sources of inequality, oppression, and injustice, her approach empowers human beings to shape an egalitarian, voluntarist political system that is based on authentic consent and philosophic reflection. Moreover, like Sarah Grimké, Mott also reflects important aspects of early Quaker constitutionalism by emphasizing the importance of human reason guided by the inner light and the role of debate and deliberation in fashioning a government based on true consent.

Of all the reformers examined in this book, Stanton, the focus of chapter 6, has been most widely recognized and analyzed by political theorists. Not only was she at the center of the *History of Woman Suffrage*, but, unlike many of her contemporaries, Stanton also left behind a considerable body of work, including extended theoretical reflections as well as the more conventional sources of communication used by women reformers, such as speeches, letters, and newspaper articles. Given the complexity of Stanton's political thought, it is not surprising that her works would include aspects of liberalism, republicanism, and ascriptive inegalitarianism.[112] The rhetorical skills for which Stanton was renowned also reflect aspects of the Scottish Enlightenment theory of sympathy. Again using the *Lectures on Rhetoric and Belles Lettres* as a frame, I demonstrate that in her speeches and writings Stanton employs indirect description and appeals to a form of sympathy similar to what

Smith envisions as the key to moral instruction. Stanton induces shame and remorse in her audience by conjuring a version of the impartial spectator for which Smith is well known. Stanton leads her audiences through various stages of argumentation, leaving them to conclude, independently, that reform is necessary. In this chapter I offer an original interpretation of Stanton by comparing the role of ridicule in her work with Smith's account. In the *Lectures* Smith devotes an unusual amount of attention to Jonathan Swift, whose writings employed ridicule in order to critique the society of his day. Interpreters of Smith have largely overlooked the significance of this powerful rhetorical tool in his moral theory, which induces shame, resentment, and desire for approbation, and which in turn opens the possibility for reform. Along similar lines, Stanton's deployment of ridicule is an essential, though unrecognized, element of her political theory. By using ridicule, Stanton is engaging in a similar method of moral instruction as Smith, yet she expands Smith's moral and political theory to specifically address women's rights. Stanton's versions of sympathy, indirect description, the impartial spectator, and ridicule undergird her relentless and unwavering advocacy for early women's rights in ways that have been unappreciated.

My analysis of Stanton raises important questions about the recent scholarly focus on her racism, exceptionalism, and elitism, which for critics severely compromise the effectiveness of her reformist message.[113] To be sure, the controversial aspects of Stanton's remarks should not be minimized. However, it is equally important to note that early versions of many of these comments are made in some of Stanton's first writings, while she employs rhetorical strategies such as ridicule. The arguments critics find objectionable also pre-date the emergence of social Darwinism and, with it, theories of racism and sexism that were based on evolutionary constructions and biological categories—theories that have frequently been used in attacks against Stanton. I explore the possibility that Stanton's comments are components of a broader rhetorical strategy that consistently argues for the equality of all people, male and female, poor and rich, black and white.[114]

The final chapter presents a brief exploration of the important yet neglected theoretical contributions of Sojourner Truth. From the explorations of the early women's rights advocates and abolitionists in this book, a rich analytical framework emerges with which to examine

Truth's life and work. Truth's most frequently deployed rhetorical tactic is ridicule, the weapon of choice of her contemporary Stanton as well. Like Wright and Mott, Truth incorporates performative elements of theorizing, as she leads her audience through speech and deed to confront the persistent injustices against women and freed slaves that are deeply rooted in the American project itself. As a freed black woman of modest means, unhindered by the race, gender, and class privilege that tainted the contributions of other women's rights advocates, Truth embodies the very concept of intersectionality about which those reformers could only write and speak. In spite of the fact that Truth, who was illiterate, left behind no writings in her own hand, her influence was sufficiently powerful to leave an indelible impression on many who saw and wrote about her. Of all the sympathetic connections early women's rights and abolitionist advocates sought to establish with their audiences, those forged by Truth were likely the most genuine and authentic.

1

# Lifting the "Claud-Lorraine Tint" over the Republic

*Frances Wright's Critique of Society and Manners in America*

In her epitaph, Frances Wright describes her life's work in sweeping terms: "I have wedded the cause of human improvement / staked on it my fortune, my reputation, and my life / humankind is but one family / the education of its youth should / be equal and universal."

In many ways, Wright's parting message rings true. She had devoted most of her adult life to radical reform, a crucial component of which was universal education. But she did so at great personal cost.

Wright's life was one of extremes. She enjoyed fame and good fortune among a variety of well known figures. The philosopher Jeremy Bentham described her first major publication, *Views on Society and Manners in America* (1821), as a "justly admired and pre-eminently interesting work."[1] John Stuart Mill declared Wright one of the most important women of her generation.[2] The Marquis de Lafayette invited her to accompany him to America and enjoyed a relationship with her so close that it scandalized his family. Thomas Jefferson, who welcomed Wright and Lafayette to Monticello, commented that her subsequent work, *A Few Days in Athens* (1822), was "equal to the best morsel of antiquity [and] the principles of the sects are beautifully and candidly explained and contrasted."[3] James Madison also entertained Wright and Lafayette at Montpelier, though he expressed skepticism about her quixotic plan for a working commune designed to help free slaves and end slavery.[4] Frances Trollope befriended Wright and, although the two women are typically considered polar opposites, they shared a number of "radical" goals for reforming American society.[5] Socialist reformer Robert Owen strongly influenced Wright's views on economic and social reform, and his own commune, New Harmony, served as a model for her abolitionist community. Owen's son Robert Dale Owen collaborated with Wright on one of the most influential newspapers in mid-nineteenth-century America. The young idealist

Walt Whitman attended Wright's lectures, read her newspaper regularly, and befriended a number of early women's rights advocates who sought to preserve her memory and whose work influenced his own writings.[6] And yet the "family" of "humankind" she had "wedded" would ultimately forsake her. After a year of suffering in excruciating pain, Wright died virtually alone, destitute, and plagued by controversy at the age of fifty-seven in Cincinnati, Ohio, her adopted home.

Wright's life was a series of "firsts," so it is fitting that this book begins with a detailed analysis of her work. Wright forced nineteenth-century America to directly confront issues of race, gender, and economic inequality—far earlier than more familiar commentators who are frequently credited with analyzing these problems for the first time.[7] Of the many travel writers who ventured to early nineteenth-century America and published their findings, Wright's visits outlasted them all. She came to America three times, in 1818, 1824, and 1835, finally settling in the United States as an American citizen. Working with Robert Dale Owen at the *Free Inquirer*, Wright was the first female editor of a major American newspaper. Together with Owen, Wright lent her support to the newly created Working Men's Party in New York, thereby becoming one of the first women involved with the burgeoning labor movement in America. In spite of the fact that Wright would distance herself from the party because it sought to equalize private property and fell short of endorsing her ambitious plan for universal education, party-backed candidates for the New York State Assembly were nevertheless derided as "Fanny Wrightists" and "Wright Reasoners" by the press.[8] She traveled to Cincinnati, New York, Philadelphia, Baltimore, Boston, Louisville, St. Louis, and other cities to lecture. As the first woman to speak to mixed public audiences in the United States in a secular setting, Wright broadened the nature of public authority for women by serving as an instructor in independent thinking, a frequent theme in her speeches, appealing not just to elites but also to laborers and working-class Americans. Although many praised her remarkable rhetorical talents and were impressed by the large and diverse audiences she drew, others were scandalized by her encroachment into the male-dominated public realm.[9]

Wright was one of the first European commentators on America to criticize the lack of educational opportunities for women and their subordination in marriage, a regressive effect of English common law that lingered in the post-revolutionary period. Although Alexis de Tocqueville is celebrated for his observations on the inequality of American women, Wright's *Views on Society and Manners in America*, published in 1821, predates the first volume of Tocqueville's *Democracy in America* by thirteen years, and the second volume by eighteen years.[10] In fact, as we shall see, many of the innovative ideas and observations with which Tocqueville is credited appear years earlier in Wright's work.[11]

Wright was also the first person to devise and implement an actual plan to end American slavery. Collaborating with Robert Owen and George and Frederick Rapp, who had formed their own communes, Wright developed a detailed strategy to establish a working community, Nashoba, in Tennessee, in which enslaved people would work to purchase their own freedom. Founded in 1825, Nashoba proved controversial and would ultimately fail. Yet it stands out as a bold early attempt to advance the abolitionist cause.

In all these ways, Wright paved the way for the many women's rights activists and abolitionists who would follow her. And yet, while Wright's pioneering efforts were impressive and her prescience in many cases was laudable, these achievements do not demonstrate in themselves that Wright offered a "first" political theory or made an original theoretical contribution. In fact, commentators have often observed the derivative nature of Wright's ideas, claiming that her work merely borrows from elements of the Scottish Enlightenment as well as utilitarianism and materialism. Specifically, the many similarities between Wright's ideas and those of predecessors such as John Millar, Robert Owen, and Jeremy Bentham have been duly noted.

Adding to the challenge of demonstrating Wright's theoretical relevance are her considerable shortcomings, which for many have obscured any useful message arising from her work. Wright's opposition to slavery was unwavering, yet through the peculiar design of Nashoba, which required that Wright purchase slaves who then performed manual labor to earn sufficient funds to secure their own freedom, she effectively became a slave owner herself.[12] The excessive optimism about the American project that tainted Wright's *Views on Society and Manners in America* finds a parallel in her perhaps equally naïve belief later on that, despite their deep roots in American culture, slavery and the oppression of women could be overcome through education and the cultivation of reason.

Wright came to acknowledge the naiveté of her early embrace of the American experiment, admitting that her "enthusiasm doubtless conspired to throw a Claud-Lorraine tint over a country which bore the name of Republic."[13] Yet in response, she plunged herself into a systematic reform effort so radical that it arguably led to her ruin. Wright's progressive views on sexuality and her withering critique of the institution of marriage as a patriarchal holdover of English common law did not stop her from marrying the father of the child she conceived out of wedlock or from remaining in the marriage despite the ill treatment and financial exploitation she suffered at the hands of her husband (she was finally granted a divorce before she died). In spite of Wright's fervent support for women's rights, she was estranged from her only daughter, who would later testify before a congressional committee in opposition to woman suffrage, arguing that it "can only bring misery and degradation upon the whole sex, and thereby wreck human happiness in America!"[14]

Wright was indeed a polymath who was undoubtedly influenced by the thinkers she met and whose works she voraciously read, and the controversial nature of her radical reform agenda is undeniable. But what makes Wright theoretically significant is that she adapts the teachings of a variety of thinkers to develop an insightful and original analysis of the American project and propose solutions—however imperfect or contentious—to the problems that plagued it. Wright "offers a philosophical system founded on a synthesis of several philosophies that are typically viewed as competing positions," namely, Owenite socialism, Benthamite utilitarianism, and Scottish Enlightenment empiricism and moral sense theory, "and her system is aimed at producing concrete social and political change."[15]

The originality and significance of Wright's political theory are demonstrated in four major ways that I examine in this chapter. First, Wright's life and work reflect a transition from republicanism to an early form of socialism, which has been largely unexplored in American political thought. With her gradual recognition of the deep entrenchment of inequality in American society—a recognition earned in part through the disappointing failure of Nashoba—came disillusionment with the republican idealism that had fueled her early embrace of America. Racism and sexism were not merely fading remnants of British aristocracy, as her original optimism led her to believe, nor was American economic development guided by a republican dedication to the common good. Instead, she increasingly focused her energies on exposing the systemic and interrelated causes of inequality that were endemic to the new republic and on developing a comprehensive plan for reform. The key component is government-sponsored universal education that would be funded through progressive taxation. Inspired by socialist reformers such as Owen, Wright envisioned a cooperative effort to mitigate inequalities of race, sex, and class.

Second, Wright can also be credited with developing one of the first accounts of American slavery through a perspective similar to what would later be termed "critical race theory," which uses the intersection of race, class, and gender to analyze systems of oppression. Building on recent scholarship that identifies elements of critical race theory in Tocqueville's thought, I show that Wright's work, which precedes Tocqueville's by more than a decade, exhibits many of the same aspects. Specifically, Wright's observations align her with several key arguments of early "criticalists" such as Tocqueville: the idea that racial identities are social constructions and not fixed biological categories; the theory of "interest convergence," according to which efforts to promote racial equality occur only when the goal of racial equality "converges" with an overarching "interest" of the dominant elite, often resulting in a "backlash" by the privileged class who resist any effort to roll back the advantages they enjoy; and the emergence of "negative externalities" for whites that result when the "psychological benefits" of a racist and sexist society blind them to the fact that the system also levies "material and moral taxes on them as individuals."[16]

Third, Wright innovates and expands on these nascent aspects of critical race theory to examine the oppression of American women, thereby contributing to the development of critical feminist theory, both of which rely on similar epistemological and ontological assumptions.[17] Whereas the similarities between Wright and Tocqueville on the issue of slavery reveal that both are early criticalists, Wright's extension of critical theory to the plight of women differs markedly from Tocqueville's writings, which remain firmly attached to republican principles. That Tocqueville chooses not to extend the principles of his relatively progressive account of American slavery to the plight of American women is even more surprising when we consider that Tocqueville's work, published in 1840, lags behind Wright's radically forward-looking analysis, which was fully developed in her first series of lectures, by ten years.[18]

In the *Course of Popular Lectures*, Wright's account of the oppression of American women adheres to the "social construction thesis" by insisting that inequalities between men and women are culturally manufactured through the denial of educational opportunities for women and perpetuated by male elites who seek to maintain their power through religious teachings, unjust laws, and other sources of misinformation. For Wright American men experience "negative externalities" as a result of the oppression of women. Although men believe they benefit from their dominant position, the corruption of American society has blinded them to the fact that they undermine their own best interests by depriving society of the intellectual, economic, political, and moral contributions of fully half of its citizens. Wright's appeal to radical reform for men and women provides another example of "interest convergence theory" and the subsequent backlash. Nothing better exemplifies the backfiring of Wright's plans than the virulent attacks she faced when expressing her radical views in public lectures.

Fourth, I argue that Wright's *Lectures* effectively transform an empirical and materialist doctrine of knowledge and morality into a method of active inquiry that forms the basis of a theory and practice of American democratic citizenship. Here again Wright makes a significant and highly original contribution to American political thought and feminist theory. Her speeches offer an experiential view of knowledge and morality that anticipate aspects of American pragmatism that would be articulated by transcendentalists such as Ralph Waldo Emerson, Henry David Thoreau, and Margaret Fuller, and developed more fully by Charles Pierce and John Dewey.[19] Moreover, Wright's speeches are not simply words on paper or orations delivered to passive recipients but performances that literally demonstrate the approach to knowledge and freethinking Wright advocates as a solution to the problems that plague Jacksonian society. Wright models freethinking and citizenship for others to emulate and make their own. In this regard, Wright offers a collaborative model of knowing that "makes us recognize our epistemological, ethical, and political responsibility as members of a community of knowers, a sense of responsibility that is a necessary accompaniment to empowerment."[20] Only by engaging in freethinking, according to Wright, can America hope to address its most challenging problems.

## Republicanism, Proto-socialism, and Wright's Evolving Critique of the American Project

Although Wright's early life was fraught with tragedy—both parents died within two months of each other—she was raised in prominent households with close ties to the vigorous intellectual community of the University of Glasgow, center of the Scottish Enlightenment. Hence it is no surprise that her views resemble those of the Glasgow community. Wright's insistence that knowledge must be validated by sensation bears the stamp of her guardian James Mylne, successor of Adam Smith as chair of moral philosophy, who was nicknamed "Old Sensation" because he believed that "we can know nothing beyond the evidence provided by our senses."[21] Wright's early views were also undoubtedly shaped by John Millar, a close friend of Mylne and professor of law and jurisprudence who was influenced by Smith and David Hume. Wright and her sister frequently visited Millar's estate and befriended his nine precocious children.

The Millar family would prove to be an important resource in the development of Wright's republicanism, which shaped her initial views on America. An "infamous" Whig, Millar supported both the French and American revolutions and opposed slavery, positions Wright would later adopt as well. Millar's daughter-in-law Robina Craig Millar served as the correspondent in the series of letters that would later become the basis of *Views on Society and Manners in America*. An ardent republican and radical Whig, Millar had emigrated to the United States with her husband but was forced to return after his unexpected death. Wright also drew from histories written by Carlo Botta, David Ramsay, and others, who provided sympathetic views of the American Revolution as an alternative to the excesses of the French Revolution and Napoleonic Wars.[22]

Wright represented a kind of "enlightened republicanism" that sought to reconcile republican politics with the needs of commercial society, in similar spirit to Smith's *Wealth of Nations* and *Theory of Moral Sentiments*. Instead of simply endorsing the traditional values of (civic) republicanism, Wright and other "enlightened republicans" believed that "human emancipation" was to be found in the creation of "communities that retained an arcadian element, most frequently located in the countryside, apart from industrial expansion."[23] The harmful effects of economic specialization and the division of labor would also be countered with increased political participation through universal suffrage and the formation of new political institutions. In her early writings, Wright "consistently used classical republican imagery to represent the heroic face and political goals of the American republic," and yet she also recognized aspects of "modern liberty" based on the "progress of knowledge" that accompanied the "growth in manufactures which she identified as desirable."[24] Wright's plan for Nashoba, itself a working farm, is emblematic of "enlightened republicanism." For Wright, slavery was an unfortunate anomaly in America, a holdover from European aristocracy that needed to be purged. The solution posed by Nashoba sought to satisfy America's lofty founding principles by offering freedom and equality for its inhabitants in an agrarian setting, on the one hand, while acknowledging the economic needs of commercial society, on the other, by developing a plan that would reimburse slave owners for their losses and ensure that the commune could financially sustain itself. Along similar lines, Wright describes American women largely in republican terms, as patriotic mothers and wives of future citizens, and yet she also insists that they receive a sophisticated education comparable to that received by men.

However, by the end of 1827, Wright grew disillusioned with the Nashoba project and turned away from her romanticized republicanism. Wright was never able to secure a sufficient number of slave workers to sustain the community and, owing to unrealistic expectations about worker productivity, the slaves were unable to purchase their own freedom and turn a profit. Nashoba's caretaker had left the community amid rumors of an extramarital affair with Wright, who in turn fell ill and left for Europe to recover. Although she transferred ownership of Nashoba to a group of trustees and sought to transform the working farm into a more racially integrated community built around a school for slave children, it still failed to thrive. The final blow came when a log written by a trustee of Nashoba was published, revealing that he and a "mulatto" woman were living together as part of a broader "free love" scheme that was openly encouraged among the inhabitants and admitting that the slave workers were subjected to inhumane treatment. Realizing that radical change was necessary to end slavery, Wright sought "a more assertive and autonomous challenge to social hierarchy, sexual convention, and racial difference."[25] This more "assertive challenge" came in the form of a plan for comprehensive change outlined in a series of lectures she delivered throughout several states.

Perhaps the strongest, most direct influence on Wright's critique of American society was the socialist economic reformer Robert Owen. Although Wright would not actually meet Owen until 1825, her unwavering advocacy of universal education and condemnation of institutional religion bear the stamp of his early writings. Both call for national support and regulation of a system of public education that would be funded by progressive taxation.

Elements of Owen's devastating critique of the effects of the manufacturing system on the working class in his book *New View of Society* (1816) and his testimony to the British Parliament in *Observations on the Effect of the Manufacturing System* (1817) reemerge in Wright's withering portrayal of American society in her *Lectures*. Owen writes in the *Observations* that, in a manufacturing society obsessed with profit, "all are sedulously trained to buy cheap and to sell dear; and to succeed in this art, the parties must be taught to acquire strong powers of deception; and thus a spirit is generated through every class of traders, destructive of that open, honest sincerity, without which man cannot make others happy, nor enjoy happiness himself." The wealthy become greedy and materialistic, and

the industry of the lower orders, from whose labour this wealth is now drawn, has been carried by new competitors striving against those of longer standing, to a point of real oppression, reducing them by successive changes, as the spirit of competition increased, and the ease of acquiring wealth diminished, to a state more wretched than can be imagined by those who have not attentively observed the changes as they have gradually occurred. In consequence, they are at present in a situation infinitely more degraded and miserable than they were before the introduction of these manufactories, upon the success of which their bare subsistence now depends.

No one is immune to the corrosive effects of commercial society. Even children "must labour incessantly for their bare subsistence." Denied the experience of "innocent, healthy, and rational amusements," they never learn "what relaxation means, except by the actual cessation from labour."[26]

Owen's economic theories are often contrasted with Adam Smith's by commentators who interpret Smith's work as an unqualified endorsement of commercial society. To be sure, Smith celebrates the benefits commercial society has brought to the poor, who "derive" from the "luxury and caprice" of the rich "that share of the necessaries of life, which they would in vain have expected from his humanity or his justice" (*TMS*, IV.I.10). Yet he is equally cognizant of the dehumanizing toll paid by low-wage menial laborers:

> The man whose whole life is spent in performing a few simple operations . . . has no occasion to exert his understanding. . . . He naturally loses, therefore, the habit of such exertion, and generally becomes as stupid and ignorant as it is possible for a human creature to become. The torpor of his mind renders him, not only incapable of relishing or bearing a part in any rational conversation, but of conceiving any generous, noble, or tender sentiment, and consequently of forming any just judgment concerning many even of the ordinary duties of private life. (*WN*, V.i.f.50)

The deprivation experienced by a laborer renders him incapable of flourishing as a human being and citizen as well: "Of the great and extensive interests of his country, he is altogether incapable of judging" (*WN*, V.i.f.50). Although these passages suggest an unexpected theoretical connection between Smith and Owen on the potentially corrosive influence of commercial society, they propose different solutions, with Owen embracing a far more expansive view of government involvement than his predecessor, a trend Wright continues in her own theorizing.

Wright begins her own critique of economic specialization and mechanization in America in similar spirit to Owen and Smith. In the preface of her *Lectures*, Wright admits that during her first trip she "mistook for the energy of enlightened liberty what was, perhaps, rather the restlessness of commercial enterprise," overlooking the "evils and abuses differing in degree rather than in nature from those of Europe."[27] Wright laments the reports emerging from various American cities of "the suffering condition of a large mass of their population" resulting from the fact that "the hardest labour is often without a reward adequate to the sustenance of the labourer." Consequently, laborers are reduced to working for mere subsistence, deprived of education and leisure, driven by necessity, and pushed into early graves. She condemns the prevailing notion among the rich that "the estimate of our own moral and political importance [is] swelling always in a ratio exactly proportionate to the growth of our purse."[28]

Wright expands the ideas of her fellow reformer to advance an early version of socialism that envisions itself as the extension and fulfillment of American democratic ideals. A framework used to examine nineteenth-century British socialism is helpful in situating Wright's contribution to the nineteenth-century American socialist tradition. Many utopian socialists of the time, such as "radical puritan" Quakers and Marx, were considered largely apolitical. Even Owen "viewed liberal, constitutional parliamentarism very ambivalently."[29] By contrast, another strand of Owenist socialism "was concerned more clearly with the extension and fulfillment of democratic ideals than with their perfectionist transcendence."[30] This politically engaged version "sought to join political means to social ends as well as to link the moral and economic analysis of socialism to republicanism" and represents "a more traditionally democratic form of socialism which was profoundly suspicious of most attempts to supersede politics or to introduce principles of order markedly different from those sought by republicans."[31]

Wright's contribution clearly falls into the category of political socialism. She applies the ideas inherited from Owen and others directly to the American project so that the country can realize its own principles and live up to the promise of representative government properly understood. Wright calls for national support and regulation of a system of universal education that would be funded by progressive taxation. Schools would be controlled by local districts with the goal of preparing the general citizenry for the task of self-government. By providing "every son and daughter in this galaxy of commonwealths" in America with equal "means of instruction," Wright proposes to end economic inequality and the exploitation of workers in America. Under the corrupt existing system, "art and science are applied, not to relieve the labour of industry, but to depreciate its value," and "human beings count but as an appendage to the machinery they keep in motion." Wealth and prosperity bring little happiness to most Americans because "enjoyment is calculated by the luxury of the few instead of the ease of the many." By contrast, Wright's education provides "the habits of healthy industry" by training future American citizens in the habits of equality. They will "be protected equally from the sufferings and the vice attendant on poverty and on riches" because they will "be trained as equals to understand and to exercise the rights set forth" in the Declaration of Independence and other founding documents. Wealth and prosperity would be redirected to provide for the common good by giving "relief to the widow, protection to the orphan, [and] guardianship of the state to every child in the land."[32] And it is clear that Wright views the American political process as an essential component of this reform:

> Let the popular suffrage be exercised with a view to the popular good. Let the industrious classes, and all honest men of all classes, unite for the sending to the legislatures those who will represent the real interests of the many, not the imagined interests of the few—of the people at large, not of any profession or class.[33]

Thus, unlike other nineteenth-century socialist thinkers who were deeply skeptical of political reforms, Wright became even more committed to a political solution through the American democratic process properly understood and appropriately bolstered through education. Although Wright was more politically engaged than Owen, she nevertheless maintains some of the "political emphases" of Owenism, including its rejection of violent revolution, dictatorship, and class conflict as instruments of social transformation.[34]

Because Wright's socialism is unique in many ways and clearly distinguishable from Marxist socialism, it offers an important yet poorly understood alternative to competing theories of the time.[35] Her ideas serve to challenge critics who see "socialism's claim to wish to extend democracy beyond parliamentary boundaries" as merely a guise for "ultimately authoritarian intentions," as well as socialists themselves, who "have far too often ignored the threats to liberty . . . embedded in the anti-political assumptions of socialist theory."[36]

Owen was not the only teacher from whose views Wright would ultimately depart. Although Bentham and Wright were enthusiastic supporters of the American project, there were some sharp differences between their respective positions that further enhance the political significance of Wright's theorizing. Both agreed that the reliance on common law was detrimental to progress in the new nation. However, Bentham categorically rejected the notion of natural rights and attacked the Declaration of Independence as a "hodge podge of confusion" because its fundamental ambiguity left it vulnerable to misinterpretation. By preferring the predictability and stability of codified statutory law over ambiguous "fundamental constitutions," Bentham effectively dismissed a central component of American civil society.[37]

By contrast, Wright consistently embraced the Declaration and other aspects of civil society as vital elements of the American project, even as her views on how to enact its principles continued to evolve. Wright repeatedly invokes the Declaration's famous claim that all men are created equal as the basis of American society that all other countries should imitate. American government is unique in that it alone possesses the "principle of improvement," namely, *the power of silent adaptation to the altering views of the governing and the governed people*" through representation.[38] "*The simple machinery of representation carried through all its parts*," she writes, "*gives facility for its being moulded at will to fit with the knowledge of the age. If imperfect in any or all of its parts, it bears within it a perfect principle—the principle of improvement*."[39] This, combined with the eternal principles of liberty and equality as outlined in the Declaration, is for Wright American republicanism rightly understood. The American principle of improvement is wholly consistent with the essential characteristic that for Wright distinguishes humankind from other beings, namely, "some vague desire of advancing in knowledge."[40] At its best, America—not Britain or continental Europe—is most compatible with her principles, and vice versa.

The importance of the founding principles for Wright also serves to differentiate Americans' understanding of patriotism. "European"—that is, British—patriotism has meant "love of country in an exclusive sense; of love of countrymen in contradistinction to the love of our fellow-creatures; of love of the constitution, instead of love or appreciation of those principles upon which the constitution is, or ought to be, based."[41]

For Wright, America has a unique opportunity to observe a more humanistic patriotism because of its devotion to human improvement generally, rather than the written Constitution as such, or to particular national interests. It is more important for Americans "to know why they honour their institutions, and *feel* that they honour them because they are based on just principles" than to simply memorize those principles or promote them in a jingoistic way.[42]

Wright concludes that it is for Americans

> to examine their institutions, because they have the means of improving them; to examine their laws, because at will they can alter them. . . . It is for them not to rest satisfied with words, who can seize upon things; and to remember, that equality means, not the mere equality of political rights, however valuable, but equality of instruction, and equality in virtue; and that liberty means, not the mere voting at elections, but the free and fearless exercise of the mental faculties, and that self-possession which springs out of well-reasoned opinions and consistent practice.[43]

And only by adopting universal education and other reforms that she proposes can Americans actualize the ideals on which their system of representation is based:

> First, that the people are enlightened judges of their own interests—or, in other words, *that they are by nature or by education, fitted to distinguish the means for which the greatest happiness may be produced to the whole population; and secondly, that the representatives, through whom the people legislate, shall, in all cases, faithfully carry into effect the views of the people whose attorneys they are.*[44]

Thus, whereas Bentham was dismissive of the Declaration and the very notion of fundamental principles, for Wright, "the great principles, stamped in America's declaration of independence are true, are great, are sublime, and are *all her own*."[45]

## Wright's Critical Theory of Race and American Slavery

Wright incorporates into her critique of American slavery and the oppression of women a key element of Owen's economic theory: that human nature is fundamentally shaped by conditions and circumstances. For Owen, any "defect of character" such as dishonesty among those who live under commercialism "ought not to be attributed to the individuals possessing it, but to the overwhelming effect of the system under which they have been trained."[46] Along similar lines, the dehumanization of laborers and the exploitation of children do not arise from the inherent evil or fallen nature of humankind. If conditions can be improved, so, too, will human nature become more virtuous. Although Owen was successful in extracting legislative reform to improve the condition of workers, he was convinced that revolutionary change in society was necessary. To advance such change, he would go on to found the utopian community, New Harmony, in Indiana, where Wright would stay and upon which she would base her own commune, Nashoba.[47]

Of course, Owen is not the first theorist to appreciate the importance of social conditions in shaping human behavior. One of Adam Smith's most notable contributions is the idea that morality is determined largely by the particular cultural context in which people live. For "the different situations of different ages and countries are apt . . . to give different characters to the generality of those who live in them, and their sentiments concerning the particular degree of each quality, that is either blamable or praise-worthy, vary, according to that degree which is usual in their own country, and in their own times" (*TMS*, V.2.7). Smith's concept of the impartial spectator is designed to be an ideal judge of moral behavior as "we remove ourselves, as it were, from our own natural station, and endeavour to view [our own sentiments and motives] as at a certain distance from us . . . with the eyes of other people, or as other people are likely to view them." However, the "other people" to which we refer are nevertheless citizens of our own communities, as imagined by ourselves. Thus "we endeavor to examine our own conduct as we imagine any other fair and impartial spectator" from our community "would examine it" (*TMS*, III.1.2). The impartial spectator, then, is still "constructed out of modes of judgment that seem essentially relative to a particular culture" and "is otherwise just like actual, partial spectators" because "it is built out of actual spectators."[48]

These influences helped lay the groundwork for Wright's adoption of an early form of the "social construction thesis," which constitutes one of several crucial "epistemological and ontological assumptions" embraced by critical race theorists who "reject the notion that there are scientifically differentiated races in favor of the view that racial identities are social constructions."[49] Detailed analysis of Tocqueville's "Three Races" chapter reveals that "he was one of the earliest white proponents of the social construction thesis."[50] Wright's observations on slavery in the *Views on Society and Manners in America* demonstrate that she, too, employs elements of the social construction thesis. According to Wright, the harsh climate of the South required workers who could withstand heat and disease, and imported Africans, who were already acclimated to similar weather, seemed ideally suited. By contrast, the temperate climate in the North was amenable to a greater variety of workers, and thus "the slave population was inconsiderable." Because slavery is "as it were grafted in the soil" of the South, "the evil yet needs years of patience, the more perfect understanding of the mischief to the master, or the more universal feeling of the injustice to the slave; the more absolute conviction of the necessity of a remedy, or the more clear insight into the mode in which it should be applied, ere this foul blot can be effaced from that portion of this great Union."[51] For Wright, it is not because Southerners are inherently immoral that they own slaves, nor is it the nature of enslaved people to be in servitude. Similarly, the fact that Northerners are free of slavery cannot be traced to any innate superiority. Rather, all are the result of external conditions. Although it will be a great challenge to uproot the pernicious institution, she unambiguously supports change: "African slavery is at once the disgrace and honor of America; the disgrace she shares in common with the whole civilized world—the honor is all her own."[52] The adaptability of all parties involved suggests for Wright that reform through a fundamental change of conditions is still possible.

There are several important parallels between Wright's account of slavery and Tocqueville's later analysis. Like Wright, Tocqueville attributes the prevalence of slavery in the South to the climate and popular misconceptions of labor: "The closer they get to the tropics, the harder

Europeans find it to work; many Americans maintain that below a certain latitude it is fatal for them, whereas Negroes can work there without danger." Whereas the North cultivates cereals, the South specializes in labor-intensive crops such as tobacco, cotton, and sugar, thereby making it more amenable to and dependent on slavery.[53] Given that the population of enslaved peoples would continue to grow significantly after the publication of Wright's book, it is not surprising that Tocqueville, writing his examination of American slavery at least ten years afterward, would also include the size of the slave population in the South as a virtually insurmountable obstacle for abolition.

As Tocqueville's apparent racism has been reconsidered in light of the situational view he adopts, so, too, do Wright's offensive comments in the *Views on Society* merit reexamination.[54] The patently racist aspects of Tocqueville's and Wright's theories cannot be wholly excused, since neither ever explicitly disavowed them. However, the parallels between Wright's ideas and those expressed by Tocqueville are striking. Wright observes the "clumsy features of a negro girl," a member of a "degraded race" that is "neither frugal nor . . . moral" but is "singularly cheerful and good humoured . . . immoderately fond of dancing . . . and exhibit a show of finery which might amaze Harlequin himself."[55] Tocqueville also laments the physical appearance of the slave who "is hardly recognized as sharing the common features of humanity. His face appears to us as hideous, his intelligence limited, and his tastes low; we almost take him for some being intermediate between beast and man."[56]

Both Wright and Tocqueville perceive less racism in American society than they might expect. Europeans, according to Wright, develop a prejudice that is perhaps even more intense than that of Americans because of the lingering effects of aristocratic class antagonism and the sharp contrast between their respective physical appearances. Wright believes that Northerners are less racist than Southerners, noting that freed blacks can be found "taught by the same master and attending the same church" as whites. And while Virginians "pride themselves upon the peculiar tenderness" with which they treat their "African vassals," they should "break the chains" and abolish slavery instead of "gild[ing] them."[57] By contrast, for Tocqueville, "Race prejudice seems stronger" in the North because lingering racism prevents freed blacks from exercising their legal rights.[58] However, both agree that proximity and interaction between blacks and whites lessen prejudice. For Wright, in the North, "So much had been said and written in favour of the unhappy African" and slavery has been practiced unjustly for so long that whites have been "gradually disposed to befriend" them and view them as political allies.[59] "In the South," Tocqueville claims, "less trouble is taken to keep the Negro apart: they sometimes share the labors and the pleasures of the white men; people are prepared to mix with them to some extent." Like Tocqueville, who concludes that "those who hope that Europeans will one day mingle with the Negroes seem to me to be harboring a delusion," Wright declares that "there must inevitably exist a barrier between the American and the negro" because both "are a distinct race."[60] Finally, Wright traces the "laxity of morals" among slaves to the fact that "man, emerging from the savage or the slavish state, seizes on the indulgencies and the tinsel of luxury, before he discovers the value of those higher enjoyments, derived from the acquirement of knowledge and the cultivation of refined and elevated sentiment."[61] Tocqueville similarly observes that freed Negroes "remain half civilized and deprived of rights amid a population that is infinitely superior to them in wealth and enlightenment; they are exposed to the tyranny of laws and the intolerance of mores."[62]

Tocqueville's choice of "language certainly reveals that the social racism that permeated nineteenth-century culture did affect" him. The same can certainly be said of Wright. However, it would be wrong to include Tocqueville among the "leading figures responsible for the rise of scientific racism in America," since his "writings from other contexts clearly repudiated the primordialist theories of racial difference that dominated white intellectual circles in the middle of the nineteenth century."[63] Wright's early commitment to ending slavery, and especially her later reform efforts to transform American society, indicate that she rejected "primordialist theories" of race as well.

Given Wright's alignment with aspects of critical race theory, the much broader controversy surrounding her involvement with Nashoba can be seen in a new light. Perhaps the most damning criticism of Wright is the accusation that, as Nashoba failed, she embraced miscegenation and co-education over colonization not because of a change of heart or overcoming of racism but, rather, because she opportunistically sought to protect her own reputation.[64] By raising questions about

Wright's perceived racism, we are in a better position to consider alternative explanations for her behavior.

In this context, perhaps the failure of Nashoba can be seen as validation of another element of critical race theory, "interest convergence," which posits that reform efforts for minority groups gain support only by appealing to the interest of elites, and yet these same efforts fail because they effectively reinforce elite privilege and inspire backlash against the aggrieved. In this case, Wright's plan was designed to appeal to the interests of whites—in the North as well as the South—by demonstrating that freed slaves could be economically productive and culturally assimilated. However, the failure of Wright's efforts inadvertently contributed to the pervasive skepticism that ending slavery could ever be economically beneficial or successful. The "sex scandal" surrounding Nashoba was surely amplified by white suspicion and resistance to radical change.[65] Wright's subsequent commitment to universal education and comprehensive reform can perhaps now be seen, not as a kind of Hail Mary pass by a radical (racist) activist, but rather as her acceptance of "the fact that interest convergence is such a ubiquitous aspect of our legal and political history," a discovery that "has convinced most critical race theorists that genuine reforms will occur only after a systemic transformation that stamps white racism out of American culture."[66]

There are indications that what seems to be a reversal is in fact an extension of a broader theory of reform that expands on her earlier views on race and gender. In the *Views on Society*, Wright is unambiguously supportive of education for emancipated slaves in the South based on the successful approach she observed in Northern states. Criticizing Southern slave owners who look to the decrepit living conditions of freed slaves in Virginia and Maryland and conclude that liberty and, by implication, education, are wasted on them, Wright asks,

> But what argument is to be adduced from this? That to emancipate the African race would be to smite the land with a worse plague than that which defaces it already? The history of the negro in the northern states will save us from so revolting a conclusion. To argue that he constitutes, even there, the least valuable portion of the population, will not affect the question. If his character be there *improving*, a fact which none will deny,

we have sufficient data upon which to ground the belief that he may, in time, be rendered a useful member of society.

She concludes: "Were the whole race emancipated, their education would necessarily become a national object, the white population would be constrained to hire their service, and they themselves would be under the necessity of selling it."[67] Wright's firm belief that freed slaves must and should be adequately prepared to enjoy the political liberties they would gain—in America—amplifies the ambivalence of her early thoughts on colonization.[68] Moreover, in the *Views on Society* Wright advocates miscegenation for whites and Native Americans on the grounds that "they have each been too violently opposed to one another." She also observes that the Spanish conquerors and their "conquered vassals" created a "mixed race" that is "remarkable no less for their intelligence than their high spirit, who are now working out the deliverance of their country from the odious thralldom of Spain and who are destined, perhaps, in the course of a few generations, to rival in strength and civilization the proudest empires of the old hemisphere."[69] These early arguments lay the groundwork for Wright's later support for miscegenation among blacks and whites and demonstrate that she took seriously the possibility—however unlikely—that marginalized populations such as Native Americans and, ultimately, freed slaves, could be integrated into American society. Along similar lines, Tocqueville entertained the improbable notion that blacks and whites could be forced to mingle by some external despot or through miscegenation.[70]

Indeed, although Wright repeatedly insists that freed slaves must receive extensive preparation for assimilating into society and that education should be introduced to them gradually, she is equally insistent that *all* Americans, regardless of race, are in need of instruction. To be sure, Wright's tone is undeniably patronizing, and her plans clearly reflect paternalistic tendencies. Yet the substance of her comments shows an early and conscious, if flawed, attempt to convey the complexities of slavery and the ways in which enslaved people are harmed by the institution itself and to offer a pathway to reform.[71] Wright's commitment to improving the conditions under which people live and thrive constitutes "a social philosophy designed to bring about social change, not just for women but also for the other oppressed groups of working-class and black Americans." Wright demands "the inclusion of the interests of these groups, and part of her ultimate goal is to give them moral agency and political empowerment." In this regard, her work represents "a fascinating amalgam of nineteenth-century feminist thought, with its emphasis on education as the solution for women's subordination, and a harbinger of modern feminist thought with her recognition that all oppressed groups—not just women—need to work together to bring about social justice."[72]

## Women and the American Republic: Wright's Call for Universal Education in Citizenship

Wright's advocacy of women's rights in America follows a trajectory similar to her views on slavery. The early influence of the Millars left Wright with a view of American women consistent with "enlightened republican" principles. Her insistence that women receive a progressive education and establish greater intellectual independence is a tacit acknowledgment of the pressing needs of a burgeoning commercial society. John Millar's *Observations on the Distinction of Ranks in Society* (1771), whose chapter, "Of the Rank and Condition of Women in Different Ages," examines the progress of society in terms of the advancement of women, likely contributed to Wright's view—from which she never wavered—that "the condition of women affords in all countries, the best criterion by which to judge the character of men."[73] Wright cites favorably the arguments of Benjamin Rush, who advocates national instruction for both men and women in republican principles such as patriotism and the workings of American government, though she notes that many American women still failed to fully understand those principles.[74] And yet, as Wright's dream of helping to free slaves dims with the decline of Nashoba, so, too, does her republican-infused optimism about American women soon fade. Undaunted by the prospect of failure, Wright would redouble her efforts to develop a comprehensive plan for radical reform that would not only end slavery but guarantee equality for American women as well.

Several aspects of Wright's early "enlightened republicanism" would later be echoed in Tocqueville's account of American women in the second volume of *Democracy in America*, which was published nineteen years after the *Views on Society* appeared in print. Wright and Tocqueville agree that women play vital roles in American society as patriotic mothers of future citizens. Wright acknowledges that America is "a country where a mother is charged with the formation of an infant mind that is to be called in the future to judge of the laws and support the liberties of a republic."[75] So, too, does Tocqueville declare that, as "there have never been free societies without mores, and . . . it is woman who shapes these mores . . . everything which has a bearing on the status of women, their habits, and their thoughts is, in my view, of great political importance."[76] Both Wright and Tocqueville admire the freedom and gaiety of young American women and celebrate the prevalence of public education in America, especially in New England.

Both also express concerns about the potential disadvantages of marriage for American women. Although American women marry relatively young and establish a "happy order of things," for Wright there is inadequate time or opportunity to pursue a substantive education. "Married without knowing anything of life but its amusements, and then quickly immersed in household affairs and the rearing of children," American women "command but few of those opportunities by which their husbands are daily improving in sound sense and varied information."[77] Tocqueville's American girl educates herself as she freely associates with men so that she can learn "how to defend herself" against sexual challenges, yet this freedom comes at considerable cost.[78] "I know too that it tends to develop judgment at the cost of imagination and to make women chaste and cold rather than tender and loving companions of men."[79] Along similar lines, "when the time has come to choose a husband," the young American woman's "cold and austere powers of reasoning," shaped and reinforced "by a free view of the world," teach her that "a light and free spirit within the bonds of marriage is an everlasting source of trouble, not pleasure."[80] Tocqueville demonstrates his ambivalence by conveying mixed messages about the fate of American women in marriage:

> I have never found American women regarding conjugal authority as a blessed usurpation of their rights or feeling that they degraded themselves by submitting to it. On the contrary, they seem to take pride in their relinquishment of their will, and it is their boast to bear the yoke

themselves rather than to escape from it. That, at least, is the feeling expressed by the best of them; the others keep quiet.[81]

The American woman "has freely accepted the yoke" of her husband. She "suffers her new state bravely, for she has chosen it."[82]

The account of American women constitutes part of Tocqueville's much broader discussion of the individualism, alienation, and self-centered acquisitiveness of democratic man and the role of compassion and sympathy in mitigating their effects. Although equality leads to increased interaction among Americans and provides ample opportunities to tap into humanity's "natural compassion," it also paradoxically loosens the various bonds between them. The era of "domestic dictatorship" in the family is finally over in America, yet the separate spheres of influence for men and women persist. Americans rightly assume, for Tocqueville, that "the constitution of men and women, clearly intended to give their diverse faculties a diverse employment," also prescribes "clearly distinct spheres of action." Although women are thought of "as beings of equal worth" to men, "their fates are different." Americans "do not think that a man and his wife should always use their intelligence and understanding in the same way, but they do at least consider that the one has as firm an understanding as the other and a mind as clear."[83]

While Americans "have allowed the social inferiority of woman to continue, they have done everything to raise her morally and intellectually to the level of man." Tocqueville concludes: "In this I think they have wonderfully understood the true conception of democratic progress."[84] Maintaining separate and socially unequal spheres and weakening sympathetic attachments between husbands and wives is a necessary evil for constructively channeling power in American democracy:

> Nor have the Americans ever supposed that democratic principles should undermine the husband's authority and make it doubtful who is in charge of the family. In their view, every association, to be effective, must have a head, and the natural head of the conjugal association is the husband. They therefore never deny him the right to direct his spouse. They think that in the little society composed of man and wife, just as in the great society of politics, the air of democracy is to regulate and legitimatize necessary powers.

By contrast, a more egalitarian view of American democracy would "destroy all power" entirely.[85]

It is precisely such an egalitarian view that Wright advances. Instead of encouraging young women to accept the confines of the feminine realm for the sake of preserving the American republic, Wright's faith in "enlightened republicanism" leads her to propose an education for American women that is on par with that of their patriotic male counterparts. For Tocqueville, the compromise of sympathy between men and women is a necessary evil in America whose effects are mitigated by separate and unequal education. For Wright, the weakening of sympathy between American men and women is a problem that is caused precisely by separate and unequal education and must be solved by instituting comparable instruction. "The two sexes have less in common in their pursuits and turn of thinking than is desirable" because "the less vigorous or the more thoughtless mind is not easily brought to forego trifling pursuits for those which occupy the stronger reason of its companion."[86] Instead, with an education on par with men, "a woman of a powerful intellect will of course seize upon the new topics presented to her by the conversation of her husband."[87]

For Wright, education is key to fostering democratic citizenship for men and women alike. She praises "the wonderful advance which [America] has made, not only in wealth and strength but in mental cultivation, within the last twenty years" and declares that this progress would be "doubly accelerated when the education of the women shall be equally a national concern with that of the other sex, and when they shall thus learn not merely to enjoy but to *appreciate* those peculiar blessings which seem already to mark their country for the happiest in the world."[88] True learning is not achieved with a European-style education in "abstract science or ornamental literature" that serves no useful purpose but, rather, through practical experience. By exercising "his rights and duties as a citizen," the American man "becomes more or less a politician and a philosopher," and his education "goes on through life." As a result, "his stock of useful knowledge increases daily, his judgment is continually exercised, and his mind gradually fixed in habits of observation and reflection."[89] Wright prescribes the same for American women, as "the mother herself should well understand those laws and estimate those liberties. Personal accomplishments and the more ornamental branches of knowledge should certainly in America be made subordinate to solid information."[90]

In the *Lectures* Wright transforms the experiential form of learning she recommends for American men and women into a broader theory of knowledge that serves as the foundation of her critique of American society and comprehensive plan for reform. Wright offers a method of inquiry that is designed to foster independent thinking for men and women alike. For the founding principles of the American republic can only be achieved if citizens can expose the self-empowering machinations of corrupt elites, thereby challenging their authority and reestablishing a genuinely democratic society in which power is shared among true equals.

## Wright's Critical Theory and the Oppression of American Women

Just as Wright anticipates important elements of critical race theory, her later views on American women serve as an important precursor to critical feminist theory, which relies on similar epistemological and ontological assumptions. Whereas the similarities between Wright and Tocqueville on the issue of slavery reveal that both are early criticalists, Wright's extension of critical theory to the plight of women differs markedly from Tocqueville's approach, which remains firmly attached to republican principles. For Wright, white male privilege is supported by an elaborate network of corrupt political and religious institutions and sustained by oppressive social and cultural practices. The *Lectures* build on the "social construction thesis" by insisting that inequalities between men and women are culturally manufactured through the continual denial of educational opportunities for women and perpetuated by male elites who maintain their power through patriarchal religious teachings, unjust laws, and other sources of misinformation. For Wright men also experience "negative externalities," another aspect of critical race theory. Although men believe they benefit from their dominant position in American society, its corruptive influence blinds them to the fact that they support positions that ultimately go against their best interests. Finally, Wright's appeal to radical reform for men and women provides another example of "interest convergence" and subsequent backlash. Nothing better exemplifies the backfiring of Wright's plans than the virulent attacks she faced when expressing her radical views on women in public speeches and writings.

For a clearer understanding of the criticalist elements of Wright's later thinking on women, it is useful to recognize that, in addition to Owen's theories, Bentham's ideas had a considerable impact as well. After Wright returned from her first trip to America and published the *Views on Society* to wide acclaim, Bentham, impressed by her work, invited her regularly to visit his home and study along with a group of "philosophical radicals" that included James Mill and others. Both Bentham and Wright were enamored of the American project and recommended the American model of government as an antidote to the aristocratic corruption of Europe.[91] Both valued a democratic society with broad enfranchisement, direct representation, and active participation by its citizens.

Wright's adherence to Bentham's utilitarianism is widely recognized. However, a relatively unexplored yet important aspect of Bentham's theory—namely, his understanding of corruption—is reflected in Wright's critique of American society and her criticalist feminist theory as well. In the *Constitutional Code* (1830) Bentham outlines several mechanisms that are used by corrupt elites to control the masses.[92] Corruption consists not only of bribery but also encompasses all the laws and regulations formed by a government that privileges the elite few at the expense of the many. "Delusion" of the masses is achieved by myths and abstractions that exaggerate the grandeur and omnipotence of the ruling elite and cloak their tyranny with an appearance of legitimacy and moral superiority. "Factitious honor" is bestowed on wholly undeserving elites by sycophants who control "the vital channels of information and opinion" and who "employ propaganda in support of the rulers." They garner "artificial respect and veneration" for the elites by using "abstract terms such as Crown, Throne, Church, Law, and Property, instead of concrete terms King, Churchmen, Lawyers, and the Rich," thereby "render[ing] criticism 'bad taste.'"[93] Together the mechanisms help create and maintain a demoralized and acquiescent public. Bentham's theory of corruption is part of a broader philosophical distinction he draws between "real" and "fictitious" entities. Real entities are those that can be demonstrated empirically, and, as the term itself suggests, fictitious entities cannot be validated by experience or observation. Among the most popular are abstract terms used by authorities in religion, politics, and law to maintain their domination over a pliant citizenry.

Wright's account of the corruption of language in her lecture "On the Nature of Knowledge" clearly bears the stamp of Bentham's ideas:

> The field of knowledge is around, and about, and within us. Let us not be alarmed by sounding words, and let us not be *deceived* by them. Let us look to things. It is things which we have to consider. Words are, or, more correctly, should be, only the signs of things. I say they *should be*, for it is a most lamentable truth, that they are now very generally conceived to constitute the very substance of knowledge. Words, indeed, should seem at present contrived rather for the purpose of confusing our ideas, than administering to their distinctness and arrangement. Instead of viewing them as the shadows, we mistake them for the substance.[94]

As we see, the "words" to which she refers here are also the "fictitious entities" or teachings of elites that are "contrived" for the "purpose of confusing" the people, passed off as sources of true knowledge when in fact they are not. These teachings gain power over people because they cannot be independently verified through empirical experience. As a result, the "words" are accepted at face value and mistaken for the "substance of knowledge."

That these "words" are "contrived" is a clear indication that whatever lessons they convey are artificial constructions devised by elites who seek to maintain their dominance in American society by whatever means necessary. For Wright, rich and powerful men deploy "hired servants" to disseminate messages that keep the American people in a state of perpetual ignorance and confusion, thereby neutralizing potential threats to their privileged status. The hired servants, in turn, are kept in a perpetual state of servitude because they depend on the elites for their livelihood and, ultimately, for their very existence. Wright explains:

> So long as the mental and moral instruction of man is left solely in the hands of hired servants of the public—let them be teachers of religion, professors of colleges, authors of books, or editors of journals or periodical publications, dependent upon their literary labours for their daily

bread, so long shall we hear but half the truth; and well if we hear so much. Our teachers, political, scientific, moral, or religious, our writers, grave or gay, are *compelled* to administer to our prejudices, and to perpetuate our ignorance. They dare not speak that which, by endangering their popularity, would endanger their fortunes.[95]

The wealthy and powerful are the "masters" of these hired servants because their interests and vanity determine the lessons of the day. "The rich and pampered few are ever spared, or so gently dealt with, as rather agreeably to tickle the ear, than to probe the conscience, while the crimes of the greatly-tempered, greatly-suffering poor, are visited with unrelenting vigour."[96] The poor, in turn, cannot overcome their subjugation because they are deprived of the kind of education that would encourage freethinking and independent inquiry—the very sort of education Wright proposes as the key to reform. The result of this dynamic is the perpetuation of gross hypocrisy in America between the founding principles of equality and freedom, on the one hand, and the radically uneven application of those principles in American practice, on the other.

Wright expands her analysis to address the corruption of elites in America through their pursuit of profit and power at the expense of truth and the apparent willingness of the American populace to accept their moral and political proclamations at face value rather than recognizing them for the self-serving platitudes that, for Wright, they clearly are. The main victims of this corruption are the most disenfranchised: slaves and women. Indeed, in the preface to her lectures, Wright explicitly links these two forms of oppression. "American negro slavery," she declares, "is but one form of the same evils which pervade the whole frame of human society. . . . It has its source in ignorance."[97] In the same passage she mentions another evil caused by ignorance in the form of "that worst species of quackery, practiced under the name of religion," namely, "the neglected state of the female mind and the consequent dependence of the female condition."[98]

Throughout the lectures Wright continually points to examples in which women are kept subordinate by a vast array of institutional mechanisms of oppression constructed by male elites and perpetuated by their hirelings. Although she is pleased by the increasing numbers of women in her audience, Wright is fully aware that true equality remains elusive, "nor is the ignorance of our sex matter of surprise, when efforts, as violent as unrelaxed, are everywhere made for its continuance." Again, it is the "appointed teachers and professional men" who are behind these "efforts."[99] One of the most destructive teachings used to subordinate American women is the biblical teaching of the Fall, in which Eve is held responsible for the sins of mankind by seeking knowledge. The woman who hears these stories is afflicted with "agitated fancy," not sober fact; she imagines hearing "the voice of a god in thunders," not the thunder itself; "she sees the yawning pit and, before behind, around, a thousand phantoms conjured from the prolific brain of insatiate priestcraft, confound, alarm, and overwhelm her reason."[100]

Wright insists that her purpose is not to replace one source of indoctrination with her own: She wishes "not to convince, [but] to *win attention*," for "could truth only be heard, the conversion of the ignorant were easy." The difficulty of her task is compounded by the fact that "the hired supporters of error understand" that their privilege relies on relatively flimsy ground as they desperately seek to maintain their position of dominance:

Well do they *know*, that if the daughters of the present and mothers of the future generation, were to drink of the living waters of knowledge, their reign would be ended—"their occupation gone." So well do they know it, that far from obeying to the letter the command of their spiritual leader, "Be ye fishers of men," we find them everywhere *fishers of women*. Their own sex, old and young, they see with indifference swim by their nets; but closely and warily are their meshes laid, to entangle the female of every age.[101]

Given the pervasiveness of socially constructed sources of inequality and oppression, it would not be surprising that a criticalist like Wright would describe a number of "negative externalities" for men as well. Whatever "psychological benefits" men receive in such a corrupt society blind them "to the fact that the system also levies material and moral taxes on them as individuals."[102] By describing members of the educated classes as "hired servants," Wright makes clear that these men fancy themselves to be all powerful when in reality they are completely dependent on those who supply their "daily bread." Turning her sights to ordinary men who are complicit in this scheme of corruption, Wright declares:

> Fathers and husbands! Do ye not also understand this fact? Do ye not see how, in the mental bondage of your wives and fair companions, ye yourselves are bound? Will ye fondly sport yourselves in your imagined liberty and say, "it matters not if our women be mental slaves?" Will ye pleasure yourselves in the varied paths of knowledge, and imagine that women, hoodwinked and unawakened, will make the better servants and the easier playthings?[103]

In the lecture, "Of Free Inquiry," Wright again highlights the false consciousness that arises among men who subordinate women: "Those who arrogate power usually think themselves superior *de facto* and *de jure*. Yet justly might it be a question whether those who ostensibly govern are not always unconsciously led." The oppression of women ultimately violates the self-interest of men as well: "Whenever we establish our own pretensions upon the sacrificed right of others, we do in fact impeach our own liberties, and lower ourselves in the scale of being!"[104] She appeals to men who delude themselves into thinking that the subordination of women "ensures their utility," explaining that the same argument is "employed by the ruling few against the subject many in aristocracies; by the rich against the poor in democracies; by the learned professions against the people in all countries."[105] Men are unwitting hypocrites when they use the very same arguments to oppress women that are used by elites to oppress ordinary men like themselves.

Critical race theory asserts that the expectation of privilege causes antagonism between lower-class whites and blacks.[106] Wright's criticalist account of women's oppression also observes the various tensions among men and women that are created and stoked by elites as another mechanism of domination. Wright explains that the ignorance arising from a reflexive reliance on received authority results in destructive resentment that needlessly pits men against women. She laments:

> How prone are we to come to the consideration of every question with heads and hearts preoccupied! How prone to shrink from any opinion, however reasonable, of our own! How disposed are we to judge, in anger,

those who call upon us to think, and encourage us to inquire! To question our prejudices, seems nothing less than sacrilege; to break the chains of our ignorance nothing short of impiety!

The same anger and resentment leads people to "deem it both a presumption and an impropriety for a woman to reason with her fellow creatures"—a woman, of course, like herself. The irony, explains Wright, is that "my sex and my situation tend rather to qualify than to incapacitate me for the undertaking" of calling for "the equal distribution of knowledge."[107] Men should realize that women are honest brokers. Women derive no tangible advantages from the teachings of male elites, Wright explains, so they are ultimately beholden to no one, in spite of their subordinate status. Yet men are blinded to the fact that women are their most trustworthy companions. In spite of their privileged status, men are beholden to the very same teachings that invest them with a false sense of superiority.

Throughout her criticalist account of the oppression of women, Wright continually draws from a kind of "interest convergence" theory as she tries to persuade men that it is in their best interest to secure equality for women. To a considerable degree, her efforts were successful. Wright's lectures were widely attended and discussed favorably in the American press. Her rhetorical prowess earned the admiration of commentators who marveled at her ability to speak extemporaneously to mixed audiences who were mesmerized by her boldness and acuity. Perhaps not surprisingly, however, she also experienced a devastating backlash from the established powers when their dominance is challenged and reforms are proposed. Critics labeled Wright "The Red Harlot of Infidelity," "the whore of Babylon," and even the "priestess of Beelzebub." A New York editor described her as a "bold blasphemer, and a voluptuous preacher of licentiousness . . . impervious to the voice of virtue, and case-hardened against shame!"[108] The epithet "Fanny Wrightist" was hurled at any public figure, female or male, whose ideas were deemed too unconventional or radical. One of the most devastating critiques came from an unlikely source, another female education reformer. Reflecting on Wright's stage presence, Catherine Beecher denounced her nemesis as one who "stands, with brazen front and brawny arms, attacking the safeguards of all that is venerable and sacred in religion, all

that is safe and wise in law, all that is pure and lovely in domestic virtue." Beecher concluded, "I cannot conceive any thing in the shape of a
woman, more intolerably offensive and disgusting."[109] It is notable that,
in her influential tract, *A Treatise on Domestic Economy* (1841), Beecher
draws extensively from Tocqueville's work to advance a view of feminine
domesticity in opposition to Harriet Martineau, the focus of chapter 2,
and other women's rights advocates, presumably including Wright.[110]
Like Tocqueville, who seeks to maintain hierarchical power dynamics
in American society, Beecher seeks to preserve traditional gender roles
among American men and women for the sake of the stability and security of the new nation. These examples of resistance among elites serve
as important reminders that although the critical feminist theory principles foreshadowed in Wright's analysis seem commonplace today, this
was certainly not the case in Jacksonian America.

## Wright's Method of Inquiry as Performative Pragmatism

Whereas Tocqueville's realization that racism is so deeply embedded
in the American project led him to view the possibility of reform in
extremely pessimistic terms, Wright's awareness of endemic racism
and sexism in America caused her to develop a comprehensive plan for
reform and to instruct mixed secular audiences throughout the country
in the art of independent thinking.

The "false consciousness" that accompanies white males' privileged
status "obscures [their] ability to live by the core values of the American
creed."[111] The results, Wright recognizes, are devastating: "We speak of
equality, and we are divided into classes; of self-government, and we fit
not ourselves to govern. We hear of law and legislation, and the mass of
the people understand not the one, and take no interest in the other." For
Wright, "equal representation" is impossible without "equal instruction."[112]
The evils of slavery and women's oppression have only one possible cure:

> The spread and increase of knowledge alone can enable man to distin-
> guish that the true interests of each point to the equal liberties, equal
> duties, and equal enjoyments of all; and that then only, will the principles
> set forth in the first national instrument of American government, the
> declaration of independence, be practically exhibited—when the law of

force shall give place to the law of reason, when wealth shall be the reward of industry, and all things shall be estimated in a ratio calculated in
the order of their utility.[113]

In her lectures, Wright portrays in vivid detail the vast system of
corruption in America and its impact on virtually every aspect of life.
She describes not only the mechanisms of oppression and their effects
on American society but the way in which corruption takes root in the
minds of individual citizens as well. Wright returns to the fundamental
confusion people experience when they are bombarded with "opposing
creeds and systems," each of which sustains elite privilege by "asserting
its claim to infallibility, and rallying around its standard pertinacious
disciples, enthusiastic proselytes, ardent apologists, fiery combatants,
obsequious worshippers, conscientious followers, and devoted martyrs."[114] The system of education in a corrupt society is part of the problem, not the solution. Its teachers are among the "hired servants" who
pass themselves off as experts and offer up useless abstractions as fundamental truths. Left vulnerable by a "pernicious education," individuals
are overwhelmed by the sheer variety of opinions and ideologies offered
by elites and are forced to accept these ideas at face value. Thus

> the more regularly a youth is trained in fashionable learning, the more
> confused is usually his perception of things, and the more prostrated his
> reason by the dogmatism of teachers, the sophism of words.[115]

When mere "words" or, in Benthamite terms, "fictitious entities" are
mistaken for "things" or empirically demonstrable "facts," individuals
are unable to distinguish between fact and opinion. As a result, "false
principles" or opinions are "engrafted by means of pretended science"
and misrepresent themselves as objectively true, and natural or "real
science" is "erroneously imparted" because it is "ostentatiously incul-
cated" through "the disguise of oral and written lessons instead of being
exposed, in practical illustrations, to the eye, and the ear, and the touch,
in the simple, incontrovertible fact."[116] Along similar lines, women fall
sway to the "useless investigations" and "fruitless inquiry" of religious
doctrines "which never can be answered" because they cannot be independently verified.[117] The knowledge women need to be full participants

in democratic society cannot be found through religious indoctrination but, rather, through experiential learning and observation.

Although we might expect that Bentham and Wright would reject the validity of "fictitious entities" altogether, given their pernicious effects on individuals and society, they do not. For Bentham, many important general terms and key concepts pertaining to law and to government, including justice, are "fictitious" because they acquire meaning through cultural practices and traditions, not through empirical experience.[118] Fictitious entities can have practical utility in buttressing "traditionalism and legitimacy," but they should never be considered "real" or factual.[119] Like Bentham, Wright urges her audience not to dismiss "fictitious entities" out of hand but, rather, to understand them properly, as opinions that can be independently verified to varying degrees. By applying Wright's method of inquiry, individuals know where opinions stand on the scale of demonstrable knowledge. For "exactly in proportion to the extent and accuracy of our knowledge, must be the justice of our opinions; and *vice versa*, that in equal proportion to our remissness in collecting, and carelessness in weighing, examining, comparing, and arranging facts, must be the error of our opinions."[120]

Only after understanding the distinction between facts and opinions are we in a position to "carry our investigations into the other branches of knowledge, according to our leisure, taste, and opportunity."[121] Wright claims that with adequate preparation we can

> engage in general reading with little risk of taking facts for granted without evidence, or receiving the visions of weak understandings for the lessons of wisdom. We may then, too, examine our opinions with some hope of discriminating between the erroneous and the correct; we may then change or form our opinions with good security for basing them on a solid foundation; we may then exercise our reason, for we shall have facts to exercise it upon; we may then compare popular creeds, and investigate unpopular doubts; we may then weigh all things in the balance of reason, seat our judgment on her throne, and listen to her decisions.[122]

We are also in a better position to evaluate the opinions of others. Friends "of tried veracity and approved judgment" are more reliable sources of opinion than those who are not adequately educated. Although trust can be established among individuals trained in inquiry, any secondhand knowledge should be "in a measure accorded," but it will be "considerably weakened" because it is removed "from the original sensations of the reported spectators."[123]

Wright's theory of knowledge redefines morality as well. Religious and political elites have in effect perpetrated a fraud by presenting moral truths as abstractions that appeal "only to the mind, or directly to the feelings"—as fictitious entities that are vulnerable to corruption—instead of "facts" that can be verified through individual experience and observation. Nowhere can we find a better example of this kind of moral corruption than the destructive effects of religious indoctrination on women who live in a constant state of fear of the unknown and the unverifiable.[124] Religious hypocrites in the form of overzealous "northern religionists" contribute further to the corruption of America. They viciously attack Southern slave owners, not because they truly want to end slavery, but rather because "denunciation against the vice of the south risks no patronage and wins cheap credit for humanity."[125] Referred to as a "religious physician," the abolitionist extremist "arraigns, tries, convicts, condemns—himself accuser, jury, judge, and executioner; nobly immolating interests which are not his, generously commanding sacrifices which he has not to share, indignantly anathematizing crimes which he cannot commit, and virtuously kindling the fires of hell to consume sinners, to whose sins, as he is without temptation, so *for* whose sins he is without sympathy."[126] The religious zealot panders to the emotions of his audience instead of actually doing something to end slavery, thereby avoiding any moral responsibility for his actions. For Wright, he has no real desire to "cure" his "patient" or rescue the enslaved. In fact, the corrupt abolitionist's diatribes, which alienate Southerners and appease Northerners, virtually guarantee that the original sin of slavery is left untouched.

Wright insists that morality should be founded, not on unverifiable abstractions, but on shared experience. No one can truly know the intentions or motivations of others because they cannot be proven. Empty assertions cannot be refuted. What can be verified, however, are the effects or consequences of individual action. For the "varying degree of sensibility evinced by individuals towards the joys and sorrows of others is apparent *to every observer* . . . [and] forms the basis of virtue; and when by means of experience we have distinguished painful from pleasurable sensations in our own case, this sensibility assists us to estimate them in the case of others."[127] Thus it is not the imagined motivations that determine morality, as elites would have it, but rather the observable "consequences of *our* actions" that are accessible to all.[128] Wright's reconfiguration of morality shifts power away from the elites and toward the people who are bound together by the simple ability to feel and observe. And it is "in this seeking of our own pleasure through the pleasure of others" that "the highest degree of active virtue" is found.[129]

Much like the American pragmatists who succeeded her, Wright's model of experiential learning is designed precisely to equip individuals with the tools they need for independent thinking and inquiry so that they may properly evaluate the teachings of others. Thus it is not merely an empirical body of knowledge that Wright offers, or some utopian scheme based on universal truths. Rather, Wright provides the foundation for a mode of inquiry that is consistent with American principles and that can help those principles inform action.[130] Wright's education provides training in an essential skill for a self-governing republic, namely, the ability to rely on one's own judgment in order to challenge self-serving elites. Wright is ultimately proposing an intensive method of inquiry and self-scrutiny that will best equip citizens—rich and poor, male and female, black and white—to enjoy the equality, freedom, and prosperity at the heart of the founding American principles. Wright's aim is not simply to create a new mindset but to inform political action as well. She provides the tools with which Americans can bridge the gap between the principles they profess to believe and the life they actually live, with all of its injustices. Only through experiential education can America actualize its own principles and change when needed. Key components of this reformed society are equality between men and women, the abolition of slavery, and economic justice.[131]

A final point that further highlights Wright's originality is the performative aspect of her theorizing. Her speeches were not treatises but, rather, performances that literally demonstrate the approach to knowledge and freethinking Wright advocates as a solution to the problems that plague Jacksonian society. Wright models freethinking and citizenship for others to make their own. The spectacle of Wright's performative knowledge, I believe, is the source of Whitman's admiration and the inspiration for his view of America as a spectacle of diversity. At the beginning of her first lecture, "On the Nature of Knowledge," offering herself up as a model for inquiry, Wright cautions:

> Let not the present audience imagine, that I am about to add one more to the already uncountable, unnamable systems, which distract the understandings of men, or to draw yet new doctrines and precepts from the fertile alembic of the human brain. I request you to behold in me an inquirer, not a teacher; one who conceives of truth as a jewel to be found, not to be coined; a treasure to be discovered by observation, and accumulated by careful, persevering industry, not invented and manufactured by learned art of aspiring quackery, like the once fashionable elixir of immortality and philosopher's stone. My object will be simply to *take with you* a survey of the field of human inquiry.[132]

For Wright, the proper role of an instructor is not to proselytize but, rather, "to fertilize the intellect with knowledge, and to leave it to draw, on all subjects, its own free, fair, and unbiased conclusions."[133]

Let us take Wright at her word, for the sake of argument, and reflect on the didactic effect of her theorizing on her audience. By the simple act of coming to hear Wright speak, the audience would already have to confront prevailing opinions and prejudices that they themselves doubtless held about women's traditional roles. Speaking confidently, clearly, and logically the tall Scottish redhead stood before them, as a direct challenge to the notion that women should not and could not speak in public. That she expressed herself so eloquently—a fact even her critics grudgingly admitted—discredited the pervasive idea that women were incapable of reasonable argument. As she drew from male theorists to devise her own ideas, Wright co-opted the male voice of the public realm and made it her own. The audience would rely on their own experience of perceiving Wright in order to challenge these preconceptions for themselves firsthand. Wright did not simply tell her audience that women could and should speak in public. Rather, the audience taught themselves this truth by experiencing and internalizing the powerful force of her example. Moreover, Wright served as a role model for those who wished to enter the realm of public speech but had hitherto been excluded—men and women, black and white. And she modeled the very approach to inquiry that she encouraged for others. Her descriptions of the plight of slaves served to remind those with firsthand experience of slavery and to provide a secondhand kind of experience, admittedly imperfect, to those who had never directly encountered its evils.[134]

Spectators were released from the authority of elites and the doctrines they sought to impose. Armed with the experience of hearing and seeing Wright, the audience was better positioned to examine, from the perspective of their own experiences and perceptions, the doctrines they received through formal education and especially from religious and political authorities. As they reflected on these teachings, individuals would be better able to assess their veracity. Although Wright clearly despised organized religions, dogmas, and ideologies, her aim was not simply to replace authoritative teachings with her own doctrines. Rather, her goal was to help others put these teachings in their proper place, namely, to recognize them as opinions, not facts, that could in turn be evaluated in terms of the benefits they offer and the happiness they provide to society as a whole.

Wright establishes a confluence between the thought process and social practices she prescribes, on the one hand, and the founding principles of America, on the other. From this standpoint, individuals would be in a better position to embrace freedom and equality not as a doctrine but, rather, as an actual experience and "fact of life." Her audience would be more open to granting greater rights and opportunities to women. Clearly, slavery would be scrutinized as well, with a view to ending it. We have already seen that Wright challenges the authorities that legitimize and perpetuate slavery by holding their arguments up to close scrutiny. For Northern audiences, Wright reminds her listeners of the experience of actually seeing freed slaves as the very kind of perception and observation that constitutes a fact and thereby challenges abstract and unfounded proslavery arguments. Even if their perceptions and experiences were not wholly sufficient to dispel the view of enslaved people as other, as less than equal, the audience would likely be more open to the possibility of seeing them as equal human beings because the authorities that have argued otherwise have been forcefully challenged in a way they had never experienced.

## Wright's Legacy Reconsidered

Given the complexity of Wright's theory, and the active power of her example, perhaps now we can better appreciate Whitman's seemingly extravagant reflections on Wright and her critics years after her death:

> She was a brilliant woman, of beauty and estate, who was never satisfied unless she was busy doing good—public good, private good . . . a woman of the noblest make-up whose orbit was a great deal larger than theirs— too large to be tolerated for long by them: a most maligned, lied about character—one of the best in history though also one of the least understood . . . we all loved her: fell down before her.

Whitman adds, "I never felt so glowingly towards any other woman. She was one of the few characters who excite in me a wholesale respect and love; she was beautiful in bodily shape and gifts of soul."[135] For Whitman, it is as if Wright quite literally embodied the union of the physical and the spiritual, which forms the basis of his own understanding of democratic citizenship.[136]

In a fitting epitaph that rivals Wright's own, Ernestine Rose declared that

> Frances Wright was the first woman in this country who spoke on the equality of the sexes. She had indeed a hard task before her. The elements were entirely unprepared. She had to break up the time-hardened soil of conservatism, and her reward was sure—the same reward that is always bestowed upon those who are in the vanguard of any great movement. She was subjected to public odium, slander, and persecution. But these were not the only things she received. Oh, she had her reward—that reward of which no enemies could deprive her, which no slanders could make less precious—the eternal reward of knowing that she had done her duty.[137]

In Whitman's admiration of the "brilliant" spectacle that was Wright's performative inquiry, and in Rose's celebration of her perseverance in the face of adversity, we realize the scope and significance of Wright's contributions to the struggle to end slavery and the oppression of women—and the true nature of the controversies that surrounded her. Through her words and deeds, Wright broke the "time-hardened soil" of moral, intellectual, and political complacency in America and laid a path for reformers and activists who would follow. Her defiant insistence on lifting the "Claud-Lorraine tint" shrouding the disjunction between America's professed ideals and the reality of systemic oppression advances our understanding of the American project. And indeed, her stubborn sense of duty to the cause of women's equality would reward her with a place on the frontispiece of *History of Woman Suffrage*, the first formal account of the early women's rights movement in America.

## 2

# Harriet Martineau on the Theory and Practice of Democracy in America

Frances Wright was not the only female European visitor who would offer a penetrating critique of Jacksonian America. Harriet Martineau, an English writer, traveled to America in 1834, as Wright retreated to an unhappy private life in Paris with her husband and newborn daughter, roughly two and a half years after Tocqueville's visit. Like Wright and Tocqueville, Martineau wrote to wide acclaim about her journey, publishing a three-volume study, *Society in America* (1837), a sequel, *Retrospect of Western Travel* (1838), and a treatise explaining her theoretical approach, *How to Observe: Morals and Manners* (1838). Like Tocqueville and Wright, Martineau was an ardent opponent of slavery and developed a comprehensive approach to reform that would tap into America's foundational principles properly understood. Martineau counted the work of Adam Smith as one of many influences on her political thought, as did Wright.

Like Wright, Martineau was a staunch advocate of women's rights and a path breaker in her own right. One of the most prolific professional female writers in the nineteenth century, Martineau wrote over two thousand articles in her lifetime, published over a dozen books on a wide range of topics, and earned sufficient income from her work to support herself financially. This, in spite of struggling with health problems so severe as to leave her bedridden for several years, only to recover with the intervention of mesmerism, all of which she carefully documented in her writings.

Martineau's life and work were in many ways a series of contradictions, which have spurred competing and equally contradictory interpretations. Martineau was virtually a celebrity in her lifetime, in spite of her constant self-effacement. Like many other female thinkers of the time, she was characterized—and even categorized herself—as a "popularizer" of the ideas of others. Her *Illustrations of Political Economy*

(1832)—which sought to make the complex ideas of Robert Malthus, David Ricardo, James Mill, John Stuart Mill, and Adam Smith more accessible to popular audiences—was enormously successful. Martineau also translated and condensed Auguste Comte's six-volume work *Positive Philosophy* to widespread acclaim. Yet critics have seized upon her popularity and self-proclaimed status as a "popularizer" to undermine her reputation as a serious and original thinker.

The sheer number of thinkers who influenced Martineau, combined with the staggering volume of writings she produced in her lifetime, contribute to the view of Martineau's ideas as merely a derivative hodge-podge of theories lacking any coherent or comprehensive worldview. Martineau's *How to Observe* is perhaps "the first book on the methodology of social research in the then still unborn disciplines of sociology and anthropology."[1] And yet even one of her most sympathetic commentators contends that, contrary to the book's title, it "devotes far more space to what one should observe in a society . . . than to the philosophical foundations of social investigation."[2] Along similar lines, Martineau's *Illustrations of Political Economy* has often not been seen as a theoretically sophisticated analysis of political economy but, rather, as an edifying tale to allay popular fears about economic progress.[3]

Similarly contradictory views have been expressed about *Society in America*. Hailed as "among the most thorough sociological studies of a society in the nineteenth century," Martineau's three volume work

> investigated government and politics, all sectors of the economy and the social institutions, "Civilization" as she called them. She described the structure or "apparatus" of each institution and then analyzed the actual functioning or operation of these structures, particularly in terms of the values and principles which were being articulated.[4]

But for others, *Society in America* "did not much rise above a party pamphlet. . . . The book was something of a hybrid, part social treatise, part moral tract, with chapters on the economy, rural labour, and religion." Martineau's "chapters on government were strangely inconsequential, given that she had talked to leading American politicians, including James Madison." And in spite of the fact that "Martineau was, in fact, far ahead of" her contemporary Tocqueville "on the issue of women's rights and more engaged in the campaign to abolish slavery . . . as she said of herself, she could popularize but had limited powers of the imagination and 'nothing approaching genius.'" Therefore, "one cannot look to her for a theory of US society, which perhaps explains her neglect of the more speculative Tocqueville," whose "expansive analysis of the United States was to have provided repercussions for transatlantic attitudes."[5]

Faced with this divergence of views, it is important to recognize that Martineau occupied a unique position that overlapped several cultural realms and that her work drew from different genres that observe conflicting norms as well.[6] An important part of her "popularizing" was to combine the intellectually rigorous "objective" style of male-dominated public writing in her reviews and essays with elements of "feminine" writing, especially didactic fiction. In *Illustrations of Political Economy*, for instance, Martineau appropriates the genre of the "little book," a "short, didactic tale offering a simple life history, or segment of history, told in lively language and set within a clear interpretive framework," thereby rendering complex theories of political economy accessible to popular audiences.[7] Thus Martineau

> demystified upper-class, "masculine" language, and she achieved this by introducing "feminine" language to it. By publishing narratives that made economic principles comprehensible to the average reader, Martineau demonstrated that theory was deficient without narrative and, in the process, toppled the hierarchy of "masculine" and "feminine" language initially taken for granted by her contemporaries and by recent critics.[8]

Martineau also "constructed a contradictory role for the woman activist that was neither strictly public nor private." By "writing in the privacy of her own home, she could make a living and participate in public debates while still avoiding the accusation of egotism and personal bias. At the same time, by participating in public debates as a journalist, she could influence the direction of society as a whole."[9] Thus Martineau "stands out as deviating from the dominant model of women's authorship: she writes on topics traditionally disallowed; enters the arena of politics dominated by men; and thus represents a new style of woman writer" who was deplored by male "professional authors" because she "disrupted" professional norms.[10] Martineau "conceived of her work as *visibly* engaged in shaping legislation and government policy. The *Illustrations* . . . treated topics of current political interest" that were well received not only by broad swaths of the public, but by British politicians who sought her advice as well. This led Martineau to believe that "her *Political Economy Tales* had an impact on the Reform of 1832 and on subsequent reforms of the poor laws and laws of taxation."[11]

Martineau's complex insider-outsider status has also deeply influenced the ways in which her contributions to the early women's rights movement have been perceived.[12] "Although Martineau was a lifelong advocate of women's rights, she disapproved of feminists who drew attention to their personal lives in their work," including Wollstonecraft (and presumably Wright), whose intellectual contributions had been overshadowed by her scandalous reputation. Martineau "actively sought anonymity and objectivity in her work as a means of distancing her gender and identity from her writing," not necessarily to deny her femininity, but rather to allow her "to express a more 'objective' perspective on women's issues and to communicate her ideas to a mixed-gender audience." Thus "through various forms of low-profile activism, Martineau defined feminism as an activity, rather than as a public identity, which would enable women to criticize oppressive social conditions without having to assume roles as 'public women.'"[13]

In spite of her best efforts to steer clear of controversy, Martineau's apparent support for Malthus's theories, such as delaying marriage and childbirth, combined with her own decision to remain unmarried, invited vitriolic attacks by critics who saw her, among other things, as unfeminine.[14] The accuracy of Martineau's "popularized" versions of Malthus's work has come under scrutiny as well, as "many of his supporters, Martineau included, likewise misread him and took his theories to extremes."[15] However, the extent to which Martineau is culpable for Malthus's compromised reputation has been questioned by interpreters who see far more ambiguities and complexities in her work. It is plausible that Martineau raises as many questions about the reforms as she answers in her writings, which "show the texture of pressures and loyalties that surround the poor law illustrating the complex web of social debts and responsibilities that are transacted through relief."[16]

My examination of Martineau's work expands on these trends. Like many commentators, I see deeper purpose in Martineau's "popularizing" that allows her to make important and original theoretical contributions while acknowledging her debt to other thinkers. The combination of genres and perspectives in Martineau's writings is not a sign of intellectual inconsistency but, rather, an indication of the sophistication and complexity of her thought. Martineau's didactic tools are designed to actively engage a variety of audiences on multiple levels. Although her ideas have an underappreciated theoretical depth, they are also geared toward pragmatic change.

In this chapter I show that Martineau's "popularization" of Adam Smith's works extends far beyond merely summarizing his economic principles for a popular audience. Indeed, Martineau expands on Smith's moral theory of sympathy and uses it as a tool to analyze the intractable problems facing American society with the hope of solving them. Smith's writings, like Martineau's, draw from multiple genres and perspectives to engage his audience in a process of moral reform. However, Martineau augments Smith's moral theory by adding a fundamentally and explicitly dialectical component to the concept of sympathy and by applying this revised understanding of sympathy specifically to the study of American democracy. Martineau's explorations of the relation between sympathy and America's founding principles, such as majority rule, provide the foundation of her insightful critique of slavery and the status of American women. By developing a theory of sympathy that is explicitly dialectical, Martineau advances an appropriately sophisticated understanding of morality that can shed important light on the complexities of Jacksonian America, with its increasing plurality and diversity, and on other developing cultures as well.

The first part of this chapter explores the ways in which Martineau expands Smith's moral theory into both a powerful tool for sociopolitical analysis and a foundational principle of democratic practice. The chapter examines how Martineau applies her theory to the study of American democracy, focusing on the relation between her view of sympathy and America's founding principles, her understanding of majority rule, and her critiques of slavery and the status of American women. By exploring Martineau's analysis of American democracy in detail, this study honors the spirit of her original intention to title her three-volume work

*Theory and Practice of Society in America*, namely, her desire that the work be seen as a serious attempt to link her moral and political theory to American democratic practice.[17]

## Martineau's Moral Theory: Beyond Smith's Moral Sentiments

Martineau's reliance on the economic principles espoused by Adam Smith in *An Inquiry into the Nature and Causes of the Wealth of Nations* (1776) has been widely recognized.[18] This is not surprising, given the admiration for Smith she expresses in her earlier work *Illustrations of Political Economy* and her explicit reference to Smith early on in *How to Observe*, where she borrows his comparison of the economies of Spain, Portugal, and Poland to explain the ways in which economic systems affect the structures of particular societies. Overlooked, however, is Martineau's theoretical and methodological reliance on the moral philosophy advanced by Smith in *The Theory of Moral Sentiments*. In *How to Observe*, Martineau goes on to critique the theory of the moral sense and elaborate on the concept of sympathy—themes that are also explored in great detail by Smith in *Moral Sentiments*. Martineau even cites Smith as a model of the "philosophic observer," whose perspective she adopts throughout the rest of the book, noting that he "sets out with a more philosophical belief" than his rivals.[19] But in engaging Smith's philosophical principles outlined in *Moral Sentiments*, Martineau improves on his moral theory as well.

Martineau opens *How to Observe* with a critique of the popular notion of the moral sense, the view that moral principles are "fixed and immutable" and therefore "all ought to agree as to what is sin and virtue in every case."[20] The problem with the moral sense, for Martineau, is that, in positing a universal and absolute system of moral principles, it fails to account for the wide range of differences across historical ages and cultures, thereby blinding the observer by forcing her to disapprove of behavior that is foreign to her experience instead of trying to understand it. The adherent to the moral sense doctrine sees "sin" where there is only "difference" and suffers the "agitation of being shocked and alarmed" at strange sights rather than preserving her "calmness," "hope," and "sympathy."[21] Smith also criticizes the theory of the moral sense in the concluding section of *Moral Sentiments* (*TMS*, VII.iii.3). Underlying Smith's ultimate rejection of moral sense theory is his acute recognition of the complexity and diversity of human behavior (*TMS*, VII. iii.3.15–16).

In rejecting the theory of the moral sense, Martineau argues that "every man's feelings of right and wrong, instead of being born with him, grow up in him from the influences to which he is subjected." Yet she maintains that "knowing that some influences act upon the minds of all people in all countries, [the observer] looks every where for certain feelings of right and wrong which are as sure to be in all men's minds as if they were born with them." Thus, for example, it "is considered wrong all over the world . . . to torment another without any reason, real or imaginary." By contrast, "to make others happy is universally considered right."[22] By replacing the traditional basis for universal morality, an inborn sense of right and wrong, with another source, a universality of certain general influences that affect people in similar ways, Martineau takes virtually the same step as did Smith, according to whom the human reaction to circumstances forms the basis of universal moral principles. For both, morality is "part of humanity's adaptation to the circumstances in which it happens to find itself."[23]

Equally important to human experience in Martineau's moral theory is the unifying principle of human nature, the desire for happiness. "The external conveniences of men," Martineau writes, "their internal emotions and affections, their social arrangements, graduate in importance precisely in proportion as they affect the general happiness of the section of the race among whom they exist."[24] There are, however, myriad ways in which different cultures pursue happiness. Martineau insists that the observer "must not allow himself to be perplexed or disgusted by seeing the great ends of human association pursued by means which he could never have devised, and to the practice of which he could not reconcile himself."[25] Rather, the particular practices of a given society should be evaluated in terms of their role in advancing the happiness of the members of that society. "To test the morals and manners of a nation by a reference to the essentials of human happiness," she concludes, "is to strike at once to the centre, and to see things as they are."[26] For Smith, as well as for Martineau, assessing the morality of any action requires a view of how the motives, reactions, and consequences contribute to "the happiness either of the individual or of the society" (*TMS*, VII.iii.3.16).

The most important element of convergence between Smith and Martineau is the central concept of sympathy. For Martineau, sympathy—or "openness" to "hearts and minds"—when "untrammeled and unreserved," allows the observer to recognize underlying universal predispositions in others who may appear to be vastly different from herself but who nevertheless exhibit "hearts, generous or selfish, pure or gross, happy or sad." Through sympathy, "the action of the heart will meet a corresponding action, and . . . the nature of the heart will meet a corresponding nature." Sympathy thus opens the way to interaction, as "openness and warmth of heart [are] greeted with openness and warmth."[27]

For Smith, the moral sentiments of mankind are founded upon acts of the imagination in which, through sympathy, we share in the emotions that motivate the actions we observe and in the emotions of those who are affected by those actions (*TMS*, Introduction, 9). Smith's related concept of the "impartial spectator" explains how people determine what constitutes proper behavior for themselves by distancing themselves from a given situation. Although complete detachment is implied in Smith's explanation, sympathy nevertheless mitigates this detachment because we must view our own sentiments and motives "with the eyes of other people, or as other people are likely to view them" (*TMS*, III.1.2).

Although the concept of sympathy occupies a central role in the moral theories of both Martineau and Smith, their respective understandings of the concept differ. Smith's theory emphasizes imaginary rather than actual experience. Observers must assume that they have sufficiently understood the perspective of the other to make appropriate moral judgments. There is not necessarily any real interaction between observer and observed. The act of sympathy is primarily an internal, psychological, speculative process that emphasizes the role of the self over the other as the former adopts the position of the latter in her imagination. This is why, as Smith himself admits, the feelings of those who sympathize are by necessity "weaker in degree" than the feelings of those who actually experience them (*TMS*, I.i.2). Given the role of speculation and the relative subordination of the other in Smith's principle of sympathy, it is likely that behavior and actions that are familiar to the observer will inspire happiness and approval, while behavior and actions that are unfamiliar will arouse unhappiness and disapproval. Thus, when it comes to discovering underlying principles of goodness and evil in cultures that are vastly different from one's own, Smith's moral theory is limited. Smith's sympathetic observer may encounter difficulties in placing oneself in the shoes of someone of the opposite sex, or of a different race, or of a radically different socioeconomic status and accurately understanding that person's position. Although the impartial spectator is designed to allow individuals to engage in self-reflection from the relatively detached standpoint of society at large, it, too, can foster a kind of "echo chamber" in which individuals confuse their personal biases with those of society.[28] Martineau's theory of sympathy explicitly preserves the integrity of the self and the other to a greater degree than Smith's. Since Martineau's observers do not simply imagine themselves in the other's shoes but instead seek greater understanding of the other through direct engagement and observation of "corresponding openness," there is a greater opportunity to acknowledge the other's identity in the act of sympathizing. Martineau's observers do not have to reconcile themselves to imagining that they accurately understand the position of those who are observed. Instead, the observed are actually recognized largely on their own terms.[29]

To better understand why this is so, it is important to recognize the centrality of discourse, and its relation to sympathy, in Martineau's moral theory. To be sure, the *Lectures on Rhetoric and Belles Lettres* show that Smith's moral theory includes a theory of rhetoric. However, as with other elements of his moral theory, his views on rhetoric still focus primarily on the effects of various rhetorical practices on the imagination. Martineau understands discourse broadly to include not only actual speaking but listening to and observing "the instructive commentary on all the facts of life."[30] The importance of dialogue in Martineau's moral theory is underscored in the penultimate chapter, aptly titled "Discourse." There, she proclaims, "The Discourse of individuals is an indispensable commentary upon the classes of national facts which the traveller has observed." Martineau is careful to emphasize that discourse must be supplemented with a solid understanding of the "facts" of that society. Otherwise, the observer will soon be overwhelmed by the "diversity that there is in men's minds" and "the narrowness of the mental vision of each as he stands in a crowd." But "general facts" provide "certain fixed points . . . round which testimony may gather."[31]

For Martineau, discourse serves as "an instructive commentary" on society also because it shows "what interests the people most," but only if the observer "goes with a free mind and an open heart" and "commits himself to his *sympathies* . . . with those about him."[32] This combination of sympathy and discourse is powerful enough to overcome even government-imposed restrictions on "communication." For Martineau insists that human beings "cannot but speak of what interests them most to those who most share the interest"—that is, those who are sympathetic.[33] The interrelation between sympathy, dialogue, and objective "facts" provides a rich and accurate view of the pressing issues faced by a given society. Clearly, Martineau's theory goes beyond speculation and entails active engagement with others whose perspectives are largely preserved.

Martineau later underscores the rewards of open discourse in gaining insight into the fundamental questions that preoccupy a given society.[34] Moreover, the advantages of "conversing with the leaders on both sides of great questions," those who have reflected most on "all the facts of the case," are immeasurable. For

> there is, perhaps, scarcely one great subject of national controversy which, thus opened to him, would not afford him glimpses into all the other general affairs of the day; and each time that his mind grasps a definite opposition of popular opinion, he has accomplished a stage in his pilgrimage of inquiry into the tendencies of a national mind.[35]

Finally, at the conclusion of *How to Observe*, Martineau reiterates the importance of sympathy and applies the principle specifically to her own authorial action, namely, the act of discoursing about discourses. The purpose of a travel journal, for Martineau, is not simply to "record facts" but, rather, "to reflect the mind of a traveller, and give back to him hereafter the image of what he thought and felt day by day," guided by his queries but not limited by them.[36] Explicitly connecting the moral principle of sympathy to the "mechanics" of observation, namely writing, Martineau draws her book to a close:

> Sympathy by itself may do much: with fit intellectual and mechanical aids, it cannot but make the traveller a wise man. His journey may be

but for a brief year . . . but if, by his own sympathy, he grasps and brings home to himself the life of a fresh portion of his race, he gains a wisdom for which he will be the better for ever.[37]

These remarks suggest that Martineau's written account of America is itself an extension of the moral principle of sympathy. Although Martineau's journals and notebooks no longer exist, *Society in America* strongly resembles a journal, with its relatively loose organization and abundance of colorful anecdotes and descriptions. Specifically, *Society in America* can be characterized as a deliberate effort on Martineau's part to apply her moral theory for her readers, who may not be able to visit America themselves or have the experiences she had. Martineau allows the general characteristics and tendencies of American society to emerge by presenting all types of Americans speaking their minds and revealing their genuine interests, which in turn reflect the interests of the nation as a whole. Martineau appeals to the sympathy of her audience by opening her mind and provoking corresponding openness. She wants her readers to hear private conversations as if they were actually present, to corroborate the "facts" of American culture and society with the behavior they observe indirectly through Martineau's compelling descriptions and directly as she inserts herself into her own narrative. She reminds them of the underlying shared values of humankind, such as the desire for happiness, so they are not forgotten in the overwhelming diversity of human behavior. This is what allows Martineau to provide a compelling defense of majority rule, abolitionism, and greater rights for American women.

Smith's moral theory does not explicitly privilege the role of discourse or engagement in the same way that Martineau's does. As a result, his theory is more limited in addressing the social and political challenges of a given society. There is no equivalent in Smith's moral theory of the Socratic dialogue, for instance, which allows individuals to directly confront "misleading preconceptions," "prejudices," and "ignorance" and which would provide a necessary supplement to Smith's theory by helping individuals "evaluate the social or political system as a whole" and thereby transcend the limits of their particular groups to form a larger moral community.[38] With its emphasis on interaction and discourse, Martineau's approach incorporates precisely the dialectical, discursive elements that are lacking in Smith's work.[39]

A closer look at Smith's treatment of issues such as slavery and the status of women reveals even more clearly the potential limitations of his theory in addressing the challenges the young American republic would face. Instead of applying his moral principle of sympathy directly to attack slavery, Smith chooses to condemn it on vaguely utilitarian grounds (*WN*, III.ii.8–9). Nor does Smith clearly employ his moral theory to better understand the inequality of women, restricting his comments to a brief exploration of the relation between female virtue of humanity and the male virtue of generosity (*TMS*, IV.2.10). And although the virtue of the "fair sex" appears inferior when compared to its masculine counterpart, Smith later distinguishes barbarous and civilized societies based on the feminine criterion of humanity, not generosity (*TMS*, V.2.7–9). Yet he does not explore the larger ramifications of this analysis in any further detail. Smith's understanding of sympathy encourages observers to assume they understand the position of the other without necessarily verifying their knowledge through interaction or "discourse." As a result, Smith's observer, who must place himself in the shoes of the other largely through an act of imagination, is more captive to his own prejudices and more likely to lose sight of the integrity of the other. And because the position of the impartial spectator largely reinforces the status quo, it is equally unlikely to challenge the beliefs of societies that oppress slaves and women. It is possible, therefore, that the passivity of slaves and the acquiescence of women will be mistaken for acceptance of their unequal treatment.

Martineau's moral theory is more explicitly dialectical than Smith's, both literally and figuratively. Martineau's theory of sympathy rests on the claim that discourse serves as a window into the fundamental characteristics of a given society. It allows the diversity of a given community to reveal itself, freely and directly, even in the most despotic of circumstances. As shall become clear, Martineau's *Society in America* demonstrates how American discourse quickly reveals the essential tensions over slavery and the oppression of women, which in turn raise fundamental questions about the "social or political system as a whole." Thus, when Martineau appeals to the imagination through her writing, it is not merely to demand that observers or readers, through their own devices, place themselves in the shoes of another but rather to reproduce the experience of interaction with others for her readers through examples, anecdotes, and conversations. Martineau's strategic deployment of the first person reproduces this experience for her readers in a direct and poignant way. Martineau uses the imagination as a tool through which those who are observed share their experiences with readers so that they may be better understood.[40]

Unlike most commentators on early America who appeal to Scottish Enlightenment philosophy—specifically, Adam Smith's theory of economics—to mitigate the effects of an increasingly diverse commercial society, Martineau appeals to Smith's moral theory and applies it directly to America, with intriguing results.[41] Through the innovations she makes to Smith's work, Martineau improves upon competing accounts of American democracy, such as Tocqueville's concerning majority rule, slavery, and the role of women.

## Sympathy, Majority Rule, and Democracy in America

Martineau's moral theory animates *Society in America* from the outset. Her goal is "to compare the existing state of society in America with the principles on which it is professedly founded; thus testing Institutions, Morals, and Manners by an indisputable, instead of an arbitrary standard."[42] The fundamental American principles are, of course, "the inalienable right of all the human race to life, liberty, and the pursuit of happiness." America's devotion to the pursuit of happiness coincides directly with Martineau's moral theory in *How to Observe*, which posits that all human beings desire happiness but pursue it in different ways. Martineau notes that America is the first example in history of a government "deduced from the principles of human nature" as well as the "experience of man in governments," including "despotisms, oligarchies, and the mixtures of these with small portions of democracy."[43] Because America uniquely combines the fundamental principle of human happiness with the "small portions" of past experience in democracy, it is the first country to have developed "the capacity of mankind for self-government," which had hitherto been impossible.[44] America's capacity for self-government is based on the golden rule, "Do unto others as ye would that they should do unto you."[45] As we shall see, this capacity for self-government is, for Martineau, rooted in the moral principle of sympathy, as the observance of the golden rule itself suggests.

Martineau applies her theory of sympathy to her account of American democracy by observing American democracy on its own terms as well as her own.[46] She engages in extensive "fact finding" about America by consulting the Constitution; the Declaration of Independence; the *Federalist Papers*; correspondence between the Founders, especially James Madison and Thomas Jefferson; Jefferson's *Notes on Virginia*; and of course, her own extensive personal experiences.[47] One of Martineau's most important sources of information on American institutions is the tutorial she received from the frail Madison at the twilight of his life.[48] Indeed, the problems examined in Martineau's study of America mirror those that troubled Madison himself.[49] Finally, the dialectical aspect of Martineau's theory allows her to insert herself directly into the narrative by using the first person at key points in discussions of majority rule, slavery, and American women, thereby heightening the poignancy and effectiveness of her account.

At the core of Martineau's account is her understanding of the principle that "the majority will be in the right," which is buttressed with the concept of sympathy.[50] A key weakness of democratization and majority rule Martineau observes among Americans is a kind of social conformism and general "deficiency of moral independence" resulting from an overreliance on public opinion. Rather than thinking for themselves, Americans often seek a surrogate for the vigorous moral leadership provided in former ages by the aristocracy or the feudal sovereign. Thus majority tyranny for Martineau does not arise within the majority per se but rather stems from an aristocratic minority steeped in the teachings of "the remains of feudalism" that dominates public opinion by squelching dissent.[51] In this way, the vocal minority constitutes an "anomaly" that is the exception to majority rule.

Martineau illustrates this concept with an anecdote aimed at defending majority rule against critics, especially Europeans, who long for the reestablishment of aristocratic preeminence in what they perceive to be a young, disorderly nation. In describing the case of an attack on William Lloyd Garrison by a violent mob in Boston, which she witnessed firsthand, Martineau challenges the notion that the people at large are to blame. To provide a full picture of the incident, Martineau puts her discourse-based understanding of sympathy into practice, relaying the conversations she had about the attack with a university president, a leading Boston lawyer and two of his students, and a prominent judge.[52] From these interactions, she discovers that it is in fact a minority, the wealthy Northern elite who have economic and social ties to the slave-owning South, that engages in antiabolitionist lawbreaking, while it is the majority of people whose liberties, especially free speech, are actually threatened.[53] Thus while it might appear that the abolitionists are the minority faction and that the destructive mobs who oppose them reflect the will of the majority, Martineau argues that the reverse is true, based on her personal observation and open interaction with others.

How does the true majority reassert its supremacy? For Martineau, Americans must reject their reliance on these aristocratic minorities and instead tap into their sympathetic virtues: "mutual respect and deferences" and "mutual helpfulness." More in keeping with their democratic character and their nation's founding principles, these resources will ultimately lift Americans "above their personal selfishness and mutual subservience."[54] As the "disturbance" over Garrison suggests,

> If there be any anomaly among the institutions of a republic, the function of the law is certain to be disturbed sooner or later: and that disturbance is usually the symptom by the exhibition of which the anomaly is first detected, and then cured.[55]

For the true will of the majority to be expressed, however, it is crucial that these disturbances and anomalies be brought to the attention of the American people, presumably by writers such as Martineau and other like-minded activists:

> It takes some time to awaken the will of the majority; and till it awakes, the interest of the faction is active, and overbears the law. The retribution is certain; the result is safe. But the evils meanwhile are so tremendous, that no exertion should be spared to open the eyes of the majority to the insults offered to its will.[56]

Martineau's account of majority rule appeared less than two years after Tocqueville's description in volume 1 of *Democracy in America*. There is no evidence that Martineau read Tocqueville's first volume at that time.[57] And although Tocqueville was aware of Martineau's book, he refused to read it.[58] Nevertheless, like Martineau, Tocqueville describes the tyranny of the majority in terms of excessive conformism and selfishness. And Tocqueville, too, proposes a kind of sympathetic engagement as part of the solution to the problem of majority tyranny. For Tocqueville, service on juries teaches men "equity in practice" because "each man, when judging his neighbor, thinks that he may be judged himself."[59] Along similar lines, regular participation in governmental and other associations serves to instruct Americans to attach themselves to their respective communities.[60] Religion serves to preserve majority rule by encouraging a kind of tolerance of the variety of religious practices observed in America that nevertheless rests on "the same morality in the name of God."[61] Religion also instills in the American man the "habit" of "regulating his opinions and his tastes" by mirroring the stability and order he finds in his own marriage and family.[62] Religion thus serves as a limit to the imagination, which would otherwise run rampant in the face of the constant upheaval in American law.[63] Tocqueville characteristically balances these democratic solutions with a more aristocratic one by portraying lawyers as an elite influence on the people through their mastery of the law and legal tradition. For Tocqueville, the American people create binding ties through activities that transcend self-interest through association. These ties both facilitate majority rule and limit it by creating intermediary associations between individual and state. Yet limitation of majorities goes only so far.

The final chapter of the 1835 volume of *Democracy in America*, "The Three Races," demonstrates the challenges posed to American sympathy by the fundamental injustices of slavery and racism.[64] Whatever sympathetic understanding is gained through formal institutions such as jury duty is not extended to slaves, whose mores seem to be utterly different from those of white Anglo-Americans. Christianity has been used to abolish and reestablish slavery in a "restricted" way, according to Tocqueville, so the power of religion to provide a clear-cut message against slavery is severely compromised.[65] The general "enlightenment" of American society, whether from the elite influence of lawyers or the well-grounded character of the common man, is incapable of eliminating lingering prejudice against slaves.[66] In the face of these intractable problems, Tocqueville concludes with a less than satisfying assurance that the American republic based on majority rule properly understood will ultimately prevail somehow—even if the Union does not.[67] As I have discussed in chapter 1, it is because Tocqueville envisions racism as endemic to American culture that he is so deeply skeptical of any possible solution short of "a complete dismantling of the system."[68]

Martineau's understanding of the shortcomings of American majority rule is no less clear-eyed or critical. However, she applies her interpretation of Smith's theory of sympathy to majority rule in America to provide an alternative understanding that does address intractable problems such as slavery. If a vocal minority imposes its will on an apathetic majority, the potential solution rests in awakening the sentiments of the majority and encouraging it to appeal to its own sympathetic virtues. As the subsequent sections show, Martineau applies her discourse-based understanding of sympathy by relaying various anecdotes and conversations dealing with contentious issues to remind Americans of their nation's founding principles. In so doing, she implicitly encourages citizens to reconsider the nation's oppressive ways, thereby drawing on their own fundamental virtue of sympathy.

## Sympathy and Slavery in America

There are several similarities between Tocqueville's and Martineau's accounts of slavery in America. Both argue that slavery corrupts slave as well as master. Both deplore the lingering prejudice against freed slaves in the North and the self-destructive adherence to slavery in the South. Both express misgivings about the feasibility of colonization, a popular idea among antislavery advocates at the time. And both appeal to the economic interests of North and South in arguing against slavery. Indeed, Martineau should be added to the list of early "criticalists" who lay the groundwork for critical race theory that includes Tocqueville and Wright. In their own lives, Tocqueville and Martineau devoted considerable efforts to the abolitionist cause. Yet it is Martineau's application of her moral theory to the problem of slavery in America that ultimately distinguishes her account from Tocqueville's.

Martineau powerfully illustrates how slavery dehumanizes slave and master, young and old, male and female, black and white. In virtually every aspect of her attack on slavery, she provides vivid anecdotes, examples, conversations, and case studies that are designed to persuade readers of diverse perspectives that, in order to live up to its own fundamental principles, which are themselves images of the fundamental principles of humanity, America must abolish the institution. By building her argument around conversations about slavery, Martineau personalizes an otherwise abstract argument about principles in a way that brings the issue alive for the reader. She refuses to dismiss the arguments she encounters, no matter how nonsensical or hypocritical they may seem to her, and allows the reader to engage in the conversation. "Whenever I am particularly strongly convinced of anything in opposition to the opinion of any or many others," Martineau writes, "I entertain a suspicion that there is more evidence on the other side than I see." Professing to have heard "every argument that can possibly be adduced" both for and against slavery, she declares, "I know the whole of its theory;—a declaration that I dare not make with regard to, I think, any other subject whatever."[69] Her remarks correspond closely with the concluding passages of *How to Observe*, where she insists that the observer examine all aspects of a "national controversy" to gain a better understanding of the fundamental problems facing a given society.[70] By contrast, Tocqueville includes only one anecdote in the "Three Races" chapter that leaves the reader with a tragic sense of resignation and despair.[71] The deep racial conflict woven into American culture is lamentable yet virtually unsolvable.

Steadfastly eschewing such fatalism, Martineau is relentless in her pursuit of a deeper understanding of this seemingly intractable conflict, with the ultimate aim of breaking down barriers to reform. Thus, for instance, she uses the mob attack on the abolitionist Garrison as an opportunity to gain a fuller picture of the complex social forces driving the slavery debate by discussing the incident at length with a range of Boston citizens. She recounts a typical dialogue with a member of the Colonization Society in order to show why colonization advocates are mistaken.[72] Martineau relates her discussions with Chief Justice John Marshall, a slave-owning Virginian, in which he expressed hope that America would soon follow the example of England by abolishing slavery.[73] She goes to the trouble of recording five separate arguments justifying slavery, which were provided to her by "eminent men" of America, as well as a summary of a proslavery speech given by a South Carolina senator, and an editorial from a "highly esteemed southern newspaper."[74] Martineau even includes a section titled "Morals of Slavery," in which she reluctantly concedes that slave-owning societies unwittingly encourage the development of mercy, indulgence, and patience—although the vices of the society far outweigh its virtues. Martineau broadens the appeal of her abolitionism still further by providing a detailed economic critique of slavery, which targets those who would defend the practice on economic or pragmatic grounds.[75]

Martineau's moral theory, whose principle of sympathy encourages the use of concrete examples and anecdotal evidence to illuminate larger principles operating in American society, allows her to bring to life in poignant and revealing detail the central premise of the abolitionist argument: Slaves are human beings who deserve all the rights and benefits of American citizens.[76] Although Martineau observes numerous cases in which slaves behave in undesirable ways that may make emancipation unimaginable to some, she also relates important instances in which slaves flourish when freed from their oppressive circumstances. Through this juxtaposition, the true humanity of slaves is allowed to emerge, and it becomes immediately clear that their nature has been systematically distorted by the repressive conditions in which they live. Their full humanity is masked by their inhumane environment.[77] Martineau thus appeals to abolition opponents and skeptics by acknowledging their fears and concerns, then works to whittle away their prejudices by depicting the potential effects of abolition in a new light. By providing unforgettable examples of slaves as flourishing human beings, Martineau offers her readers clear evidence that Negroes would thrive in American society as fully functioning, productive citizens if given sufficient opportunities, especially education.[78]

Martineau addresses the perceived "impossibility of giving people of colour any idea of duty." She admits that "slaves will often leave their infants to perish . . . that they will utterly neglect a sick parent or husband." But "the reason is obvious. Such beings are degraded so far below humanity" due to their "circumstances." Clearly, whatever "want of natural affection" or sympathy there is among slaves is caused by their dehumanizing environment, not by any natural deficiency. Moreover, Martineau adds that "there are perhaps yet more instances of domestic devotion" among slaves than there are examples of degradation.[79]

Another example of the fundamental humanity of slaves is provided in a discussion about a slave owner who finds a way around the laws prohibiting the formal education of slaves by instead offering the indirect "moral training of task-work" supplemented with a considerable amount of free time. Martineau claims that the plan "succeeded admirably. . . . [The slaves'] day's task was finished by eleven o'clock. Next, they began to care for one another: the strong began to help the weak:—first, husbands helped their wives; then parents helped their children; and, at length, the young began to help the old." In this, Martineau sees "the awakening of natural affections which had lain in a dark sleep."[80] Even slaves who have been dehumanized by their deplorable situation are capable of regaining their natural disposition of sympathy. And an observer need only be open to such examples to recognize the true nature of slaves.

Perhaps the most important aspect of the humanity of slaves, according to Martineau, is their innate love of freedom. Applying the discursive aspect of sympathy directly, Martineau recounts in the first person a conversation she had with a woman about a relatively benevolent slave owner in Montgomery, Alabama, whose slave had nevertheless tried to escape. "She turned round upon me," Martineau writes, "and asked what could make the ungrateful wretch run away a third time from such a master?" Inserting herself into her own narrative to emphasize the point, Martineau responds, "He wanted to be free. . . . From any master."[81]

Martineau's descriptions of slaves show the principle of sympathy at work. Her openness allows her to observe the diverse behaviors and circumstances of slaves, which ultimately reveal their true selves. Tapping into the power of sympathy to engage in a dialogue with her readers, Martineau initially appeals to members of her audience whose unexamined views of slavery would most likely be tinged by racism and proceeds to lead them through counterexamples that challenge their opinions and show that social reform is possible.[82] Although Martineau is deeply aware of the systemic nature of racism in American society, her moral theory helps her avoid the resignation that arises in Tocqueville's account.[83] Martineau places readers in a position to contemplate equality between the races as a genuine possibility, making them more likely to accept her bold and unambiguous proposal: "There must be an immediate and complete surrender of all claim to negro men, women, and children as property."[84]

## Sympathy and the Oppression of American Women

Martineau's extensive analysis of the lamentable plight of American women in *Society in America* contrasts sharply with Tocqueville's relatively brief account. As with her critique of slavery, Martineau deploys a rich understanding of sympathy that engages her readers through the use of example, anecdote, and dialogue to wage a devastating attack on the oppression of American women. At the heart of her analysis is a condemnation of the notion of implied or tacit consent and the misunderstood acquiescence of women who do not perceptibly resist their social, moral, and political inequality to men. The target of her attack is precisely the image of the American woman that arises from Tocqueville's account. If Tocqueville's discussion of slavery is plagued with regret because the sympathetic ties that bind Americans cannot bridge the gap between the races, then his portrayal of the American woman is crippled by sympathetic deficit as well. Tocqueville's insistence that the separate spheres of influence and "social inequality" between American men and women are necessary to maintain stable power structures undermines the ambivalence in his description of American women, who seem to voluntarily resign themselves to their fate.

Guided by her view of sympathy, which requires that discourse be combined with a thorough knowledge of the "facts" at hand, Martineau compares the facts of American political life as expressed in the founding documents, especially the Declaration of Independence, with the facts about life for American women, particularly their status under the law, to reveal the true nature and extent of their oppression. American women are denied equal liberty and equal opportunity in the pursuit of happiness. The principle of self-government fails when it comes to women because they are not asked to consent to the rule of law. Thus women are unjustly held accountable to laws they had no role in shaping. In this regard, the situation of American women is analogous—but by no means identical—to that of slaves.

The solution, for Martineau, is clear: The principle of sympathy demands fundamental openness to others, with special importance given to discourse. It requires that women have the opportunity to speak their minds, to reveal what is most important to them, and to act of their own accord. They must be given opportunities to expressly consent to the laws that govern their societies. Religion, marriage, and the relations between the sexes must also be reformed to coincide with the moral principle of sympathy.[85]

In the chapter "The Political Non-Existence of Women," Martineau demands that the reader acknowledge the hypocrisy reflected in the incongruity between the political status of women, on one hand, and the core principle that governments derive their just powers from the consent of the governed, on the other. "Governments in the United States have power to tax women who hold property; to divorce them from their husbands; to fine, imprison, and execute them for certain offenses," she notes. "Whence do these governments derive their powers? They are not 'just' as they are not derived from the consent of the women thus governed."[86] As the punishments against women who break the law are unjust because they were not agreed to by the majority of all Americans, so, too, are the laws in certain states that grant women certain rights and protections insufficient for Martineau because they were made without the consent of women. Women have never been asked what they think, so their acceptance of the rule of law cannot be inferred. Martineau demands at the outset that the perspective of those who are observed must be engaged directly.

That these circumstances are unjust according to the basic democratic principle requiring the "equal political representation of all rational beings" is, for Martineau, a case "so plain" that she might "close it" after these initial remarks. Realizing, though, that argument alone is insufficient to make her case, Martineau inserts herself directly into the conversation with her readers:

> I, for one, do not acquiesce. I declare that whatever obedience I yield to the laws of the society in which I live is a matter between, not the community and myself, but my judgment and my will. Any punishment inflicted upon me for the breach of the laws, I should regard as so much gratuitous injury; for to those laws I have never, actually or virtually, assented. I know that there are women in England . . . [and] in America who agree with me in this. The plea of acquiescence is invalidated by us.[87]

Martineau presents herself to the reader as an individual before the law who can choose to consent to it or not and, in an act of openness, invites others to acknowledge her position. Just as no one will speak for her in the debate over women's rights, she suggests, the acquiescence of any woman should never be mistaken for consent.[88]

Singling out actual examples like Angelina Grimké for praise in "rousing into life and energy many women who were unconscious of genius, and unvisited by calamity, but who carry honest and strong human hearts," Martineau acknowledges that America is blessed with many powerful and intelligent women who desire to become abolitionists because of their moral outrage against slavery.[89] But these courageous women are violently denounced and discouraged from following their interests. Martineau recalls the women who were persecuted for supporting Garrison's presence in Boston and a successful female writer who was shunned by society after becoming an abolitionist. Also in the background is Martineau's personal experience of being confronted by frightening mobs outside the Boston Female Anti-Slavery Society meeting in 1835, where she agreed to speak.[90] Clearly, the inability of women to promote reform through speech and action constitutes a moral crisis in America that must be recognized through sympathetic openness and rectified accordingly.

Martineau reinforces the message that it is the moral imperative of women to act on their moral indignation toward slavery by appealing to her readers through dialogue. She relates a conversation with a woman who refused to act because, as a woman, she could have little influence. Drawing from her Christian faith, the woman insists that there is no need to work toward freeing the slaves, since they would be rewarded with freedom in the afterlife. And yet, Martineau leads the woman to concede that her sense of Christian charity did propel her to break up a fight on the street between two boys. Martineau again inserts herself directly into her own narrative and responds, "Well: if there are a thousand strong men in the south beating ten thousand weak slaves, and you can possibly help to stop the beating by a declaration of your opinion upon it, does not your Christian duty oblige you to make such a declaration, whether you are man or woman?"[91] By relating this conversation, Martineau appeals to Christian women who may support the abolitionist movement but do not feel obligated to act on their convictions. She seeks to encourage these women to look inward, to recognize their own hypocrisy, and to become more outspoken. For it is only by acting upon their convictions, Martineau argues, that men and women become fully moral beings.

Martineau extends her sympathetic appeal to pious women with a detailed commentary on the role of women as it emerges from Scripture. "The morals of woman are crushed," Martineau laments, by "the prevalent persuasion that there are virtues which are peculiarly masculine, and others which are peculiarly feminine." Based on this fallacy, believers create a "separate gospel for women, and a second company of agents for its diffusion." Not only is Scripture itself cheapened by this erroneous assertion, but virtue itself is compromised. "Men are ungentle, tyrannical," Martineau writes. Conversely, women are, "as might be anticipated, weak, ignorant and subservient." Those who distinguish sharply between male and female virtues, Martineau contends, fail to recognize that "the character of Christ" is "the meeting point of all virtues," and therefore "all virtues nourish each other, and can not otherwise be nourished." Thus as the "manly character" must become more "gentle" in order to approach true, Christ-like magnanimity, so to does the "gentle" character of women need to become more brave.[92] Capitalizing on the sympathetic engagement she has achieved with the reader, Martineau encourages her more devout audience to consider the often neglected scriptural teachings that emphasize egalitarianism.

Martineau also takes aim at the corrosive effects of the condescending nobility with which American men purport to elevate women, but which masks their actual degradation.[93] Although her discussion is similar to Mary Wollstonecraft's in A Vindication of the Rights of Woman (1792), Martineau redescribes the problem of chivalry and its solutions according to her own moral theory.[94] Chivalry is an example of sympathy gone awry. American men believe they provide a "paradise" for women to inhabit, but in reality, they construct a world that systematically denies women opportunities to grow and thrive as moral and political individuals. As a result, "Indulgence is given [them] as a substitute for justice."[95] Men develop a kind of false consciousness: They believe they are doing what is best for women, when in reality, they simply treat women as the Other rather than as individuals like themselves who deserve similar treatment. Likewise, women cannot place themselves in the shoes of men, since they are deprived of opportunities to envision themselves in positions of equality. Among both sexes, self-reflection of any kind is virtually nonexistent; both blindly embrace habits and traditions instead of listening to their hearts and minds. By inferring, rather than observing, the perspective of others, misunderstandings can arise that serve to perpetuate injustices instead of rectifying them. By contrast, a stance of fundamental openness to others is more likely to lead to equal treatment among individuals. Again the advantages of Martineau's conception of sympathy become apparent.

To address the problem of chivalry, Martineau realigns the concept of marriage in American society to conform to her moral principle of sympathy. Although she concedes that marriage in America is "more nearly universal, more safe, more tranquil, more fortunate than in England," it is nevertheless plagued by problems arising from "the inequality of the parties in mind and in occupation."[96] Describing the fundamentally unequal marriage between a licentious slave owner and his wife, Martineau observes,

> Where the generality of men carry secrets which their wives must be the last to know; where the busiest and more engrossing concerns of life must wear one aspect to the one sex, and another to the other, there is an end to all wholesome confidence and *sympathy*, and woman sinks to be the ornament of her husband's house, the domestic manager of his establishment, instead of being his all-sufficient friend.[97]

The unmarried Martineau makes a plea for marriage based purely on love among equals and emphasizes the importance of sympathy in securing it.

As I mentioned in chapter 1, Tocqueville's account of American women appears in the second volume of *Democracy in America*, which was published three years after Martineau's *Society in America*. Tocqueville declined to read Martineau's study, and Martineau would comment on Tocqueville's work a number of years after it appeared in print. But the parallels—and distinctions—between Martineau and Tocqueville's account of women in America were not lost on Catharine Beecher, who, in her influential tract, *A Treatise on Domestic Economy* (1841), draws extensively from Tocqueville's work to advance a view of feminine domesticity in opposition to Harriet Martineau and other women's rights advocates such as Frances Wright.[98] Whereas majority tyranny was the primary concern that framed his discussion of slavery in volume 1 of *Democracy*, Tocqueville's relatively brief discussion of women in volume 2 is part of a much broader reflection on the ways in which sympathy might curb the effects of excessive individualism in America. As a result of their newfound equality, Americans enjoy greater interactions, yet for Tocqueville they remain aloof and detached from one another.[99] The gulf between master and servant is undeniably narrowed in democratic America, yet a separation between them persists. "In democracies," Tocqueville writes, "servant and master are very close; their bodies constantly touch, but their souls remain apart; they have occupations together, but they hardly ever have common interests."[100] Sympathy, compassion, and the "temporary and freely made agreement" only go so far in bridging the gap between master and servant. Each prizes his freedom and nominal equality, but masters "do not claim their [servants'] love or devotion; it is enough if [the servants] are punctual or honest."[101]

The tide of egalitarianism has profound effects on the American family as well. The "relations between fathers and sons become more intimate and gentle; there is less of rule and authority, often more of confidence and affection."[102] And "the affectionate and frank intimacy of childhood easily takes root among" brothers in American democracy.[103] Whereas self-interest drives Americans to help one another, it is "not interest" but, rather, "common memories and the unhampered sympathy of thoughts and tastes" that bind brothers together.[104] Tocqueville's emphasis on the "brotherhood" that emerges not only between brothers but between fathers and sons is unambiguous and telling.[105]

Tocqueville's initial impressions of American girls and young women show that they, too, enjoy some of the benefits of democratic egalitarianism. Unlike their aristocratic counterparts, American girls do not languish in seclusion. Indeed, they seem to experience a gender-neutral upbringing and enjoy relatively free interactions with boys.[106] Because young girls enjoy the same easy relations that give rise to sympathy and compassion among men, it would stand to reason that American women would share in the same sympathetic interaction with men in their respective "brotherhood." Yet the qualifications of Tocqueville's descriptions of egalitarianism reemerge, as girls and women are ultimately excluded from the American "brotherhood."

Like the master and servant whose distance is veiled by their consensual contract, the American woman "has freely accepted the yoke" of her husband.[107] Yet, unlike the master and servant, whose roles for Tocqueville at least in principle might be exchanged and whose contractual arrangement is a temporary one, men and women never share or switch marital roles, and their nuptial agreement in principle lasts in perpetuity. One wonders how much these arrangements compound the effects of the potential conflict between husband and wife. The combination of the weakening of social bonds and the strengthening of familial ones paradoxically contributes to an unbridgeable gulf between men and women, husbands and wives, one that is masked, moreover, by inferred consent. The separate spheres dictated by puritanical religious teachings and necessitated by industrialization further erode the sympathetic interaction between men and women—interaction they are otherwise raised and educated to enjoy and that is otherwise facilitated by the equality of conditions in democratic society.[108]

## Martineau's Sympathetic American Democracy

In *How to Observe*, Martineau advances a view of morality that recognizes both a universal drive toward human happiness and the overarching importance of diverse human experience. At the core of her theory is the principle of sympathy. Rooted in a broad understanding of discourse, which includes both speaking with others and observing their speech, Martineau's unique conception of sympathy allows openness and flexibility in the face of cultural diversity and encourages understanding of the similarities and differences among groups and individuals. In *Society in America*, Martineau translates her moral theory into practice. In a sustained act of sympathetic discourse, she relates her interactions and experiences in America to her readers, often in the first person, encouraging them to act on the moral principle of sympathy and engage those who are unlike themselves.

Key components of Martineau's approach—her criticism of the rigid absolutism of moral sense theory, her focus on the diversity and complexity of moral judgments, and, of course, her emphasis on sympathy—parallel important aspects of Smith's analysis in *The Theory of Moral Sentiments*. But Martineau advances Smith's theory in several important ways. She expands upon Smith's relatively brief discussion of cultural diversity, placing the issue at the center of *How to Observe*. Whereas Smith's theory, by relying on the imagination as the primary vehicle for sympathetic engagement, leaves the observer vulnerable to mistaking her own perspective for that of another, Martineau's view of sympathy, which promotes open engagement with the other through observation and discourse, fosters cultural understanding by helping observers to transcend the limits of their own perspectives.

Martineau is able to evaluate the gravest challenges confronting American democratic society with depth and clear-sightedness by utilizing an innovative interpretation of Smith's moral theory that strengthens the power of sympathy to bridge cultural differences and promote social reform. Martineau offers a view of majority rule empowered with important tools to remedy its wrongs concerning slaves and women by appealing to its fundamental principles of sympathy. She urges her readers to adopt her sympathetic stance of openness that recognizes the diversity of moral perspectives while retaining the ability to make informed moral judgments. Careful examination of her writings reveals a serious but neglected attempt to encourage people to engage those who are dramatically unlike themselves and transcend the customs and traditions that lead to and perpetuate oppression. Her work thus provides an early example of a progressive political theory that seeks to accommodate the increasingly pressing needs of plurality in an evolving democratic society.

3

# Facing the "Sledge Hammer of Truth"

*Angelina Grimké and the Rhetoric of Reform*

In a public letter to education reformer and critic Catharine Beecher, Angelina Grimké writes: "Thy friend remarked, after an interview with an abolitionist, 'I love truth and sound argument; but when a man comes at me with a sledge hammer, I cannot help dodging.'" She continues:

> I presume thy friend only felt the truth of the prophet's declaration, "Is not my work like as a fire . . . and like a *hammer* that breaketh the rock in pieces?" I wonder not that he did *dodge*, when the sledge hammer of truth was wielded by an abolition army. Many a Colonizationist has been compelled to dodge, in order to escape the blows of this hammer of the Lord's word, for there is no other way to get clear. We must either *dodge* the arguments of abolitionists, or . . . be willing to be broken to pieces by them.[1]

Grimké's *Letters to Catherine E. Beecher* (1837) are part of the highly charged public battle over abolitionism and women's rights between Grimké and Beecher. Grimké's *Appeal to the Christian Women of the South*, along with Sarah Grimké's *Epistle to the Clergy of the Southern States*, served as the opening salvo unleashed by the sisters in 1836 against the "sins of slavery." In response to the *Appeal*, Beecher sent several private letters directly to Grimké, which were published in book form the following year. Grimké responds in turn with her own series of letters that were published first in the *Liberator*, the *Emancipator*, and the *Friend of Man* and later in book form.

Grimké was already well known for her passionate appeals. In a letter written privately to William Lloyd Garrison the year before, Grimké expressed a zeal for abolitionism so compelling that he published the message in the *Liberator* without securing her permission, explaining that "we cannot, we dare not suppress it." Grimké's letter to Garrison is filled with apocalyptic visions, exhorting reformers to "be *prepared* to meet the Martyr's doom" and "be willing to suffer the loss of all things." She includes herself among abolitionists who should believe that "*this is a cause worth dying for.*"[2] The fervor of Grimké's written appeals was matched by the ardor of her abolitionist activities. The public battle with Beecher did not deter her from continuing a speaking tour so controversial that it culminated with the burning of the Pennsylvania Hall for Free Discussion by an antiabolitionist mob after she had delivered a rousing speech there. Yet not even Grimké could endure so much turmoil. After the fire, she retreated from the public stage, settled into married life, and taught at a school she founded along with her husband and fellow abolitionist, Theodore Dwight Weld. Although Grimké continued to support women's rights and abolitionism, her efforts were conducted far from the public stage.

The use of powerful, violent imagery by a woman, the conflation of the word of God with the teachings of abolitionism, and the melding of divine and human punishment for the "sins" of slavery in the passage quoted above indicate broader themes underlying the acrimonious struggle between the two women over the role of rhetoric in bringing about political change and over the relation between reason and emotion, logic and passion.

The moral principle of sympathy, which animated nineteenth-century debates over slavery and women's rights, is a key component in the conflict between Beecher and Grimké. To encourage observers to empathize with others, rhetoric took its cue from Enlightenment discussions about the relation between reason and emotion and their role in persuasion. Whereas Lockean Enlightenment teachings ultimately advocated the power of reason over emotion, Scottish Enlightenment thinkers sought to balance reason with emotion in theories of the moral sense and, with it, the moral principle of sympathy.[3] And yet, with the popularization of Lockean and Scottish Enlightenment theories, sympathy became associated with sentimentalism and the emotional aspects of domesticity and increasingly isolated from the seemingly rational operations of public and political life.[4] At the heart of Beecher's critique is the charge that Grimké misunderstands and misuses sympathy by appealing to the passions and emotions of her audience in ways that alienate rather than persuade.[5] Her "sledge hammer of truth" obliterates whatever sympathetic bonds might be established between reformers and their intended audience. Equally important, Beecher accuses Grimké of abusing the power of rhetoric and transgressing the boundaries of feminine domesticity by using emotional language in the public realm of logic and reason. As a result, Grimké cannot possibly achieve her goals of abolishing slavery and expanding the rights of women. For Beecher, sympathy, while necessary, is inadequate in providing the moral compulsion to enact change in the political realm.

Beecher's critique sheds light on the broader criticism of Grimké and her deployment of sympathy as well. In fact, of all the women I examine in this book, Grimké is perhaps the most frequently targeted by critics for her sentimentalism.[6] Instead of fostering an authentic understanding of the plight of enslaved people and instilling the moral courage to act, commentators observe that Grimké and others "increasingly conflated feeling the pain of slaves and fighting slavery," and, as a result, "activism was simply active sympathy for suffering."[7] Thus "talking about cruelty allowed whites to criticize slavery without asking tough questions about human rights, racial equality, or African Americans' place in society."[8] Grimké's direct appeal to women's sympathies has also come under particular scrutiny for serving to elevate her authority as a female public speaker at the expense of those for whom the sympathetic appeals are actually made, especially enslaved and freed black women. Grimké and others imply that they "have particular authority to speak for female slaves" in spite of the fact that none of them actually experienced the horrors of chattel slavery and few, if any, had direct contact with enslaved women or freed black women. Moreover, by addressing women as a class, "white female abolitionists" such as Grimké "suggest that they are authorized to appeal to them in terms of their shared femininity, even those who oppose their views." Thus "Grimké's *Appeal* creates an authority for herself and other well-to-do white women while erasing the influence of other women."[9]

As a female public speaker and writer, Grimké had to draw authority from the traditional, circumscribed role she played in society in order to advocate for change by appealing to women as a woman. And yet she had to do so in a way that did not raise suspicions that she was "pushing the agenda of women's rights," which risked alienating men and women alike. As a result, Grimké's approach "draws rhetorical power from the hierarchy" dominated by men "even as it preserves its influence." We might expect that Grimké's new public role would serve as a pathbreaking model for other women, but it actually has the unintended effect of "leaving unchallenged hegemonic definitions of womanhood that limit white women and restrict their roles in society."[10] Although many of these critics would likely be loath to align themselves with Beecher's traditional and conservative worldview, they essentially draw similar conclusions about Grimké's rhetoric by deeming it inappropriate according to various standards.

Not everyone takes such a dim view of Grimké's life and work, however. It is important to note that both sisters consistently sought to qualify their comparisons between white women and slaves. Unlike other reformers, such as Frances Wright, the sisters also enjoyed close personal relationships with freed black men and women such as the abolitionist Sarah Douglass, which gave them greater insight into the unique challenges facing enslaved men and women.[11] Equally important, the Grimkés also experienced slavery differently from Northern white women, both as oppressors who directly benefited from the institution as daughters of a wealthy South Carolina slave owner and as subjects of oppression because, as children, they were effectively compelled to participate in the enslavement of others. Rather than ignoring the intersectional tensions of race and gender, the Grimkés decided early on to combine women's rights and abolitionism and thereby "raised the question of the relations, or intersections, between the two causes, as well as that of the relations of hierarchy existing between them." The sisters developed an early understanding of intersectionality by tracing systematic oppression in all domestic relations. For them, slavery was supported by a view of domination that pervaded other aspects life in various ways.[12]

In this chapter I expand on the notion that Grimké's understanding of the intersection of race and gender is more complex and that her understanding of sympathy, while still problematic, is more sophisticated than critics contend. I use Adam Smith's moral theory of rhetoric and his concept of propriety as a helpful frame of reference to recast aspects of Grimké's theory in a new light. This allows us to reexamine the controversies surrounding Grimké apart from Beecher's criticisms and those of contemporary critics. We see that, while Grimké's rhetoric might not be defensible according to Beecher's criteria, a case can be made that her rhetoric meets the requirements of propriety as outlined in Smith's moral and rhetorical theory. Specifically, we find that Grimké's rhetoric can be determined to be suitable to its deeply controversial subject matter, namely, slavery and the inequality of women, and that it is appropriate to the character of the speaker, namely, a young, ardent Southern Christian abolitionist. Grimké thus provides an example of how to deploy powerful, often deeply emotional rhetoric while maintaining moral and intellectual legitimacy. Her *Appeal* also makes more important contributions to political theory than we might expect. Specifically, Grimké redefines human rights in an inclusive way so as to apply to free and enslaved peoples, male and female alike. By redefining human rights in this way, Grimké is able to forge sympathetic bonds without necessarily obliterating the integrity of enslaved peoples or robbing them of human agency. Her worldview therefore reflects a greater degree of intersectionality than typically assumed, consistent with her own unique life experience. However, the ability of Grimké's rhetoric to appeal to broader, more diverse communities is ultimately limited because it is still deeply rooted in a progressive Christian worldview. Although Sarah Grimké's worldview is also shaped by her religious faith, I argue in chapter 4 that she is better able to transcend the limits of her theological inclinations and offer a foundational theory of women's rights that accommodates greater diversity. Yet the case against Angelina Grimké is not as clear-cut as we might think, nor should we prematurely dismiss her ability to advocate for genuine reform. At the very least, I hope to add a layer of complexity to the ongoing debate surrounding Grimké's theoretical and political contributions.

## Framing the Terms of Debate: Beecher's Critique

Beecher's goals in writing the *Essay on Slavery and Abolitionism* (1837) were complex. She desired to initiate a radical social movement in which American women studied in schools such as her own so that they might educate the nation's children and thereby reform society. To achieve this aim, Beecher had to persuade women to transfer their ambitions from speaking out in public against slavery and the oppression of women to preparing themselves as inculcators of morality and virtue in the domestic sphere as mothers and teachers. To discredit potentially dangerous

role models for ambitious women to emulate, Beecher targeted brazen female abolitionists and early women's rights advocates who dared
express themselves publicly, including Grimké.[13] Given the heated
interchanges between the two women, it is all the more surprising that
Grimké had written to Beecher in 1831 asking to visit Hartford Female
Seminary, the school Beecher established for women to train as teachers, with the hope of studying there. Although Grimké wanted to attend
Beecher's school, she was dissuaded by the Quaker elders of the Fourth
and Arch Street Meeting, whose acceptance she, along with her sister,
had eagerly sought but ultimately failed to secure.[14]

In the *Essay* Beecher explains that she agrees with the goals sought by
Grimké and other Garrisonians but vehemently opposes the means used
to achieve them. Specifically, Beecher objects to the incendiary language
used by Garrisonian abolitionists, which she contends only fosters antagonism and alienation among slavery supporters. Instead, she argues,
abolitionists should follow the example of the British antislavery leader
William Wilberforce by seeking to persuade opponents gradually, privately, and quietly, with logical, rational, evidence-based arguments.[15]
Not only is the Garrisonian style of speech objectionable for Beecher,
but she also criticizes its use of particular words as misleading audiences
and obscuring the overall message. The inappropriate nature of Garrisonian speech falls short theoretically, it seems, because it fails to articulate
a comprehensible view of sympathy. The opposing sides simply cannot
connect to one another either in speech or in action, as Southern slavery
supporters become even more obstinate and Northern reformers even
more self-righteous. Without such a connection, reform is impossible.

To be sure, Grimké's *Appeal* and *Letters*—the latter published in response to the education reformer's attack—together constitute a tour de
force in abolitionist and early women's rights literature. In the *Appeal*
Grimké capitalizes on her unique position as a transplanted Southerner
to reach out to her female cohorts and exhort them to transcend the limits of their subordination and struggle mightily against slavery. She offers an exhaustive exegesis of biblical teachings to undermine scriptural
justifications for slavery and provides powerful images and examples
to encourage readers to sympathize with enslaved people, not merely
as passive victims of injustice, but as fellow human beings who deserve
freedom and equality.

The *Letters* include a large share of emotional outbursts, as Beecher duly notes, as well. The final missive ends with a dramatic parting shot hurled directly at Beecher: "Hast thou ever asked thyself," Grimké asks, "what the slave would think of thy book, if he could read it? Dost thou know that, from the beginning to the end, not a word of compassion for *him* has fallen from thy pen? Recall, I pray, the memory of the hours which thou spent in writing it! Was the paper once moistened by the tear of pity? Did thy heart once swell with deep sympathy for thy sister *in bonds*?" Delivering the final blow, Grimké declares that Beecher's work "bespeaks a superior intellect, but [is] paralyzed and spell-bound by the sorcery of a worldly-minded expediency" that produced "its cold and heartless pages."[16]

Grimké declares that "intellectual greatness cannot give moral perception—therefore, those who have no clear view of the irresistible-ness of moral power, cannot see the efficacy of moral norms."[17] She laments that Beecher has fallen victim to a larger phenomenon that "as a nation, we have too long educated the *mind*, and left the *heart* a moral waste."[18] Grimké claims to possess the very calmness sought by Beecher, but her demeanor does not arise solely from pure reason and logic, nor does it appeal exclusively to emotions. Grimké's dedication is based on "solemn calmness which is the result of conviction and duty" and which, I contend, combines reason and emotion.[19]

Beecher begins by attacking Grimké and others for failing to com-municate their thoughts to Southerners directly, instead choosing to express themselves indirectly through emotionally charged writings that merely stoke "party spirit, denunciation, recrimination, and angry passions."[20] Garrisonians have made a "false deduction" from the expe-rience of Wilberforce and the British abolitionists, who are successful because "they collect facts, they arrange statistics, they call public meet-ings, they form voluntary associations, they use arguments, entreaties, and personal example, and by these means they arrest the evil."[21] Based on their example, Beecher proposes that Grimké and the Garrisonians should "collect all the evidence of this supposed hurtful tendency, and privately, and in a respectful and conciliating way, to have presented it to the attention of the wise and benevolent men, who were most inter-ested in sustaining this institution." If their efforts continue to be un-successful, the Garrisonians would be justified in bringing a "temperate statement of facts, and of the deductions based on them, drawn up in a respectful and candid manner."[22]

The Garrisonians' use and abuse of language for Beecher extends further, to "their indiscreet and incorrect use of terms" such as "man-stealer," which appears interchangeably with "slave-holder."[23] Garrisonians are "guilty of a species of deception" because they ignore the fact that the two terms are not used interchangeably in American society at large.[24] Beecher also accuses Grimké and other abolitionists of using the term "immediate abolition" in a fundamentally misleading way. Abolitionists do not really care if their actions are most likely to succeed in a particular time and place.[25] Moreover, "immediate abolition" is defined and understood as a "legal act" by which slavery is abolished through a political process.[26] Yet, for Beecher, Grimké and the abolitionists have a far more vague conception of emancipation, which extends beyond political policy making to encompass broader moral and religious prescriptions, according to which "every man is bound to treat his slaves, as nearly as he can, like freemen; and to use all his influence to bring the system of slavery to an end as soon as possible."[27]

Beecher continually advocates "expediency" through her gradualist approach over any misleading sense of "immediacy," reinforcing the irony that the abolitionist position urges "immediate" change yet employs a method that is for her least likely to succeed in a timely fashion. Insisting that she is not justifying proslavery prejudices, Beecher explains that "it is a certain consequence of throwing men into strong excitement," especially with overheated rhetoric, "that they will act unwisely and wrong."[28] By contrast, "the more men are treated as if they were honest and sincere—the more they are treated with respect, fairness, and benevolence," Beecher concludes, "the more likely they are to be moved by evidence and arguments."[29]

## Beecher, Grimké, and Smith on the Propriety of Rhetoric

Smith's discussion of propriety in *The Theory of Moral Sentiments* describes a scenario that is remarkably similar to the conflict between Beecher and Grimké. An individual who has experienced a "misfortune" or "injury" is dismayed by the lack of "correspondence of sentiments" between her and a spectator, who experiences the situation only indirectly, as an observer, and thus is affected less intensely. Writing in the first person and addressing the reader directly, Smith declares:

> If you have either no fellow-feeling for the misfortunes I have met with, or none that bears any proportion to the grief which distracts me; or if you have either no indignation at the injuries I have suffered, or none that bears any proportion to the resentment which transports me, we can no longer converse upon these subjects. We become intolerable to one another. I can neither support your company, nor you mine. You are confounded at my violence and passion, and I am enraged at your cold insensibility and want of feeling (*TMS*, I.i.4.5).

Smith insists that the spectator "endeavor, as much as he can, to put himself in the situation of the other," but he also contends that "the emotions of the spectator will still be very apt to fall short of the violence of what is felt by the sufferer" because complete identification with another person is literally impossible (*TMS*, I.i.4.6–7). And while Smith regards the frustrations of the sufferer as perfectly legitimate, he maintains that the sufferer must realize that the experience of the spectator will "always be, in some respects, different from what he feels, and compassion can never be exactly the same with original sorrow." In short, "though they will never be unisons, they may be concords, and this is all that is wanted or required" (*TMS*, I.i.4.7).

The sufferer "can only hope to obtain" sympathy with the spectator "by lowering his passion to that pitch, in which the spectators are capable of going along with him," by "flatten[ing] the sharpness of its natural tone, in order to reduce it to harmony and concord with the emotions of those who are about him." Thus a kind of moderation is necessary, not only to forge a sympathetic bond between sufferer and spectator, but also to preserve "the harmony of society" itself (*TMS*, I.i.4.7).

In spite of the similarities between the Grimké-Beecher conflict and the sufferer-spectator experience, the fact that Grimké is not actually experiencing the suffering of slavery limits the applicability of Smith's theory to her perspective. In fact, critics have argued that Grimké conflates her own suffering with that of the enslaved and encourages her audience to do the same, thereby glossing over the enormous differences between women and slaves. Yet even in the absence of direct experience of suffering, Smith allows for powerful fellow feeling to emerge. Sympathy "does not arise so much from the view of the passion," in this case, the actual suffering of another or, by implication, the actual experience of suffering, "as from that of the situation which excites it." For "we sometimes feel for another, a passion of which he himself seems to be altogether incapable; because, when we put ourselves in his case, that passion arises in our breast from the imagination." For example, a "poor wretch" who is "altogether insensible of his own misery" still inspires "anguish" within a spectator because he imagines "what he himself would feel if he was reduced to the same unhappy situation" (*TMS*, I.i.1.10–11). It is not the actual experience of suffering, by oneself or another, that is at stake. Nor is Smith demanding that actual suffering take place. As we see, Smith's moral theory of rhetoric requires that the rhetorician is able to depict the experience of the affected so the audience as spectators can establish fellow feeling. The duties of the spectator in both situations are the same: to establish fellow feeling with the sufferer. A sense of duty by the spectator, combined with the expectation of fellow feeling on the part of the sufferer, forms the basis of a moral society, according to Smith, which the rhetorician shares responsibility for maintaining.

Clearly, for Smith, sympathy is deeply dependent on the situation in which the affected and the spectator interact. Smith's emphasis on the importance of social and cultural norms in determining the propriety of sympathy is also apparent in his conception of the "impartial spectator," which is not truly impartial but, rather, shaped by the particular society in which it arises. We "examine our own passions and conduct, and . . . consider how these must appear," not just to anyone in general, but to other members of our society. As we consider "how they would appear to us if [we were] in their situation," we become "spectators of our own behavior and endeavor to imagine what effect it would, in this light, produce upon us" (*TMS*, III.1.5).

According to Smith's account, Beecher must try to the best of her ability to relate to Grimké's plight and, by implication, that of the slave. However, Grimké must also realize that Beecher will never be able to fully understand her grievances, or those of the slave, not only because of Beecher's overreliance on logic, but also because of the fundamental limitations of sympathy itself. Equally important, Grimké is obligated to "lower" and "flatten" her pleas to meet Beecher and her audience halfway, in accordance with nineteenth-century American social and cultural norms. If she fails to do so, Grimké threatens the very fabric of society itself by permanently alienating her audience. From Beecher's perspective, Smith's scenario simply reinforces the deeply problematic character of Grimké's intemperate, inappropriate abolitionist rhetoric.

However, Smith not only tells us how to determine the propriety of a sympathetic encounter but also how to convey our ideas and actions properly through the use of moral rhetoric. For Smith, the propriety of rhetoric must not only take into account the subject matter itself, but also the relevant context of the message, especially the norms of the particular audience and the character of the rhetorician himself. Proper rhetoric occurs when "the words neatly and properly expressed the thing to be described," but also when it conveys "the sentiment the author entertained of it and desired to communicate . . . by sympathy to his hearers" (*LRBL*, i.96). Propriety in rhetoric arises when the communicator "never seems to act out of character but speaks in a manner not only suitable to the Subject but to the character he naturally inclines to" (*LRBL*, i.136). Smith's remarks indicate that the propriety of Grimké's appeals must be determined not only by her audience but by her own character and the subject matter at hand. If Grimké's appeals are sincere expressions of her sentiments, and if slavery is the abominable institution she portrays it to be, Beecher's case against her would be weakened, according to the standards of Smith's moral and rhetorical theory.

Moreover, Smith makes clear that by "lowering" or "flattening" the tone he does not necessarily mean moderating in terms of lessening the emotional impact. It is true that "extreme moroseness and gravity . . . would not be admired," nor would extreme levity. But Smith clarifies that "it is *not* in the middle point betwixt these two characters that an agreable [*sic*] one is alone to be found, many others that partake more or less of the two extremes are equally the objects of our affection" (*LRBL*, i.98; emphasis added). Again, the propriety of rhetoric depends, not on moderation for its own sake, but rather on important contextual factors, the subject matter, the audience, and the standpoint of the speaker. Beecher's insistence on logical, rational discourse when it pertains to slavery resembles either "extreme moroseness or gravity" or an almost mathematically determined middle point between reason and emotion, which may not be appropriate to the subject matter or the speaker.

Thus Smith leaves open the possibility that a more emotional appeal like Grimké's could be justified under certain circumstances.

Smith's relatively permissive views on rhetoric are further reinforced in his depiction of the ideal orator who, in contrast to the historian, "treats of subjects he or his friends are nearly concerned in . . . and uses all his art to prove what he is engaged in" and who "insists on every particular, exposes it in every point of view, and sets off every argument in every shape it can bear." Again, it is clear that Smith is not opposed to passionate rhetoric if it is consistent with the orator's true sentiment and the subject at hand: "The orator frequently will exclaim on the strength of the argument, the justice of the cause, or any thing else that tends to support the thing he has in view; and this too in his own person" (*LRBL*, i.81–82). Indeed, for Smith, "the proper expression of just indignation" by an impassioned orator "composes many of the most splendid and admired passages both of ancient and modern eloquence" (*TMS*, VI.iii.9). Along similar lines, metaphors, allegories, and hyperboles are acceptable and even encouraged if they demonstrate a genuine "connection" or "allusion" and avoid lapsing into "bombast" or "burlesque" (*LRBL*, i.64–v.66).

In the next section I show that Grimké's *Appeal* is consistent with several important aspects of Smith's moral theory of rhetoric. As Smith emphasizes the importance of social and cultural context, so, too, does Grimké draw from the norms of the Christian community with which she is deeply familiar. Grimké's task is particularly challenging because of the gross hypocrisy and deep complacency of her target audience in the face of injustice. "Southern women sit down in listless indifference and criminal idleness," Grimké laments, as they enjoy the fruits of enslaved labor.[30] Grimké's challenge, as Beecher recognizes, is to deploy rhetoric in a way that is appropriate to the controversial subject matter and urge reform without causing alienation. Grimké clearly believes, however, that drastic measures—in this case, powerful rhetoric—are required to awaken the consciences of these complacent women. To accomplish her goal, Grimké effectively constructs a kind of "impartial spectator"—in this case, an ideal form of the Southern Christian woman—to instill shame and remorse in her audience and thereby open the possibility for contrition and reform. Grimké's efforts consist of a systematic attempt to create rhetorically appropriate scenarios in which the fundamental injustice of slavery is exposed through the imaginations of her audience. Grimké, in Smithean terms, taps into the human desire for fellow feeling to argue against slavery and the oppression of women.

Although Grimké turns the tables on her "sisters in faith" by using Christian doctrine against them, she also draws from Christian teachings to help guide them. Based on her biblical interpretations, Grimké re-creates in speech a community of Christian women who share a common interest in Scripture yet who are encouraged to interpret it independently. Biblical teachings shape the norms of this community and thus determine the parameters of propriety when it comes to controversial subjects such as slavery. Grimké's encyclopedic knowledge of Scripture, combined with her detailed account of the legal oppression of women and slaves, resemble the meticulous accounting of the arguments pertaining to the subject matter by Smith's orator, as do Grimké's frequent exclamations of indignation.

Objections can be raised about the idea that Grimké's primary audience is Southern Christian women. Her direct appeal to "Christian women of the South" like herself had little practical effect because censorship of abolitionist literature in the South would likely prevent many women from reading her work, so Grimké's actual target audience must have been complacent Northern Christians. Equally important, Southern women were in no position to abolish slavery legally or otherwise, as Grimké herself admits, but Christian Northern abolitionists could make the case to Southern white men, who were in positions of power. Indeed, Beecher criticizes Grimké not only from the perspective of Southern Christian women but also from the point of view of Northern abolitionist men and women, with whom Beecher was far more familiar. Because Northerners had already abolished slavery, the rhetorical measures used to address them must be fundamentally different from those used to castigate Southerners. This is why, for Beecher, a more measured tone was necessary.

However, from Grimké's perspective, the intersectionality that exists between Northerners and Southerners on the issue of slavery is undeniable. As someone who has experienced slavery from both perspectives, she has insight that Beecher, who lacks such experience, fundamentally lacks. Grimké condemns the fact that Northerners benefit financially from slavery in the South, that their interests are "very closely combined." She also condemns the fact that many Northerners, like Southerners, "refuse the colored people in this country the advantages of education and the privilege, or rather the *right*, to follow honest trades and callings merely because they are colored."[31] Even a freed black woman admitted to Grimké in a letter that she had experienced "apathy and indifference" and lived in "selfish darkness" before allying herself with abolitionism.[32] Although the institution of slavery does not exist in the North, for Grimké, hypocrisy and complacency surely do, as freed black men and women are denied the free exercise of their rights and continue to face discrimination. As Beecher seeks to pry apart the interrelations between North and South, men and women, enslaved and free, Grimké engages in the much more difficult, perhaps ultimately impossible task of balancing them.

Nor does Grimké believe that Southern women are utterly helpless in the fight against slavery, especially compared with Northern women. Although Beecher is renowned for her celebration of the private realm of women, Grimké elevates the power women wield in that realm, and through it their influence on civil society, even further. "I know you do not make the laws," she proclaims, "but I also know that *you are the wives and mothers, the sisters and daughters to those who do*, and if you really suppose you can do nothing to overthrow slavery, you are greatly mistaken." Southern women can "read," "pray," "speak," and finally, "act on this subject." Women who own slaves should free them and, if that is impossible, pay them wages and teach them. They should also engage in civil disobedience because laws allowing slavery contradict divine law.[33] By placing herself in the position of intercessor between Northern and Southern Christian women, Grimké expands the potential pool of participants in "fellow feeling."

## Grimké's Universal Human Rights and Human Agency

Grimké's progressive religious beliefs contribute to an understanding of human rights that allows for fellow feeling among a wide variety of individuals, including women and enslaved peoples, to a greater degree than we might expect. By including enslaved peoples in her view of human rights, Grimké grants them a measure of agency that is comparable to that of other men and women.

Underlying Grimké's belief in universal human rights is her understanding of human law that, in the case of slavery and the oppression of women, is deeply flawed, and of the law of God that, according to her biblical interpretation, does not support slavery. Along similar lines, Grimké distinguishes between human rights and the responsibilities and obligations that come with them, which are universal and inalienable, on the one hand, and gifts of God, which are beyond our comprehension and solely in his power to give or revoke, on the other. In her response to Beecher's *Essay*, Grimké declares:

> Woman's rights are not the gifts of man—no!—nor the *gifts* of God. His gifts to her may be recalled at his good pleasure—but her *rights* are an integral part of her moral being; they cannot be withdrawn; they must live with her forever. Her rights lie at the foundation of all her duties; and, so long as the divine commands are binding upon her, so long must her rights continue.[34]

Moreover, human rights are integral to all human beings regardless of sex. For "whatever it is *morally* right for a man to do, it is *morally* right for a woman to do. I recognize no rights but *human* rights—I know nothing of men's rights and women's rights; for in Christ Jesus, there is neither male or female." For Grimké, human rights are truly inalienable. No other human being, nor even God, can permanently revoke them. When Grimké claims that rights cannot be permanently taken away unless someone renounces completely the "divine commands" of God, she means that, because God makes rights an integral part of our identity as human beings, we are obligated to exercise and develop those rights in order to become fully human and that to renounce God would also mean renouncing the very possibility of human rights, along with the duties and obligations that come with them. Grimké makes this argument because she wants to establish moral responsibility firmly in the human realm. We cannot blame God if human rights are violated or renounced. Equally important, moral responsibility falls to men and women alike. "Our duties originate, not from difference of sex," or, by implication, from different human natures, as determined by God or otherwise. Rather, specific duties may differ because they are shaped by "the diversity of our relations in life, the various gifts and talents committed to our care, and the different eras in which we live."[35] If these differences are constructed by human beings and determined by the circumstances in which they live, human beings are also responsible for reconstructing them in accordance with evolving views on equality.

Grimké specifically extends human rights to enslaved peoples, insisting that enslavement is not natural but rather a deeply unjust social and cultural construction that can and must be changed. Human rights "may be wrested from the slave" by circumstance or by other human beings, "but they cannot be alienated" or permanently destroyed. On Grimké's view, only the enslaved person herself can decide to give up her rights and turn away from her moral responsibilities as a human being.[36]

The exhaustive biblical exegesis with which she opens her *Appeal* emphasizes that all human beings are obligated to educate themselves and expand their rational capacities so that they may become fully moral beings. Exhorting Southern slave-holding women in particular, Grimké explains: "It is the *duty* of all, as far as they can, to improve their own mental faculties, because we are commanded to love God with *all our minds*, as well as with all our hearts." She insists that Christian Southern women "read then on the subject of slavery" and "search the Scriptures daily" so that they may determine independently "whether the things I have told you are true."[37] Consistent with her Christian understanding of universal human rights, enslaved peoples as part of their freedom must be given the opportunity to educate themselves as well, "and we commit a great sin, if we *forbid* or *prevent* that cultivation of the mind in others, which would enable them to perform this duty."[38] By implication, only a freed slave who is given every opportunity to exercise moral responsibility and to fully develop her human capacities is in a position to freely choose to renounce her rights. Whites cannot offer a Hobson's choice by which enslaved peoples choose to refuse the education and opportunities that were never given to them in the first place and use that allegedly free choice to deprive enslaved peoples of their human rights.

To emphasize the importance of human agency in shaping the social and cultural circumstances in which we live, Grimké categorically denies that divine intervention alone will ultimately bring about radical reform such as the abolition of slavery. "Will the wheels of the millennial car be rolled onward by miraculous power?" she asks. "No! God designs to confer this holy privilege upon *man*; it is through *his* instrumentality that the great and glorious work of reforming the world is to be done."[39] For Grimké, human agency is key to any form of change. By contrast, it is her opponents, presumably including Beecher, who deprive enslaved peoples of agency because they "regarded the colored man as an *unfortunate inferior*, rather than as an *outraged* and *insulted equal*," and by denying "the principle of *equal rights*."[40]

For critics, Grimké's command that slaves be allowed to educate themselves would constitute a destructively racist form of paternalism. By advocating assimilation through education, Grimké, like others, would be offering "a social vision that encompassed both a melding of peoples and a firm sense of hierarchy—an invitation to Others to participate (as almost-but-not-quite Anglos) in the body politic." However, Grimké, like other reformers I discuss in the book who advocate universal education, does not support "evolutionary constructions of racial progress," on which this racist hierarchy is based. As someone who explicitly rejects notions of racial inferiority, she cannot be considered among the reformist "civilizers of racially inferior peoples." [41] Committed to a non-doctrinal, non-hierarchical, egalitarian form of Christianity, she would reject any forms of racist imperialism or colonization. If Grimké's view of human nature is truly universal, everyone is under equal obligation to educate themselves and provide opportunities for others to be educated as well.

Isolated from her views on human nature, Grimké's insistence that Southern women should free their slaves in spite of the consequences appears troubling as well. "Consequences, my friends, belong no more to you, than they did to these apostles," Grimké explains. "Duty is ours and events are God's." She continues:

> If you think slavery is sinful, all you have to do is to set your slaves at liberty, do all you can to protect them, in humble faith and fervent prayer, commend them to your common Father. He can take care of them; but if for wise purposes he sees fit to allow them to be sold, this will afford you an opportunity of testifying openly against slavery.[42]

Behind Grimké's convoluted logic is the separation between humanly duties and God's control over "events" and "gifts," the rationale for which is unknowable to human beings. Grimké is trying to establish equality among all human beings and to empower human beings—especially Southern Christian women—by placing responsibility for maintaining their duties and obligations to others firmly in their own hands. Grimké does not want these women to use the mystery of God as an excuse to avoid action. Along similar lines, she does not want the differences in social and cultural roles between men and women to be used as an excuse for women to evade responsibility for their own actions. It cannot be denied that Grimké does not mention the slave's perspective, nor does she consider the slave's ability to exercise independent agency. Yet she does not depart from the idea that, while human beings may thwart the development of duties and responsibilities in others, as in this case slave owners prevent slaves from developing their full potential, no person can be stripped of their human rights, which are permanent and inalienable.

## Grimké's Community of Reformers

In her *Appeal* Grimké offers a series of parallels between those involved with abolitionism, on the one hand, and figures found in Scripture, on the other. These parallels are designed to show that, if Southern women would act to oppose slavery, they would not be alone; instead they would be joined with "English and Northern philanthropists" acting under the same divine obligations, and with the biblical community of fellow Christians. "Wrestling Jacobs" would continue to fight for emancipation. "Pauls" are asking for divine advice to guide their actions. "Marys" are "ready to arise and go forth in [Christ's] work" when they receive the word. "Marthas" have "already gone out to meet Jesus" and lamented over the biblical Lazarus. The allusions Grimké draws between followers of Christ and her readers would appeal to a particular segment of her audience, namely, progressive Christian women who would be receptive to revisionist interpretations of Scripture that emphasize overlooked commonalities between biblical figures and antislavery activists, especially women.[43] Because they suit the audience and the character of the speaker, these comparisons would be appropriate according to Smith's moral theory of rhetoric.

However, Grimké's allegory continues in a more troubling direction, as the "Marthas" must now confront and grieve "over the politically and intellectually lifeless slave, bound hand and foot in the iron chains of oppression and ignorance." Grimké urges her readers "to take away the stone which has covered up the dead body of our brother, to expose the putrid carcass, to show *how* that body has been bound with the grave-clothes of heathen ignorance, and his face, with the napkin of prejudice."[44] The comparison between Lazarus and a slave is among the most controversial in Grimké's works. To conceive of a slave as a dead man is clearly to strip him of all human agency and to dehumanize him. Grimké's rhetoric in this passage certainly does not "lower" or "flatten" itself to a level at which others who are not devoutly Christian may sympathize easily.

However, if we consider the intended audience, namely, Southern Christian women who have done nothing to end slavery and who do not see slaves as fellow human beings, the allegory could also mean that these women must confront their own deep-seated aversion to slaves, which dehumanizes them by transforming them into an "other." Instead, Christian women must act and "take away the stone" of enslavement, free the slave from the shackles of "oppression and ignorance," remove the "grave-clothes" of heathenism, as enslaved peoples are denied the opportunity to develop and act upon their own faith, and lift the "napkin" of prejudice that has masked his identity as an individual. Through this powerful allegory Grimké urges Christian women to recognize the effects of their own deep-seated racism, to which they are oblivious, and a vivid symbol is needed to penetrate their veneer of respectability and righteousness. The slave's "death" is imposed upon him, and solely the responsibility of slavery and oppression. These women will need to transcend the loathsome history of slavery and their culpability in it. They must see that their "Lazarus" is another human being and faithful Christian like themselves. Only then will he rise up from his "politically and intellectually lifeless" state and join the ranks of faithful followers of Christ. Grimké clearly believed that only by deploying a familiar and dramatic image such as Lazarus could she shake Southern Christian women from their moral complacency. Critics might still be right in arguing that the Lazarus allegory is disempowering to the slave. However, Lazarus is not a particularly empowering exemplar of human action generally because his fate is controlled by God, who chooses to resurrect him. There is no doubt, however, that, like Grimké's allegorical slave, Lazarus is equally human to the followers whose humanly efforts are still required to free him from the cave.[45]

Grimké's graphic portrayals of the suffering of martyrs are also seen by Beecher as indications of her inability to modulate her rhetoric to suit her audience. Analyzing Grimké's allusions to martyrs, critics have charged her with masochistic indulgence and the celebration of vicarious suffering at the expense of concrete action or genuine compassion. It is true that in all the examples Grimké provides, women endure physical pain or stand up to harsh opposition through speech and action. And yet Grimké is clearly not insisting that women must become martyrs or presume to feel the same pain as these unfortunate individuals. Rather, Grimké's overall goal is to instill "moral courage" and "bear faithful testimony for the truth" among Southern white women who do not see themselves as capable of facing "persecution."[46] It is also notable that Grimké follows with a discussion of the actual women who have stood up for emancipation, such as Elizabeth Heyrick, whose writings inspired Wilberforce to act, and other women who "labored assiduously to keep the sufferings of the slave continually before the British public" through "needles, paint brushes and pens, by speaking the truth, and petitioning parliament."[47] These women are clearly not suffering in the same degree as the martyrs of the past, nor are they sharing the same fate. Their motivations and fortitude, however, are the same. For Grimké, Southern Christian women should not act simply to gain the esteem of men, but rather out of a sense of "duty as *women*," which includes others such as Heyrick.[48] Whereas Beecher's reference to Heyrick and Wilberforce characterizes their activity in terms of fact finding, statistics gathering, and using logical arguments to make their point, Grimké highlights the power of their courage, persistence, and passionate devotion to the cause of abolition, as they emphasize the suffering of slaves.

In one of the most provocative passages of the *Appeal*, Grimké addresses slave owners, including women, who justify slavery by arguing that those who are born into enslavement "are accustomed to it, their backs are fitted to the burden," whereas "the yoke of bondage would be insufferable" to whites who were born free.[49] Grimké responds with a shocking image:

> Well, I am willing to admit that you who have lived in freedom would find slavery even more oppressive than the poor slave does, but then you may try this question in another form—Am I willing to reduce *my little*

*child* to slavery? You know *if it is brought up a slave* it will never know any contrast, between freedom and bondage, its back will become fitted to the burden just as the negro child's does—*not by nature*—but by daily, violent pressure, in the same way that the head of the Indian child becomes flattened by the boards in which it is bound.[50]

The denial of human rights and human agency is justified, according to the logic of the argument, because neither children nor enslaved people have ever experienced freedom, so they will not mourn their servitude. Along similar lines, Native Americans and their children have no experience of normal development, so they will not lament the disfigurement.

Again inviting criticisms of sympathetic excess, Grimké presses her audience to place themselves directly in the position of a slave. Southern Christian women, enslaved women, and Native American women are conflated into Grimké's image of the mother, thereby ignoring the fact that their respective situations are unique. Moreover, under American slave laws, the children of slaves are born into servitude; white children are not. Unlike Smith, Grimké here allows for no weakening or "lowering" of the sympathetic bond between two people. Recall, however, the rhetorical challenges facing Grimké as she confronts women who deny or ignore the plight of the enslaved peoples upon whom they depend every day. To the unwitting eye, enslaved people often appear content, and their servitude even appears "natural." In Grimké's example, the child cannot speak for herself and give voice to her plight, and the slave mother may appear to relinquish the child voluntarily, especially if neither is protesting. The devastating moral and psychic effects of enslavement remain invisible. A powerful rhetorical tool is therefore needed to rupture the veneer of respectability that is attached to slavery in conventional society.

Grimké renders visible that which cannot otherwise be perceived: The child represents the total deprivation of freedom and denial of human agency for the oppressed. Added to the direct connection between white women, enslaved women, Native American women, and children is an implicit association between Grimké's audience of white Southern women and male supporters of slavery. Both deploy the same justifications for their actions, namely, that the enslaved individual is ignorant of, and therefore undeserving of, freedom. The reference to

Native American children contributes another layer because their visible deformity mirrors the invisible yet "daily, violent pressure" imposed by the burden of slavery, which is in turn made visible to Grimké's readers as spectators.

By exposing the specious arguments and veneer of acceptability used to comfort and assuage those guilty of committing injustice, Grimké's image appeals to something akin to Smith's idea of the impartial spectator. It is both as potential agents and spectators that white women are led to feel "horror and indignation" in contemplating slavery. Grimké shatters the artificial wall between whites and slaves by declaring that *"it is not by nature"* that they and their children differ from one another. By commanding her audience to "try" themselves by "Divine precepts" such as the golden rule, Grimké recreates the experience of using the impartial spectator to evaluate oneself and others.[51] Only by seeing oneself through others' eyes can a person begin to feel indignation toward oneself.

A final example of Grimké's complex deployment of sympathy is the parallel drawn between freed blacks and the Northerners who wish to deprive them of the opportunities associated with freedom. "Great numbers" of whites "cannot bear the idea of equality," she writes, "and fearing lest, if they had the same advantages we enjoy, they would become as intelligent, as moral, as religious, and as respectable and wealthy, they are determined to keep them as low as they possibly can." The ultimate source of this prejudice is the fear of amalgamation. Grimké wishes that prejudiced whites would "put their souls in the stead of the free colored man's and obey the apostolic injunction, to 'remember them that are in bonds as *bound with them.'"*[52] Grimké can perhaps be criticized here for not asking prejudiced Northern whites to establish a sympathetic connection with actual enslaved people, presumably because it was unimaginable to them, but, rather, with freed blacks who most closely resembled whites. However, it might also be argued that the critique most likely to succeed against the specific fear of amalgamation and the prejudice that accompanies it would focus on those who most closely resemble one another in a particular culture, in this case, whites and freed, educated blacks. If whites fail to extend opportunities to freed blacks, they would have to confront the kind of deprivation they would themselves have experienced if they had been treated the same way. Perhaps in this regard

Grimké is "lowering" her "passion to that pitch, in which the spectators are capable of going along" (*TMS*, I.i.4.7). The potentially homogenizing and normalizing effects of this example of sympathetic rhetoric should also be considered in the larger context of Grimké's view of human rights, which allows for the heterogeneity and integrity of all human beings, and the rhetorical challenges of addressing an audience who turns a blind eye to the injustice that lies just beneath the surface of Northern society, all the while congratulating itself for its moral superiority in abolishing the institution of slavery. Whites should not only place their "souls" in the "stead" of freed blacks but also imagine a situation in which they themselves, deprived of opportunities to which they are accustomed, feel shame and seek justice accordingly. The callousness with which whites regard the plight of enslaved people is not natural, Grimké's rhetoric implies, but, rather, arises from the selfishness that comes from living in societies corrupted by slavery. Through her unique rhetoric of sympathy, Grimké forces her readers to confront their own callousness and culpability head on and, in so doing, points the way to reform.

## Grimké's Sympathetic Rhetoric of Reform

A detailed analysis of Grimké's work shows that her understanding of sympathy is theoretically sophisticated and sufficiently rich to merit extended examination on its own terms. Smith's moral theory offers a useful framework that places abolitionist and early women's rights conceptions of sympathy such as Grimké's in sharp relief, allowing their unique contributions to emerge. Grimké's work expands on aspects of Smith's theory by demonstrating specific uses of rhetoric and moral theory that may be more capable of bringing about political and social change than critics of sympathetic rhetoric would allow. Upon closer inspection, Grimké's understanding of sympathy does not necessarily deprive enslaved peoples of individual agency by sentimentalizing their plight. Nor does it necessarily oversimplify the complexities of identity or deny the limits of human connection. Seen in this light, Grimké's sympathetic rhetoric of reform, culminating in her dramatic exchange with Beecher, helps us better understand the power, and potential shortcomings, of rhetoric and moral philosophy to bring about political change.

4

## Sarah Grimké's Quaker Liberalism

For some, the title of this chapter might seem a contradiction in terms. Yet it indicates my attempt to examine two schools of thought that are often considered in tension with one another and that nevertheless have been applied to nineteenth-century abolitionist and early women's rights advocate Sarah Grimké. Along with her younger sister, Angelina, Grimké was one of the first female speakers in America to address mixed audiences in public arenas, the first being Frances Wright. Her *Letters on the Equality of the Sexes and the Condition of Woman* is seen as "the first book written by an American presenting a fully developed woman's rights argument," emerging "ten years before the first woman's rights convention in Seneca Falls, NY."[1] The 1838 book was composed of a series of letters written by Grimké in 1837 to Mary S. Parker, president of the Boston Female Anti-Slavery Society, that had been published first in the *New England Spectator* and again in the *Liberator*.

In spite of the fact that Quakers drafted two constitutions in colonial America, wrote a number of political treatises, and regularly served in public office, Quakers are typically seen as non-political. Described as "quietists" and "withdrawers," the Quakers' pacifism has been interpreted as passivity, and their observation of conscientious objection has been simplistically conflated with acts of civil disobedience. For these reasons, as Jane Calvert notes, historians have declared that "Quakers can be 'safely neglected' in the study of constitutionalism [because] 'they took no great part in political agitations of any kind.'"[2]

The historian Gerda Lerner is largely responsible for bringing to light Grimké's contributions to the history of Western feminist thought, writing a definitive biography of the Grimké sisters and overseeing the reappearance of their works in print, including previously unpublished material.[3] Lerner acknowledges the importance of Grimké's religious beliefs in the formation of her views on women's rights, explaining that "her stance was that of a sectarian of the radical left-wing of the Reformation in her insistence on her right to judge the meanings of the biblical texts for herself."[4] However, Lerner's desire to situate Grimké within the development of modern feminism leads her to emphasize aspects of her thought associated with Enlightenment liberalism, especially its privileging of reason over revelation and its reliance on the ideal of the rational autonomous individual over those associated with religion.[5] "Reasoning by way of a close reading of the scriptural text and relying only on her own judgment and interpretations," Grimké "defined the difference between sex and gender and stated, in terms which would not be as clearly stated again until late in the 20th century: gender is a culturally variable, arbitrary definition of behavior appropriate to each of the sexes." For Lerner, "feminist Bible criticism had reached the point where it led directly to a feminist world-view. It remained for feminist criticism to step entirely outside the bounds of the Christian world-view and to become skeptical, *rational*, even agnostic."[6] Lerner's approach is emblematic of many interpreters of the early women's rights movement who emphasize the movement's "progress" toward a rational secularism and effectively downplay the importance of religion because of its role in imposing a patriarchal worldview that oppresses women.

In an attempt to reconcile Grimké's Enlightenment liberalism with her Quaker beliefs, Alison M. Parker acknowledges that, for Grimké, Christian faith "could lead women not just to salvation after death" but also to a political "awareness of their equality and rights in this world."[7] Grimké's religious principles "confirmed woman's necessary participation in politics and government."[8] Calling for what she would refer to as a "Christian Community," Grimké "believed that only with women's full political participation could an ideal nation be created, for their ability to mother ensured that their votes would be based on what was best for the entire community."[9]

For Parker, Grimké and her sister Angelina initially abided by the apolitical perfectionism and "no-human-government" position articulated by William Lloyd Garrison and other reformers that complemented their Quaker faith. However, they came to realize that legal and political reform was necessary to end slavery and improve the status of women. Their support of petitioning efforts reflected an understanding of "the role for the federal government in enacting legislation and passing constitutional amendments that could promote the changes they sought."[10] In the decade before the Civil War, the sisters also campaigned for moral reform through the passage of regulatory laws that would increase the power of local and state governments to restrict the behavior of individuals, such as protemperance dry laws. During the war and Reconstruction, "they supported federal amendments to the U.S. Constitution to abolish slavery and to enfranchise black men and black and white women, thereby ensuring their status as true citizens."[11] Grimké's major works, such as the *Epistle to the Clergy of the Southern States* (1836), the *Letters on the Equality of the Sexes and the Condition of Woman* (1837), and *American Slavery as It Is* (1839), which highlighted the deprivation of any legal status to slave women, provide a detailed account of women's "legal disabilities." In her later essays, written in the 1850s, Grimké "advocated women's suffrage and went farther than many other woman's rights activists of her time by demanding that women should have literally equal representation in the state and federal legislatures."[12] As with Lerner's account, we see that the secular aspects of Grimké's life and work—in particular, her support for an expansive role for the federal government in achieving reform through legislation and constitutional amendments—would ultimately take precedence over her religious views.[13]

The most extreme portrayal of Grimké as a secular liberal feminist is based on her rejection of English common law, an important element of her critique of the legal oppression of women and a key development in the emergence of liberal feminism.[14] On this view, English common law defines women's legal, political, and social roles in terms of coverture, by which women are held subordinate to men. Because common law is unwritten, its application to women is subject to the will of male authorities who apply the principle of "equity" in whatever way they see fit, bound only by the precedents other men have set. By rejecting common law, the main source of women's identity for centuries, and embracing liberalism, early women's rights advocates including Grimké were left without norms to help determine their new roles in society. No women had actually experienced the rights and responsibilities that would be required of them under liberalism because those rights and responsibilities were conceived from the male perspective, by men. This led to the creation of "the abstract woman," a concept of the ideal individual who is unencumbered by any cultural, historical, or contextual influences and unfazed by experiences; a rights-bearing individual whose existence is prior to all subsequent obligations and duties.[15] Although liberal feminists believe that common law is incapable of reforming itself by expanding women's rights, "liberalism's abstract principles" create other problems that also hinder change. Because they "are removed from experience," liberalism's abstractions "can overlook the sites of subjection and invite the assumption that they have liberated the oppressed from that subjection."[16]

It is true that the legacy of liberal feminism is mixed. Alongside the various developments that expanded women's rights—such as greater access to education and vocational opportunities, protection of private property, suffrage, and marriage reform—there remained lingering inequalities based on patriarchal assumptions about women's traditional roles in society. However, the portrayal of Grimké and others as liberal feminists itself glosses over a reality that is far more complex and nuanced.[17] Like other advocates, Grimké's support for women's rights emanates precisely from her own unique personal and spiritual experience. As the daughter of a wealthy Southern slave owner, Grimké experienced slavery firsthand in a way no Northerner could have. She permanently relocated to the North and converted to Quakerism, only to find herself alienated from her church, which surely contributed to her independent thinking and disdain for male interpreters of Scripture.[18] Grimké was a woman who was deprived of a formal education or choice of profession but who took full advantage of her father's extensive library and benefited from the instruction of her brother, who was trained as a lawyer. Thus it is not surprising that she would support women's education and access to professions. Although Grimké's public speaking was overshadowed by Angelina's superior oratorical skills, both women were ultimately driven from the stage by the storm of controversy that surrounded their activities, which would explain her advocacy of women in the ministry and speaking in public generally. In short, Grimké would surely be puzzled by the characterization that her efforts to expand women's rights were based in "abstractions."

Grimké's work is not simply secular or "radically" liberal. Nor can her contributions be purged of their religious underpinnings without serious distortion. To highlight the unappreciated political implications of her theory while not losing sight of its religious foundation, I expand on the analysis of Grimké's understanding of the American Constitution and its role in protecting the rights of black and white women by drawing from recent research on Quaker constitutionalism, as exemplified by William Penn and the life and work of frequently overlooked founder John Dickinson.[19] Because Dickinson is best known for his contradictory stance of refusing to sign the Declaration of Independence while advocating colonial rights, he is not typically credited with holding a coherent constitutional doctrine. Penn's achievement of founding the colony that bears his name typically overshadows whatever theoretical contributions he might have offered.[20] Along similar lines, although Grimké might have supported an expansive view of the federal government, she is not seen as articulating a comprehensive constitutional theory.

While it is true that Dickinson and Penn offered far more advanced conceptions of constitutionalism than commonly believed, I do not intend to argue that Grimké held a fully developed constitutional theory of her own. Rather, I want to show that Grimké's life and work reflect several characteristics of Quaker constitutionalism. In particular, Grimké outlines a view of women's rights that is part of a larger constitutional framework that does not require a total revolution or the creation of a completely new concept of the individual, namely, an "abstract woman" that is utterly detached from reality. Instead, Grimké portrays the emergence of women's rights as a continuum of the fundamental constitution, namely, the law of nature that comes "directly to man through God" through synteresis. A defining element of Quakerism, synteresis refers to a kind of intuition or inner light that provides immediate human access to the word of God. Through synteresis, the first principles of the fundamental constitution are "immediately discernable" and include "founding ideals of liberty, unity, and peace."[21] Through the application of human reason and collective discernment, the fundamental constitution in turn forms the basis of written constitutions. On this view, the Declaration of Independence and the American Constitution are based on the fundamental constitution insofar as they correspond to the word of God as discerned through synteresis and the collective understanding of all Americans.[22] Because human reason is fallible, however, misinterpretations arise, which requires a return to the first principles and reexamination through synteresis and collective discernment. "Thus while a return to first principles did destroy the corrupt aspects of the government," including the oppression of women and slavery, "the fundamental constitution of the people remained intact and the power to reconstitute the government lay within them."[23] For Quakers like Grimké, therefore, women's rights understood as extensions of the fundamental constitution that underlie the American Constitution could never be considered ex nihilo developments. And if Grimké envisioned an expansive role for federal government in her plans for reform, those institutions would have to be grounded on the first principles of the fundamental constitution as well.

Although many early women's rights advocates and abolitionists would adopt the rhetorical technique of portraying reform as a natural outgrowth of the American founding in order to lend legitimacy to the movement, Grimké's approach is unique because it is substantively informed by her Quaker faith and reflects aspects of Quaker constitutionalism.[24] By weaving women's rights into the fabric of the American founding, Grimké demonstrates more than mere rhetorical expertise, lending additional credibility to the founding of the women's rights movement as she challenges the notion that women's rights must be created from whole cloth. Using Quaker constitutionalism as a frame of analysis, we gain a greater appreciation for the theoretical and political implications for Grimké's founding treatise on women's rights.

## Quaker Constitutionalism: A Primer

To understand the Quaker contribution to the American Founding, several misconceptions must be addressed first. Although Quakerism grew out of the Puritan Revolution, it differed significantly from Puritanism, especially in its "greater degree of spiritual egalitarianism, the authority of immediate revelation equal to or above Scripture, and the possibility of human perfection."[25] Nor should it be collapsed into the "secularized Puritanism" or reformed Calvinism that provides the basis for "the republican ideology at the American Founding," for in fact "Quaker political ideas in the late-eighteenth century were far from 'secularized.'"[26] Because Quaker constitutionalism differs significantly from the secular Whig perspective characteristic of Enlightenment liberalism, it cannot be lumped into the amorphous category of "liberalism." But neither can it be seen as an endorsement of common law or Tory support of divine rights. Indeed, although Grimké's advocacy of women's rights reflected a strong religious commitment, her views differ sharply from those of conservative evangelicals such as Beecher, especially regarding the "separate spheres" of men and women.

In accordance with the principle of synteresis, Quakers are called upon to speak if and when they are inspired to do so by the inner light or revelation. Because the light, as the word of God, aims at perfection, it allows for and necessitates change for the sake of improvement.[27] Whereas Enlightenment rationalism observed the notion that the word of God was accessible to human beings indirectly, through natural law that is ultimately discerned by reason, Quakers believed that human reason was fallible. Used alone, reason was an untrustworthy guide for divine teachings because it was subject to excessive self-interest.[28] Religious doctrine based on human interpretation of Scripture was therefore suspect and subject to correction by synteresis. Collective discernment of the true meaning of God's word is crucial to avoid mistakes.[29] Political deliberation required universal involvement as well: "Popular participation in a civil or ecclesiastical polity was a process of collective discernment through synteresis."[30] For Quakers, synteresis and reason were not mutually exclusive but, rather, complementary. Indeed, many Quakers used rational natural rights language to describe synteresis. By the mid-nineteenth century, Hicksite Quakerism defined itself by, among other things, the blending of reason and synteresis.[31]

Synteresis forms the basis of Quaker constitutionalism. Synteresis requires constant review of human decision making and insists on a return to first principles when considering reform.[32] Thus the "civil constitution . . . was rather created by God and then discerned through synteresis and transcribed by men."[33] Quaker constitutionalism thus offered "the idea of perpetuity of a fundamental constitution along with an internal process of amendment."[34] It allowed for "peaceful change that made use of the existing system—nonviolent protest of various sorts, including civil disobedience"—that was a precursor to judicial review.[35] From the Hicksite perspective, which is profoundly non-doctrinal, synteresis is presented as non-denominational, and many progressive Quaker reformers, including Grimké, intended their views to be accessible to anyone who believed in God. Thus it would be possible to apply

Quaker constitutionalism on a broader scale, to the American Constitution and the Declaration of Independence.

Synteresis also underlies the Quaker concept of "corporate witness," which requires that members of the deliberative body be unified, not by sharing the same ideas, but rather by fundamentally committing themselves to the good of the community and, ultimately, to the will of God. Thus "legal discernment could come only through the unity of the body" forged by synteresis.[36] Collective discernment was premised upon the belief that all human beings were created equal by God and had "equal opportunity to receive, discern, and express God's Light in their consciences." As a result, "while every member of the meeting had a voice, not all voices had equal weight."[37] Ensuring that everyone would be heard required delicate balancing between individual inclinations and group preferences. Although "dissent within the body was desirable," it was "a matter to be handled very delicately," requiring dissenters to express their views clearly and carefully so as to ensure the greatest accuracy of synteresis and to avoid jeopardizing the fundamental unity and harmony of the group. If a dissenter fails to persuade or convince the group, he "must submit his will to that of the collective rather than try to obstruct it" and "support the body in its goals."[38] A dissenter might submit, but she is not simply giving up or being silenced against her will, according to Quaker principle. Because human reason is fallible, a dissenter must be aware that the source of disagreement might be misunderstanding or misinterpretation of synteresis. According to Quaker belief in "an idea of progressive revelation" by which "some individuals may have had a more advanced understanding than the group," God would continue to reveal the truth to all, so the dissenter would know that there would be other opportunities to be heard. "Dissent thus should be a slow process of persuasion, convincement, and gradual revelation, not coercion."[39]

In the process of collective discernment, Quakers could use additional tools as guides, such as "common law proven reasonable and valid through induction or practice . . . that had become custom" and "the physical experiences that are recorded in [secular] history."[40] Specifically, "if the reasonable customs established through worldly experience were valid, they should comport with revelation." However, "customs based solely on practical reason were dangerous in that they led to the establishment of pernicious traditions—the blind acceptance of practices that were enemies of truth."[41]

Quaker constitutionalism differs from liberal Enlightenment constitutionalism in several important ways. Under synteresis, reason would never supersede the direct voice of God when in conflict, as John Locke proposed in his *Letter concerning Toleration*. Although individual autonomy and independent thought were highly valued, Quaker constitutionalism fundamentally required collective discernment and deliberation. Political deliberation entailed a decision-making process informed by synteresis, which may or may not arrive at the same conclusions as a decision-making process guided by reason alone. Whereas majoritarian decision making by "consensus reveals a willed decision found through a (reasoned) competition of ideas," the sense of the Quaker meeting "reveals a willingness to be led, to listen, to weigh."[42] Government was not defined in negative terms of protecting rights but, rather, as providing the conditions that would enable individuals to live a life of benevolence and good works as informed by the word of God.[43] Natural rights were not sacrificed in order to gain the protections provided by government. Rather, "man 'contributes' his rights" through the "active engagement in the polity for the good of all."[44] Only the aspects of custom, tradition, common law, and experience that comported with the word of God rightly understood through synteresis and collective discernment would be considered legitimate. Dissent was not merely tolerated, but actually encouraged, as Quakers felt compelled to discern the word of God as accurately as possible. Political obligation was not understood in purely contractual terms, nor could it simply be dissolved and begun anew because it was fundamentally rooted in the Quaker decision making process and, as such, "a 'trust' given by Heaven."[45] Rather, the fundamental agreement to form a Quaker community imposed a permanent obligation on that community that required and allowed for reform and change, returning to fundamental principles in order to readjust course when necessary. Quaker constitutionalism does not support the Enlightenment liberal view that the constitution of the people and the constitution of the government were fundamentally separable, according to which "the people were first constituted as a body" and "then created a written constitution that embodied fundamental law and limited the government." On this view, "a nation's government" is derivative of the original constitution of the people, and thus "any acts of government to which the people consent are subordinate to that [original] constitution."[46] By contrast, synteresis forges a permanent connection between the people and their government based on the word of God.[47] The notion of an "ancient constitution"—according to which fundamental principles formed "an all-inclusive civil government that was comprised of a written constitution, a government, and a system of positive law"—more closely resembles the Quaker view insofar as the collective deliberation informed by synteresis, and ultimately the word of God, allows Quakers to form an all-inclusive government of their own.[48] In this respect, Quaker constitutionalism is a "variation of divine right theory" but categorically rejects the notion of "the divine right of kings."[49]

Although Quaker constitutionalism offers a compelling alternative understanding of the American founding principles, its applicability in a diverse community with fundamentally competing interests seems limited. The Quaker community relies on the suppositions that "each member of the meeting seeks the best solution" and that "the group, in searching together, guided by their collective presence, can create and be constituted in concord and unity, even truth."[50] The Quaker community seems to presuppose that which makes deliberation most difficult, namely, the authentic recognition of the standpoint of the other. For it is a simple fact that, "until participants in disagreement can become interlocutors and achieve a kind of presence, there will not be deliberations"—a fact that deliberative democratic theorists continue to grapple with even today.[51] Although Angelina Grimké seeks to broaden her Southern female audience to include Christians of other denominations, this criticism would seem most directly applicable to her arguments, but not necessarily to those of other Quaker reformers. In the next section I show how Sarah Grimké leads her audience through a systematic refutation of the scriptural arguments used to oppress women and a comprehensive critique of the "legal disabilities" of women in America ultimately so that they may weigh her arguments on their own and form their own conclusions. Like Lucretia Mott, as we will see in the next chapter, Grimké seeks to encourage her audience to challenge dogmas and ideologies and think independently, thereby uniting disparate individuals, not into agreement, but rather into a common frame of mind. To varying degrees, these reformers engage in a Quaker practice referred to as "walking," according to which they proceed step by step through various arguments, inspired by their inner light, and thereby provide a "model for how to perform a reasonable dialogue with others" as well as how "to forge a practical, sympathetic network."[52] Based on the idea of "walking in the way of Christ," Quaker deliberation requires that any individual "purify himself of his own selfish motives and approach the meeting in humility as Christ's agent." If an individual is not sufficiently "heard," he must exercise "forbearance" because he is also providing an important model, or "Example," for others to follow, Quaker and non-Quaker alike.[53]

## Grimké's Civil Quakerism

Grimké begins her important contribution to the American project and the founding of feminism on a seemingly demure note. "It is not my intention," she proclaims, "nor indeed do I think it is in my power, to point out the precise duties of women." Rather, she calls for her "beloved sisters" to begin the process of self-reflection and independent thinking guided by synteresis.[54] What follows, however, is an expansive theoretical account of a civil government consistent with Quaker constitutionalism that requires equality between the sexes and would include a written constitution, a government, and a system of positive law. Grimké outlines a kind of "civil Quakerism," a broader set of cultural beliefs and practices that would complement the scriptural teachings pertaining to men and women and that are discerned through synteresis.[55] In effect, Grimké's *Letters* serve as founding documents of the early women's rights movement, written from a uniquely Quaker perspective, and to which other advocates would make their own contributions.

Grimké's *Letters* reflect the style and substance of Quaker speaking. The epistolary style resembles the measured, direct speech one might find at a Quaker meeting and advocated by Penn and Dickinson. That the letters were published in a widely read newspaper and later in book form suggests that a broader audience including men and non-Quakers was intended as well. Although the term "synteresis" had already fallen out of favor by the time Penn wrote his major works, Grimké nevertheless adopts the perspective of synteresis at the outset: "I believe it to be the solemn duty of every individual to search the Scriptures for themselves, with the aid of the Holy Spirit, and not be governed by the views of any man, or set of men."[56] Although it was acceptable Quaker practice to use custom, tradition, and precedent in their collective quest to discern the word of God, Grimké cannot do so in the case of women's rights because she believes that

> almost every thing that has been written on [the] subject, has been the result of a misconception of the simple truths revealed in the Scriptures, in consequence of the false translation of many passages of Holy Writ. My mind is entirely delivered from the superstitious reverence which is attached to the English version of the Bible. King Jame's [sic] translators certainly were not inspired.[57]

Consistent with the idea that synteresis provides the basis for a proper constitution, Grimké explains that her main purpose in the *Letters* is to provide the foundation for a collective understanding of the scriptural teachings on women in order to create a more just civil society and develop a more just set of laws:

> I believe the welfare of the world will be materially advanced by every new discovery we make of the designs of Jehovah in the creation of woman. It is impossible that we can answer the purpose of our being, unless we understand that purpose. It is impossible that we should fulfill our duties, unless we comprehend them; or live up to our privileges, unless we know what they are.[58]

The first duty of women, "to think for themselves," is defined, not merely in terms of the application of (secular) reason, but rather in terms of synteresis, as Grimké urges women "to take the volume of inspiration in their hand, to enter into their closet, and to ask wisdom," so that they may understand their humanly duties as creatures of God.[59] What follows over the course of several letters is an exegesis of the scriptural teachings on women that would become commonplace in the early women's rights movement. Grimké's contribution is part of the long tradition of biblical interpretation that emphasizes its egalitarian aspects and on which much of progressive Quaker doctrine is based.[60] Grimké highlights the first account of the creation in Genesis, in which man and woman are created simultaneously, as evidence of the equality at the root of the scriptural teachings. The subsequent creation account, in which Eve is derived from Adam, does not connote the natural inferiority of women, she argues, nor does it give men dominion over women. For in fact, after the Fall, God's command that Adam will rule over Eve is "a simple prophecy," an observation of what happens in the future, not a moral verdict against women.[61] Adam is given absolute dominion over the animal kingdom, but his control does not extend to Eve; rather, both remain equal in the eyes of God. For Grimké, the most plausible reason for any subsequent domination over women after the Fall occurred because "there was no other intelligent being over whom to exercise it."[62] Moreover, the Old Testament portrays Abraham and Sarah and other men and women "engaged in the same employments," further underscoring their equality.[63] Turning her attention to the New Testament, Grimké notes that the principles expressed in the Sermon on the Mount were put forth "without any reference to sex or condition" and that female apostles were active in the early Church.[64] Grimké translates the term "helpmeet" as "helper like unto himself," not a subordinate, but rather a companion who is a "free agent" and "in all respects his equal."[65] If the Pauline epistles suggest the inferiority of women, she argues, it is only because Paul's mind "was under the influence of Jewish prejudices respecting women, just as Peter's and the apostles were about the uncleanness of the Gentiles."[66] Patriarchal interpretations later advanced by Henry VIII and Milton, she observes, have not been terribly helpful, either. The infamous Pauline command that women keep silent did not reflect a divine prohibition against women preaching. Rather, it arose when "Christian women, presuming on the liberty which they enjoyed under the new religion, interrupted the assembly, by asking questions. . . . It disturbed the solemnity of the meeting."[67] Wherever there are commands to women, she notes, there are commands to husbands as well.[68] On Grimké's reading, women served as prophets, and if all Christian ministers, not just male clergy, succeeded the prophets, then "women are now called to that office as well as men."[69]

Although many of Grimké's ideas were likely influenced by other progressive scriptural readings, especially Quaker cofounder Margaret Fell's 1666 pamphlet, *Womens Speaking Justified*, she advances original interpretations of her own as well. For example, she suggests that Adam was more culpable for disobeying God's command not to eat from the tree of knowledge. Eve "was exposed to temptation from a being with whom she was unacquainted." As Grimké explains, Eve "had been accustomed to associate with her beloved partner, and to hold communion with God and with angels; but of satanic intelligence, she was in all probability entirely ignorant." By contrast, Adam was involved, "not through the instrumentality of a super-natural agent, but through that of his equal, a being whom he must have known was liable to transgress the divine command" as much as he was.[70] Grimké further emphasizes the point by observing that "Adam's ready acquiescence with his wife's proposal, does not savor much of that superiority *in strength of mind*, which is arrogated by man."[71] Grimké's reversal of the traditional account, reminiscent of Wright's, would also be echoed years later in Elizabeth Cady Stanton's writings and speeches.

After laying the scriptural groundwork, Grimké is able to distinguish between authentic egalitarian scriptural teachings and the patriarchal customs and traditions with which they have often been mistaken, especially those that emerge from English common law. In response to the pastoral letter issued by the General Association of Massachusetts to the Churches Under Their Care, which reasserted the scriptural basis for woman's obedience to man, Grimké presents an account of the systematic oppression that results from women's "legal disabilities," an account for which she has been widely recognized.[72] Comparing the authors of the pastoral letter with Cotton Mather and others who did nothing to stop the Salem witch trials, Grimké traces the source of oppression to men who "having long held the reins of *usurped* authority, are unwilling to permit us to fill that sphere which God created us to move in, and who have entered into league to crush the immortal mind of women."[73] She rails against the "false translation of some passages" in the New Testament "by the MEN who did that work, and against the perverted interpretation by the MEN who understood to write commentaries thereon." In response, she offers the results of her own reading derived directly from "studying Greek and Hebrew."[74] Power dynamics determine the dominant messages as those in authority shape the terms of debate and define others in ways that maintain their dominance. From the fact that the Sermon on the Mount was delivered to men and women "without any reference to sex or condition," Grimké concludes that "Men and women were CREATED EQUAL; they are both moral and accountable beings, and whatever is *right* for a man to do, is *right* for woman."[75] Although Grimké concedes that men and women differ in physical strength, in no way does it follow that women are morally and mentally inferior to men. To counter the assertion in the pastoral letter that women should be "unostentatious" in their religious advocacy, Grimké refers to the prophetess Anna's service to God, which was "ostentatious" in its steadfastness, and to the command that all shall "lift up thy voice like a trumpet."[76] She reminds her audience that God is the ultimate authority over men and women—including the religious leaders who seek to impose their own authority on others.

Broadening her theological analysis into a sociopolitical critique, Grimké proceeds to describe the cultural influence of these willfully inaccurate scriptural teachings and the ways in which they affect every aspect of women's lives. In similar fashion to Wright, who traced the corrosive influence of male-dominated religion on women, Grimké explains that women

> have all too well learned the lesson which MAN has labored to teach her. She has surrendered her dearest RIGHTS, and been satisfied with the privileges which man has assumed to grant her; she has been amused with the show of power, whilst man has absorbed all the reality into himself.

As a result, women have been made "the instrument of his selfish gratification, a plaything to please his eye and amuse his hours of leisure." The subordinate position of women has led to their moral degradation: "'Rule by obedience and by submission sway,' or, in other words, study to be a hypocrite, pretend to submit, but gain your point, has been the code of household morality which women have been taught."[77]

Instead of abiding by the literal translation of Genesis in which "help-meet" is rendered an equal "helper like unto himself," men and women interact with one another "under the constant pressure of a feeling that [they] are of different sexes." As a result, "our intercourse, instead of being elevated and refined, is generally calculated to excite and keep alive the lowest propensities of our nature." Men manipulate women with flattery only to transform them into an "instrument" of pleasure or comfort, relegated to the role of housekeeper or nursemaid. Most galling to an intelligent woman like Grimké is the fact that while a man "goes abroad and enjoys the means of improvement afforded by collision of intellect with cultivated minds, his wife is condemned to draw nearly all her instruction from books, if she has time to peruse them; and if not, from her meditations, whilst engaged in those domestic duties, which are necessary for the comfort of her lord and master."[78] The undue focus on domestic chores inevitably elevates "the animal above the intellectual and spiritual nature, and teaches women to regard themselves as a kind of machinery, necessary to keep the domestic engine in order, but of little value as the *intelligent* companions of men."[79] By contrast, the egalitarian marriage Grimké envisions will allow women to become better wives, mothers, and even housekeepers, "doing her duty thoroughly and *understandingly*."[80]

Grimké notes that the inequality between the sexes also results in the devaluation of woman's labor. Presaging contemporary debates over equal pay and comparable worth, she observes that, "in those employments which are peculiar to women, their time is estimated at only half the value of that of men."[81] Widows fare especially poorly under these circumstances, forced to care for their children while barely subsisting on the meager fruits of their labor.[82]

However, female slaves suffer most acutely under economic exploitation by men. "In our slave States, if amid all her degradation and ignorance, a woman desires to preserve her virtue unsullied, she is either bribed or whipped into compliance, or if she dares resist her seducer, her life by the laws of some of the slave States may be, and has actually been sacrificed to the fury of disappointed passion."[83] The harm is not limited to enslaved women, as white women are degraded as well. Forced to stand idly by and watch as their enslaved counterparts are systematically abused, they continue to associate with men whom they know "to be polluted by licentiousness, and often [are] compelled to witness in [their] own domestic circle, those disgusting and heart-sickening jealousies and strifes which disgraced and distracted the family of Abraham."[84] It is clear that the fates of men and women are closely intertwined and often inversely related. In a corrupt society based on scriptural misinterpretation, men thrive and prosper at the expense of women at all levels.

By contrast, in a reformed society governed by the principles of Quaker constitutionalism, women would feel greater "sympathy" for others and adopt greater moral responsibility. Women who lack confidence and education would "realize they are free agents" and make their own decisions: "Pay all proper respect and deference to the opinions of relatives," Grimké advises, "but never let those opinions turn you aside from the path of duty." Likewise, women who are "glad of any excuse to relieve themselves from difficult and arduous duties" and defer to male authorities would realize that they have only one master, God, and must act of their own accord.[85]

Grimké includes in her broader outline of a "civil Quakerism" a devastating critique of the legal treatment of women in America under the influence of English common law. The laws regarding women have "been enacted to destroy [their] independence, and crush [their] individuality." Most important, perhaps, is that they violate the cardinal rule of Quaker constitutionalism, namely, that women have an equal role in crafting laws. Instead, the American woman is subjected to "laws which, although they are framed for her government, she has had no voice in establishing, and which rob her of some of her *essential rights*." As a result, "woman has no political existence" and, aside from petitioning Congress, "is a cipher in the nation."[86]

Grimké proceeds to draw parallels between the legal status of free white and enslaved women. "The very being of a woman, like that of a slave, is absorbed in her master," she writes. "All contracts made with her, like those made with slaves by their owners, are a mere nullity." In violation of Quaker constitutionalism, which requires transparency and active participation by all, men "have kept us in ignorance of those very laws by which we are governed. They have persuaded us, that we have no right to investigate the laws, and that, if we did, we could not comprehend them."[87] Women, free or enslaved, have no control over their property or income. They cannot lay claim to any damages won in court and yet are held responsible for the debts of their husbands. The American Revolution was fought over unfair taxation, but the right to "no taxation without representation" has not been extended to women.

Grimké explicitly qualifies her observations by stating, "I do not wish by any means to intimate that the condition of free women can be compared to that of slaves in suffering, or in degradation."[88] Nevertheless, critics maintain that Grimké "appropriates female slaves' experience to authorize the rhetoric of white women" like herself, "further silencing the enslaved." Because Grimké's descriptions invite her audience to engage in "vicarious sharing" of the suffering female slave, she "maintains rather than challenges white privilege."[89] Although the metaphorical connection between women and slaves "uses their shared position as bodies to be bought, owned, and designated as a grounds of resistance," it simultaneously "obliterates the particularity of black and female experience" because it makes "their distinct exploitations appear as one." According to this line of criticism, the constant threat of appropriation constitutes "the essential dilemma of feminist-abolitionist rhetoric."[90] Yet these critiques offer no guidance on how to address or solve this problem. It is equally possible that Grimké was motivated by her Quaker faith and commitment to civic constitutionalism as she was by her race and class privilege. In any case, this line of criticism would seem to raise questions about the very notion of intersectionality, since attempts to examine the interrelationship between different forms of oppression would be subject to charges of appropriation of the most oppressed class. And the fact that Grimké is careful to deny any comparability in the degree of oppression suffered by women and slaves, respectively, should at least be acknowledged.

Grimké calls for the men in power to "repeal these unjust and unequal laws, and restore to woman those rights which they have wrested from her."[91] And given that "ecclesiastical bodies" governed by men follow the example of legislatures also governed by men "in excluding woman from any participation in forming the discipline by which she is governed," Grimké insists that women also be allowed to serve in ministry and freely worship as they choose.[92]

Although Grimké clearly believes that marriage reform is necessary, her vision is decidedly Quaker in that she continues to insist that marriage is "a *divine ordination*, not a civil contract. God established it, and man, except by special permission, has no right to annul it."[93] Marriage reform would consist, not of adopting a liberal contractual approach, but rather of observing the egalitarian teachings of Scripture. Women's submission would still be possible, but would occur on a fundamentally different basis:

If she submits, let her do it openly, honorably, not to gain her point, but as a matter of Christian duty. But let her beware how she permits her husband to be her conscience-keeper. On all moral and religious subjects, she is bound to think and to act for herself. Where confidence and love exist, a wife will naturally converse with her husband as with her dearest friend, on all that interests her heart, and there will be a perfectly free interchange of sentiment; but *she is no more bound to be governed by his judgment*, than he is by hers. They are standing on the same platform of human rights, are equally under the government of God, and accountable to him, and him alone.[94]

Women and men submit themselves, not to each other, but to the marriage itself, which is based on friendship and fundamental equality. As equal human beings, both men and women ultimately submit themselves to God. Along similar lines, Grimké allows for differences between the sexes so long as they do not result in inequality. Her claim that because "duties belong to *situation*, not to sex"—for example, "a mother has duties totally different for a single woman"—may mean that Grimké ultimately maintains gender hierarchies even as she seeks to reform them. However, this observation must be seen in light of her insistence that "the rights and responsibilities of men and women as moral beings are identical, and must necessarily be so, if their nature is the same, and their relations to the supreme Being precisely similar." If this premise, arising from her Quaker faith, is taken into account, what would have been a fundamentally unequal relationship in her society would be transformed into a just and equitable partnership. Thus, on Grimké's view, in spite of situational differences, "with regard to all moral reformations, men and women have the same duties and the same rights."[95]

## Grimké's Quaker Liberalism

Grimké's *Letters on the Equality of the Sexes* offers an alternative understanding of America's fundamental constitution from a uniquely Quaker perspective in a way that requires the equality of men and women. Her work should not be understood simply as another product of the liberal Enlightenment, nor should it be pigeonholed as purely religious in nature with little political significance. The framework provided by Grimké requires reconsideration of fundamental principles such as human reason, individual rights, political deliberation, participation, representation, economic justice, and morality. I have tried to demonstrate that Grimké's portrayal of reform in terms of a natural outgrowth of the American founding is not simply a rhetorical ploy to lend legitimacy to a movement but, rather, a genuine attempt to reconsider the foundational constitutional principles of America.

It is important to gain a greater appreciation for the complexity and diversity of the early women's rights movement in America and to recognize that many of its advocates were not simply activists but thinkers in their own right who made important theoretical contributions to our understanding of the American project. Indeed, Grimké's work, along with others, serves as an important illustration of a "constituent moment" in American history in which "the underauthorized" or marginalized individuals and groups "seize the mantle of authorization, changing the inherited rules of authorization in the process," and thereby "invent a new political space."[96] Grimké saw her efforts not as an innovation but, rather, a continuation of the American Founding properly understood. On her view, America's first principles have been obscured by the fallibility of human reason, which thwarts synteresis and collective discernment. Grimké's readers, however, would be encountering her Quaker constitutionalism for the first time and would find her constitutional ideals to be "new." Thus Grimké's political theory should be seen as an important part of the "American civic constitution" because it offers a unique understanding of "governing ideals of liberty, equality, and justice" that did not clearly emerge at the Founding and were not conceived by the Framers or subsequent interpreters, such as judges and political leaders.[97]

In this sense, Grimké was among the "civic founders" who "disrupted the dominant order, refashioned democratic citizenship, and constructed civic scaffoldings for new constitutional rights and commitments." Indeed, as "cofounders of the U.S. constitution," Grimké and her fellow reformers contributed to the development of vital constitutional doctrines on suffrage, representation, federal power, freedom of speech, expression, and assembly, the right to petition government, and civil disobedience. Together, these thinkers would articulate "a vision of gender justice" that underpins feminist legal claims.[98] Informed by the unique perspective of Quaker constitutionalism, with its emphasis on egalitarianism and free inquiry, Grimké helped carve out a space within the political culture of antebellum America in which a constitutionalism that abolishes slavery and provides greater rights for women could emerge.

5

# "The Most Belligerent Non-Resistant"

## *Lucretia Mott on Women's Rights*

In her 1860 speech delivered to the Pennsylvania Anti-Slavery Society, Quaker abolitionist and early women's rights advocate Lucretia Mott proclaimed that

> Robert Purvis has said that I was "the most belligerent Non-Resistant he ever saw." I accept the character he gives me; and I glory in it. I have no idea, because I am a Non-Resistant, of submitting tamely to injustice inflicted either on me or on the slave. I will oppose it with all the moral powers with which I am endowed.[1]

The characterization offered by Purvis, an African American abolitionist, captures the paradoxical sense of Mott's life and work. The diminutive, plainly dressed, sixty-seven-year-old accepted with pride and defiance her status as a "belligerent" activist who will stop at nothing to combat injustice.

Not long after John Brown's raid on Harpers Ferry and before the outbreak of the Civil War, as fellow Garrisonians gravely reconsidered their commitment to moral suasion and contemplated supporting force to end slavery, Mott stood before the society and categorically rejected the use of violence. The paradox of Mott's non-violent "belligerence" extends beyond her particular ideas to the ways in which they were received and have been interpreted.

Mott's influential status among pivotal reformers is well known to historians and biographers, yet she remains largely unknown to political theorists. Perhaps this is because there is little indication at first glance that Mott's works offer a comprehensive theory of any kind. Mott left behind no treatises or lengthy writings to include in the canon of political thought. Instead, her extant works include forty-nine speeches and sermons that were delivered extemporaneously and later transcribed for publication as well as personal correspondence of "kaleidoscopic" breadth.[2] The equally "kaleidoscopic" nature of her commitments, combined with the lack of conventional theoretical works, has understandably led to portrayals that emphasize the moral and spiritual significance of Mott's efforts, rather than their theoretical importance.

Given Mott's progressive views and her remarkable achievements in such a tumultuous era of American history, however, the relative inattention is surprising. Mott envisioned women's rights in an expansive humanitarian context that included abolitionism, pacifism, temperance, and religious reform. Mott's prominent role in the 1848 Seneca Falls Women's Rights Convention and her 1849 speech "Discourse on Woman" constitute significant contributions to the early women's rights movement. Elizabeth Cady Stanton, whose political theory has been analyzed in detail, credits Mott for inspiring her to plan the pivotal meeting at Seneca Falls. Mott's progressive views on religion, which emphasize the equality of men and women and the importance of independent thought, precede Stanton's widely read and deeply controversial *Woman's Bible* by almost fifty years.[3] Mott's uncanny ability to maintain cordial relations among fiercely competing factions and mediate various conflicts among early women's rights activists and abolitionists provides an exemplary yet overlooked model of leadership.

Mott's tireless struggle against slavery and her unwavering commitment to equality for all African Americans distinguish her from other well-known abolitionists. She founded and actively participated in the longest-lasting interracial abolitionist organization in the United States, the Philadelphia Female Anti-Slavery Society, and her insistence on immediate emancipation pre-dates William Lloyd Garrison's commitment by several years.[4] Mott never entertained the possibility of colonization or similar compromises. Whereas Stanton's forceful and single-minded advocacy of women's suffrage after the Civil War raised serious questions about her commitment to universal enfranchisement, Mott never abandoned her conviction, rhetorically or otherwise, that racial and gender equality are inseparable. When many abolitionists, including Garrison, turned away from antislavery societies to focus on aiding freedmen after the Civil War, Mott, like Frederick Douglass, continued to support both efforts because she knew the detrimental effects of slavery did not end after the conflict and subsequent constitutional reforms.[5] Mott's deep skepticism about the ability of politics alone to enforce fundamental social change proved prescient, as brutal racial oppression persisted in the Reconstruction era and beyond.[6]

Mott's position among abolitionists and early women's rights advocates as a moral and spiritual leader was established early on and has been widely accepted. The narrative that initially emerged from the pivotal multivolume study the *History of Woman Suffrage* portrayed the early women's rights movement as a linear, unified progression from the decentralized and informal approach initiated by Mott and others to the sophisticated theory of women's equality and concrete plan of action devised by co-authors Stanton and Susan B. Anthony. Although the received account carves out an influential role for Mott, it has mischaracterized her real contributions. While giving Mott and others "the status of foremothers of the woman's rights movement," Stanton and Anthony "effectively removed them as active participants by claiming 1848 as the moment of its conception and relegating all that came before to prehistory."[7] Of course, many of Mott's abolitionist and women's rights activities preceded the Seneca Falls convention by a number of years.

Although Mott's influence on Stanton has been acknowledged by scholars, Stanton is still portrayed as ultimately surpassing her predecessor by replacing spiritual lamentations with political action. Stanton "presents a clear contrast to prominent abolitionist women" like Mott because Stanton ultimately moved beyond their religious strivings for human rights by establishing a comprehensive (and largely secular) political theory of women's rights and a concrete plan for legal and political reform.[8] Stanton surpasses Garrisonian women's rights advocates, including Mott, by developing a "notion of women as a class with the potential to develop consciousness of itself as such and to organize for radical political change."[9] The received narrative of the early women's rights movement is thereby reinforced as Mott's moral and spiritual influence is supplanted by Stanton's theoretical and pragmatic contributions.[10]

To be sure, there are significant theoretical differences between Stanton and Mott. Like Sarah and Angelina Grimké, Mott holds a worldview that is fundamentally informed by her Quaker faith, whereas Stanton is credited with introducing a secular approach to the early women's rights movement. Stanton and Mott emphasize the importance of natural rights and equality of individuals, but for Mott, these principles ultimately originate from the Hicksite Quaker view of human beings as creations of God who are guided by the inner light. Mott understands the individual holistically, created by a non-sectarian God to engage in reflective action and thereby honor her duties and obligations to others. Human beings must take active responsibility for discerning the inner light and constructing a world that allows all people to function as moral beings. Mott's Quaker understanding of justice requires extensive political, economic, social, and cultural reform that includes, but is not limited to, universal suffrage. Only in such a world would suffrage be truly effective. Mott's progressive religious values, her lifelong relationships with African American men and women, and her steady commitment to interracial reform organizations would never allow her to indulge in the kind of racist or elitist rhetoric that for many diminished elements of Stanton's thought. Mott supported Stanton's efforts to promote deeply controversial reforms of marriage and divorce and deplored the Quaker tradition of disowning those who had formed interfaith marriages or who had divorced. Yet Mott criticized as "extravagant" Stanton's divisive characterizations of marriage as a legal contract because she believed that marriage was a spiritual bond made voluntarily by equal parties and should only be dissolved in the most dire of circumstances.

The striking differences between the two women problematize the notion that Stanton ultimately surpassed Mott, theoretically or otherwise. In fact, "Mott's life suggests a more complicated, racially egalitarian history of early feminism" than Stanton's.[11] Because they were "less concerned with suffrage than with more general questions of political, economic, educational, and occupational access," earlier "pioneer feminists" such as Mott "created the foundation on which later generations of women could build antiracist, global, and multicultural coalitions." Thus, "to create a narrative of woman's rights . . . that does justice to the diversity of their origins and the complexity of their development requires . . . a broader definition of politics than is allowed by the conventional Seneca Falls-to-suffrage framing" that focuses so exclusively on Stanton.[12] In this chapter I hope to contribute to the revisionist narrative of women's rights by exploring the sophistication and complexity of Mott's comprehensive understanding of justice.

Although the strength of Mott's commitment to abolitionism cannot be overstated, accounts that portray her political ideas as a direct outgrowth of her obedience to Garrison also mislead by paradoxically elevating her status while undermining her originality and credibility as a theorist in her own right.[13] As I have explained in chapters 3 and 4, Garrisonians were notoriously skeptical about politics and believed that slavery could not be abolished exclusively through legal-political means. Instead, they employed moral suasion to appeal to individuals indirectly through petitioning, speeches, and writing. Their convictions coincided with the Quakers' rejection of coercion in all forms, political and otherwise, and their commitment to pacifism and avoidance of political involvement.

Seen in this light, Mott's hesitation to push for legal and political solutions or engage in direct political action derives simply from her religious beliefs and her support of Garrison. Like the Grimkés, Mott aligned herself early on with Garrison's apolitical stance, preferring moral suasion over political activism. Like Garrison, she viewed the Constitution as a proslavery document.[14] Moreover, the Philadelphia Female Anti-Slavery Society consistently opposed direct political participation, focusing its efforts instead on petitioning and fund-raising. Abolitionist "anarchists" such as Garrison rejected all human institutions and prepared for the "millennium—the eventual and inevitable rule of the government of God on earth." For them, "any attempt at reforming or restructuring human organizations was not only wrongheaded but wicked."[15]

Unlike Garrison, Mott does not believe that human beings should cease governing altogether. Her call for radical reform does not lead to the abandonment of political life. For Mott, "true republicanism is true Christian democracy," in which every individual is responsible for abiding by the inner light and living according to reason and reflection.[16] But while Mott supports the idea of political activism to a greater degree than previously acknowledged, she does not go as far as abolitionist "institutionalists" such as Douglass and Gerrit Smith, who supported the Liberty Party and with it the possibility of reform through direct involvement in government. Rather, I argue that Mott fits best into a third category, that of the abolitionist "reformers," who were "neither wholly opposed to organizations of any kind, nor . . . wholly supportive of institutions to promote change."[17] Reformers believed that "human governments should be reordered to correspond with God's democratic moral government" and "left a place for localized, voluntary external structures."[18] I show that Mott's support for a voluntarist, egalitarian, democratic form of political life strikes a middle ground between anarchist and institutionalist strands of abolitionism.

Not only does Mott's position among early women's rights advocates and abolitionists require reassessment, her relation to other feminist political theorists such as Wollstonecraft needs to be reconsidered as well. Mott's status as a political thinker has been elevated by her connection to Wollstonecraft. Mott "played a pivotal role in the proliferation of Wollstonecraft's ideas among prominent American women's rights advocates."[19] Yet Mott's originality is again diminished, this time by characterizing her as a "proliferator" of ideas that are not her own, as a transmitter of her predecessor's theories on women's rights.[20] Wollstonecraft's strong influence on the early women's rights movement in general and Mott in particular is undeniable. Indeed, Mott recommended Wollstonecraft's work to others and regularly defended the author's reputation, which was posthumously marred by controversy. However, Mott's well-developed and wide-ranging views were also shaped by a variety of experiences independent of her exposure to Wollstonecraft's writings. By the time Mott first came upon the *Vindication*, she had already been steeped in Quaker doctrine about the unfair silencing of women in other religious circles, the inhuman institution of slavery, the benefits of co-education and egalitarian marriage, and the importance of living a life directed by reason and moderation and free of luxury, decadence, or frippery—themes explored by Wollstonecraft as well. Moreover, Mott had been sharing these views as an official minister of the Quaker church, a position that allowed her to travel to other Quaker meetings and speak before mixed audiences in various congregations.[21] There are important divergences between the two women as well. Wollstonecraft insists that women seek "political and civil employments" and gain a "political" and "civil existence in the state," but she does not elaborate on the particular sorts of "employments" or the "existence" that women must gain in political life.[22] Mott presents a broader conception of political agency for women as well as men, one that fundamentally reconfigures political power in more egalitarian, democratic, and voluntarist directions. Comparisons with Wollstonecraft should therefore in no way detract from the originality of Mott's theoretical contributions.

I heed calls for a broader and more nuanced approach to Mott's works by carefully examining them largely on their own terms to allow their unique contributions to emerge. I provide a close reading of Mott's speeches to demonstrate that her religious critique of dogmatism forms an essential component of her broader worldview, including her understanding of women's rights. Mott extends Quaker doctrine beyond the religious realm to address all sources of oppression, political and otherwise. We see that Mott's antidogmatic approach forms the basis of a highly participatory, egalitarian, voluntarist understanding of political power. As the Grimkés offer alternative views on equality, citizenship, and political change from a uniquely Quaker perspective, so, too, does Mott's understanding of political power constitute an important yet neglected contribution to American political thought. On further examination, we find a far more radical understanding of political power in the "belligerent Non-Resistant" Quaker than we might expect, and we discover that progressive theories of participatory democracy might have deeper roots in the past than we realize.

## "Truth for Authority, Not Authority for Truth": Mott's Antidogmatic Worldview

The phrase "truth for authority, not authority for truth," one of Mott's favorites, is borrowed from a rather unlikely source, Thomas Hobbes. The saying succinctly captures the spirit of Mott's systematic attack on ideology, doctrine, and dogma and her insistence on independent reflection and freethinking. The origins of Mott's antidogmatism can be traced to her early encounter with Elias Hicks, whose influence led to the 1827 Schism of the Society of Friends. Combatting what he perceived as an overreliance by worshippers on the scriptural interpretations of Quaker elites and an undue reverence for the written word at the expense of good works, Hicks sought to reassert the importance of direct, individual encounters with scriptural teachings and the necessity of actively applying religious principles to everyday life. Concurrent with the Hicksite emphasis on practice over principle is a downplaying, and in more radical circles an outright denial, of the divinity of Christ.

Hicks also strove to reestablish the prominence of the inner light in Quaker practice, a kind of internal voice possessed by all human beings regardless of religious persuasion that nevertheless provides a direct connection to the divine. The Quaker understanding of corporate witness and collective discernment, discussed in chapter 4, which rely on the inner light, shows "an indwelling spirit working through individuals toward provisional truths" that were always subject to scrutiny and correction. The inner light can emerge when human beings engage in quiet reflection, hence the term "quietism" to describe the phenomenon. However, "since God [is] a divine force within humans rather than a heavenly force acting on them," the inner light can also emerge when people engage in good acts, such as advocating for equality and justice for all people. Thus for Quakers, "a true love for oneself [is], in effect, a love of the divine urgings within oneself *toward* the self and others."[23] The Hicksite understanding required active engagement and reasoning, not passive obedience to the word of God. Hicksites discouraged formal worship of the Sabbath in favor of encouraging, as Jesus did, good works at every opportunity, not just on high days and holy days.

Hicks influenced a number of early women's rights activists and abolitionists. Like the Grimkés, Mott innovates by taking what is primarily a religious approach and expanding it in several directions, including the political. The development and expansion of Mott's antidoctrinal approach can be seen in her earliest speeches. Virtually every speech Mott delivered after returning from the 1840 World's Anti-Slavery Convention in London, where she first encountered Stanton, and leading up to the 1848 Seneca Falls Convention, begins with a systematic condemnation of mindless acceptance of religious dogma and unreflective observance of rituals and practices. While commentators have traditionally recognized little notable activity among early women's rights activists before 1848, these speeches reveal that Mott was formulating a comprehensive worldview that contributed significantly to the movement's progress.

In an 1841 speech, Mott lays the foundation for her antidogmatic approach. She begins by forging a strong connection between truth, freedom, and independent thought.[24] Mott then provides a detailed interpretation of Scripture that elaborates on the crucial distinction she draws between sectarianism, on the one hand, and the "principles of universal obligation" that "are common to all, and are understood by all," on the other.[25] Acknowledging the controversial nature of her own actions as a female preacher in a male-dominated society, Mott challenges the common view that women should not speak in public. This view is based on Paul's First Letter to the Corinthians, which prohibits women from speaking in church. Yet Mott points to the Letter to the Galatians and other Pauline writings that declare men and women to be equal.[26] It would therefore be a mistake to interpret Paul's admonition to the Corinthian women as a blanket prohibition against preaching or to extrapolate from Scripture an absolute opposition to women speaking in public to mixed audiences.

Mott's understanding of Scripture is not original in itself. The overall framework for the theological attack on dogmatism and sectarianism was laid by Hicks. And key components of her argument were explored in great detail by the Grimkés, as I discuss in chapters 3 and 4. Throughout his long career, Garrison, too, delivered withering critiques of organized religion. What is unique about Mott's message, however, is the overarching attack on all "creeds and forms," not just theological ones. For Mott, dogmas have been used to justify all sorts of objectionable practices, including "the prevalence and the general justification of war, and slavery, and oppression . . . [and] all the vices of society."[27] If people reexamined dogmas and doctrines for themselves and thereby achieved true equality, Mott later emphasizes, "We should not see large classes, crushed by existing monopolies, laboring for their scanty pittance," or "systems of oppression which have been conformed to so long."[28] Not only should individuals familiarize themselves with sources that are used to devise a doctrine of oppression, religious and otherwise. People should also reflect on their own actions and beliefs to gain a better understanding of the pernicious effects of oppression and even of their own role in unconsciously perpetuating injustice. Thus Mott urges every woman to "look seriously at herself" and "learn how great an evil her nature suffers in being prevented from the exercise of her highest faculties."[29] Along similar lines, all people should strive for "knowledge of themselves" and true fulfillment and turn away from "theories and abstractions" and "outward observances."[30] Although Mott's attack on dogma resembles Frances Wright's condemnation of ideologies of all sorts, Wright in no way shares Mott's religious convictions, no matter how progressive they might be.

Mott does not restrict her call for self-reflection to her audience. Fully consistent with her method, she insists that her own words and deeds be subject to scrutiny as well. Instead of offering her interpretations and ideas as an alternative dogma, Mott insists that her audience test her views by studying the Bible, deciding for themselves if she is correct, and ultimately forming their own conclusions.[31] Reinforcing the importance of self-reflection as the basis of just action, Mott moves to the subject of slavery and urges those in her audience to examine their own involvement in its perpetuation, however indirect, "for we are all implicated in the transgression." Mott continues:

> Let us examine our own clothing—the furniture of our houses—the conducting of trade—the affairs of commerce—and then ask ourselves, whether we have not . . . as individuals, a duty which . . . we are bound to perform.[32]

Mott's view of social responsibility clearly places a heavy burden on human beings because it applies not only to those who actually commit injustice but also to those who tolerate or otherwise benefit from it.

Mott expands her attack on dogmatism and sectarianism still further, adapting the Quaker belief in the natural goodness of humankind and opposition to original sin to her broader purposes. "In our earnest endeavor to exalt our favorite forms and rituals," she explains to fellow Quakers, we regard "our professions of religion more than the practice of righteousness, of goodness, of truth."[33] Mott draws a parallel between Quakers who mistake habitual practice and self-celebration with true faith, on the one hand, and Christians who believe in original sin and seek absolution through rituals and ceremonies, on the other. For Mott, the self-satisfaction displayed by Quakers and the Christian notion that we are naturally "more prone to evil" are equally destructive.[34] Both doctrines compromise independent agency by encouraging adherents to place more faith in the unreflective, habitual practice of rituals than in thoughtful, deliberate actions. Mott contends that elevating Christ to an abstract level of divinity and emphasizing the miraculous aspects of his actions at the expense of his everyday practical goodness compromises the effectiveness of Christ's life as a model of behavior for mortals. Human beings are left without an accessible guide and fail to learn "dignity" and "responsibility."[35] Mott also denounces preachers within the Quaker hierarchy who, in their zeal to maintain authority, perpetuate this harmful doctrine and declare the divinity of Christ with absolute certainty while overlooking the fundamental unknowability of his divine nature.[36] Mott makes a passionate plea for true righteousness born of independent thought by proclaiming that it is "high time there was more christian boldness, more moral courage, amongst mankind to speak to the sentiment of their hearts, whether they be in accordance with the popular doctrines of the day or not."[37] Yet she pulls back when her attack on particular forms of sectarianism threatens to become yet another dogma: "Far be it from me to judge anyone for practicing such things."[38] Instead, it is up to every individual to discover the most appropriate ways to honor God and live a righteous life. Mott thereby demonstrates "an awareness of the constructed location from which someone else speaks and views interlocutors" like herself.[39]

Mott sheds further light on her theoretical approach with an autobiographical account. She begins by stating that "none can revere more than I do, the truths of the Bible." Yet she makes clear that discerning those truths demands active critical engagement with the text. The emergence of the Hicksite movement, she explains, "led me to examine, and compare text with the content" on her own to such an extent that "I scarcely noted the passage of time."[40] Yet she again pulls back abruptly, lest she encourage her listeners to embrace her enthusiasm without independent reflection. Mott's love of the Scriptures does not stop her from reexamining them, especially in light of the often destructive doctrines that arise pertaining to slavery and war. "Highly" as she "valued these ancient testimonies, they were not to take the place of the higher law inwardly revealed," namely, "the governing principle of our lives."[41] With this added step, Mott innovates on Hicksite Quakerism by offering up her own teachings to further scrutiny lest they become yet another set of dogmas. Mott shows herself to be "keenly attuned to how historical circumstances shape and reshape customs" and is "interested in improvisation as a means of discovering fluid truths."[42]

Not only does Mott want to avoid becoming another source of unquestioned authority, but she also extends her critique of dogmatism to Elias Hicks himself. Hicks's purpose was "to lead the mind to the divine teacher." Yet for Mott, no worldly educator—not even Hicks—can provide a full understanding of "the divine teacher," whose instruction by definition can never be fully grasped by mere mortals. Instead, one must go beyond or "above men's teaching" and gain insight into the inner light by one's own efforts. Mott warns against "an undue veneration of the Bible, or of any human authority, any written record or outward testimony."[43] These remarks indicate the depth of Mott's attack on ideology and her unwavering insistence on independent thinking and action, both of which are essential to her understanding of women's rights. Mott links the principle of self-scrutiny specifically to the cause of women's rights in her speech "The Laws in Relation to Women." After rehearsing the scriptural arguments challenging patriarchal interpretations of the Bible, Mott broadens her critique beyond the scriptural: "I do not want to dwell too much upon Scripture authority. We too often bind ourselves by authorities rather than by the truth."[44] Mott effectively catches herself doing precisely what her opponents have done by replacing one dogma with another. Instead, as Mott contends, the original "source" for biblical inspiration, namely, the inner light of every individual, is the most important authority. This stance provides Mott with a great deal of intellectual freedom: "It does not startle me to hear [the abolitionist minister] Joseph Barker point to some of those errors" in the Scripture. "I can listen to the ingenious interpretation of the Bible, given by Antoinette Brown," the first female ordained minister in the United States and influential women's rights advocate.[45] This openness to divergent points of view and celebration of unfettered inquiry in pursuit of truth reflect the philosophical spirit of Mott's antidogmatism. Mott "was unafraid of diverse points of view, because the voicing of these disparate approaches constituted the best hope of arriving at the soundest provisional truth." By qualifying her own truth claims, Mott "gave spectators the sense that she, herself, was under construction," thereby modeling a kind of freethinking that opens her audience to alternative antislavery ideas. Mott gave her audience "a sense of how to proceed toward a common cause," first by identifying with her, and then moving "them, through impeccable logic toward the most radical of propositions," namely, ending slavery and the oppression of women.[46]

The philosophical character of Mott's critique of ideology is further highlighted when she declares in a later speech: "I believe that such proving all things, such trying all things, and holding fast only to that which is good, is the great religious duty of our age." The ultimate religious duty for Mott is in fact also a philosophical one: the pursuit of the good through rigorous intellectual scrutiny, the replacement of dogma by the "incorruptible spirit which search[es] all things."[47]

Mott repeatedly insists that her theory is "no mere Quaker doctrine" but intended to have a universal, secular appeal.[48] For "difference of religious opinion need not prevent us from seeing the magnitude of the works of the Lord and feeling that our duty is not limited to our own particular sphere."[49] On Mott's view, one need not be a Quaker, or even a Christian, for that matter, to appreciate the good works of Jesus as a man. The antidogmatic approach Mott advocates is also fundamentally pluralistic in her view because it seeks to balance unity and diversity. "Although we should retain many of our peculiar views," she explains, "we might enjoy them without enforcing them upon others." Rather, the "petition walls of prejudice" that are based on "sectarian and sectional jealousies" must be "broken down" to allow lasting unity to be achieved among a variety of perspectives.[50] For Mott, abolitionists and women's rights advocates "did not need to agree upon particular political or religious ideologies." Rather, "they could reach consensus with others through a new route" by realizing "the ways in which particular meanings were attached to various religious or social customs," not fundamental truths, and "how their disagreements surfaced" about slavery and the oppression of women.[51]

Careful examination of Mott's early speeches reveals a multifaceted approach that extends Hicksite Quaker teachings and offers a comprehensive worldview that has important religious, philosophical, and political implications. By adopting a skeptical stance toward dogma, individuals realize the systemic nature of oppression that extends to slavery, women's equality, economic injustice, intemperance, and political violence. Oppression emerges when dogmas elude scrutiny and are accepted at face value. All people, including Mott, must engage in self-reflection and recognize their unconscious participation in and support of doctrines of oppression. In this way, the inward spirit "could attack previously unacknowledged wrongs that were protected by custom," such as slavery and the oppression of women.[52] Mott lays the groundwork for radical change by redefining autonomy and by shifting power away from traditional authorities and locating it within every individual.

Only when all men and women empower themselves in this way can they reconstruct a pluralistic society in accordance with true freedom, equality, and justice. Like Hicks, Mott offers "a performance-based, practical ministry" that "reflect[s] only the inner lights or best thinking of those gathered at that time, in that place," oriented toward greater truth and understanding, and always open to reexamination and change.[53]

### Beyond "No-Governmentalism": Participation, Suffrage, and Political Power

Mott's views on political power have been interpreted as a reflection of Garrisonian anarchism, which rejected virtually all forms of direct political involvement.[54] Garrison referred to Section 9 of Article I and the three-fifths clause of the Constitution to argue that the founding document was fundamentally proslavery. Declaring "No Union with Slaveholders," Garrison believed that any form of direct political participation represented collusion with his opponents, and he went so far as to refuse to vote even though, as a white male, he had the franchise. In spite of his aversion to direct political action, he continued vigorous efforts to influence politics indirectly through petitioning, writing, participating in antislavery societies and supporting antislavery conventions. Garrison's "no-governmentalism" was so controversial, however, that it contributed significantly to the 1840 American Anti-Slavery Society schism between those who supported non-resistance and those who began to seek political solutions to the problem of slavery.[55] Many of the latter would go on to form the abolitionist Liberty Party. Garrison's radical apolitical stance also led Frederick Douglass to distance himself from his friend and colleague, creating a rift between the two men that was never reconciled.

Not only did Garrison formulate a doctrine of non-resistance and disunion, he was also known for advocating a radically different understanding of political life. The extreme aversion to any direct political participation led Garrison and other non-resistants to conclude that only the direct rule of God through the hearts of men would be acceptable. By contrast, political rule of any kind was fundamentally coercive and tyrannical because it deprived human beings of the ability to engage in self-rule, the only path to direct contact with God. Garrisonian anarchists despised the label "no-governmentalism" imposed by their adversaries, and they "insisted that they opposed not government, but human pretensions to govern."[56] But Garrison never explained the "government of God" in detail. Violence, force, coercion, or any form of direct rule of one person over another were prohibited, yet the actual role of individual human beings in this divine government remained unclear.

Close analysis reveals important differences between Mott's views on political reform and Garrison's "no-governmentalism." Mott articulates an understanding of "superior law" that is not only informed by God but also developed through the transformative process of self-reflection and self-examination her antidogmatism requires. This "law" requires direct and indirect political participation by women and men alike. Although she acknowledges that political reform is only one of many means by which fundamental transformation is achieved, Mott does not abandon politics altogether. Instead, reformed human rule can emerge by insisting that women be given the right to vote even if the government is corrupt. Women must have a say in the laws they are asked to obey, whether by voting or serving in political office. Women should also participate in a "convention" along with men to devise a new set of rules for self-government. Finally, Mott offers an innovative understanding of citizenship for women based on the worldview that individuals rule themselves and form associations with others that are fundamentally egalitarian and voluntary. Thus it is not anarchy that Mott advocates but, rather, a radical form of democracy based on her view of autonomy.

For Mott, political injustice must be addressed by applying the very sort of antidogmatism she proposes. When religious adherents focus so intently on ceremonies and rituals for the relative security they provide, they lose sight of the "great evils which beset us as a nation," such as war, slavery, and poverty, and fail to do anything to alleviate these injustices.[57] Passive acceptance of received doctrines leads to passivity in the face of wrongdoing. For "there is a proneness in us, to put that off upon others, to say that it is because of the providential arrangements in society, the influences of circumstances over which we have no control." When people defer responsibility for injustice, they leave it to others, especially conventional politicians, to resort to force in order to enact change: "We let the destroying sword go unsheathed without the exertions we might use to enlighten the people."[58] Instead of tolerating short-term or piecemeal reforms imposed by political elites, people should focus on living reflective lives, "enlighten" others to do the same, and begin the process of fundamental change. Mott repeatedly implores her audience to work toward eliminating slavery, embracing pacifism, and alleviating poverty. Yet political action is not an end in itself. It "can only bring about a temporary relief" and "afford no permanent good" unless "the morals of the people are changed" and "we bring our christianity to our everyday life."[59] In other words, such efforts must be combined with the very sort of self-reflection and personal transformation required by Mott's approach. Only by freeing themselves from received dogmas and persuading others to do the same, as Mott's non-doctrinal Christianity requires, can individuals achieve true reform. Mott later reinforces the message that a critical stance toward dogmatism will lead to a more just political order. Examination of "the causes of . . . great evils" would place "the axe at the root of the corrupt tree of arbitrary power which has been produced by the assumption of false claims of man over his fellow-man."[60] Accepting dogma leads individuals to support traditional hierarchies that work to the detriment of all. Power is wielded unequally, oppressively, and arbitrarily; it is not shared among equals for the moral advancement of the society as a whole. By contrast, Mott envisions an egalitarian order free from injustice and oppression. Thus, rather than abandoning political life, Mott interprets political power as something that is shared among equals, not imposed by authorities on passive followers. Political reform is a necessary part of a much larger transformation of society. In light of these observations, Mott's statements on a vital source of political power—namely, suffrage—must be reexamined carefully.

Mott expresses mixed views on woman suffrage. She believes that women should not be prevented from voting, yet she is less direct than others, such as Stanton, who demand that women positively be granted the right of suffrage. Moreover, she conveys these mixed messages about the political right of suffrage while at the same time deploring politics in general as fundamentally corrupt. Voting in a corrupt society does not represent the true interests of individual citizens and fails to deal adequately with deeply entrenched injustices and oppression. People are going "to the polls and voting for warriors and slaveholders" instead of "seeking to enlighten the public mind."[61] At the Seneca Falls Convention, Mott famously discouraged Stanton from demanding the vote. Yet the convention became a pivotal event in the early women's rights movement precisely because the demand for suffrage was explicitly made for the first time, by Stanton. In her best-known speech, "Discourse on Woman," delivered the following year, Mott expresses more equivocal views. The "Discourse" reveals Mott's conviction that suffrage is a right that should be granted to all citizens regardless of race or gender for them to use as they see fit, yet suffrage alone is insufficient. Voting should be exercised within a larger context of reform efforts in religion, philosophy, economics, and culture, and it should be informed by the antidogmatic approach she tirelessly advocates. Suffrage in particular and political involvement in general are means toward a greater end, namely, the reformation of society.

Mott begins her discussion of suffrage in the "Discourse" by explaining that woman "asks nothing as favor, but as right. . . . She is seeking not to be governed by laws, in the making of which she has no voice." Women are "cypher[s] in the nation" because their views and opinions about political matters cannot be expressed openly. Garrisonians support petitioning, but for Mott this indirect tool alone is woefully deficient. Women are denied status as "moral" and "responsible" human beings because they are "deprived of almost every right in civil society," namely, the full range of opportunities to reflect on political options, express their preferences openly, and exercise informed consent in obeying laws.[62] These remarks reveal Mott's determination to expand the political involvement of women through suffrage and other means.

If the right of suffrage is granted to women, however, Mott is equally convinced that it will emerge in a deeply hostile and corrupt environment. This is why she begins her advocacy of suffrage by explaining that "it is with reluctance that I make the demand for the political rights of woman, because this claim is so distasteful to the age." It is not because suffrage is distasteful to her personally that Mott is reluctant to mention it but, rather, because it is so controversial to others. As Mott explains: "Woman shrinks, in the present state of society, from taking any interest in politics" because "the events of the French revolution, and the claim for woman's rights are held up to her as a warning." Again, it is not because women are incapable that they avoid political involvement but, rather, because they fear a backlash from opponents who profess a dread of violent upheaval. Mott's subsequent remark that the bloody revolution "was marked with extravagance and wickedness in men as well as women" highlights her pacifist conviction that radical change, though necessary, must never be pursued through force. The ends do not justify the means. To transform society, men and women alike must reflect on their actions and accept responsibility for injustice. With these remarks, Mott acknowledges the hostile environment in which women would exert political power and proposes a more peaceful and just alternative. Mott concludes this section by suggesting that, "if woman acted her part in governmental affairs, there might be an entire change in the turmoil of political life" and by asking, "If woman's judgment were exercised, why might she not aid in making the laws by which she is governed?" Although Mott supports women's suffrage, she does not demand that women vote. To do so would effectively replace one dogmatic teaching for another in a way that violates her fundamental principles. Consistent with her antidogmatic approach, Mott proposes that women be given the opportunity to choose to participate with the hope of improving political life and society generally. Indeed, she adds, "the works of Harriet Martineau . . . furnish evidence of woman's capacity to embrace subjects of universal interest" and serve as a strong indication that the contributions of other equally talented women will have similar positive effects. And yet, in a dialectical move, Mott circles back to her original skepticism. "Far be it from me to encourage woman to vote," she explains, "or to take an active part in politics, in the present state of our government." Again, Mott acknowledges the hostile environment in which women would exercise the franchise. Her opposition to political force and its reliance on coercion rather than consent is clear. In a succinct yet comprehensive expression of her position, Mott immediately reasserts that woman's "right to the elective franchise however, is the same, and should be yielded to her, whether she exercise that right or not."[63]

Through the perspective of Mott's unwavering insistence on free and independent thinking, what appears to be ambivalence toward political action is in fact a principled stance that is deeply consistent with her antidogmatic approach: Even in an extremely corrupt society, women should without question be granted the opportunity to vote and participate in politics if they wish, with the ultimate hope of transforming it.

While the right of suffrage is essential, Mott has a still broader understanding of female citizenship in mind. "When . . . a convention shall be called to make regulations for self-government on Christian, non-resistant principles," Mott explains, "I can see no good reason, why woman should not participate in such an assemblage, taking part equally with man." Mott is not abandoning the possibility of a political order. Instead, she insists that women along with men should gather and secure a more just society based on equality and self-rule. To be sure, Mott is vague about the structure and implementation of such a gathering. Nevertheless, she does not turn away from political involvement for women but, rather, expands it. Indeed, to reinforce the need for change, Mott concludes this section by emphasizing that women "have no part or lot in the formation or administration of government" and "cannot vote or hold office."[64]

While Mott is not a pure anarchist, neither did she align herself with reformists who believed that change could occur through established political institutions. Her antidogmatic stance in fact leads to a deep ambivalence about partisan organizations generally, which by their very nature encourage conformity and effectively discourage freethinking among participants. Partisan organizations, according to Mott, are supported by dogmas and empowered by unreflective followers. For this reason, sectarian societies "encroach far too much on individual rights." By contrast, "associations . . . if properly conducted," namely, by encouraging diversity and independent thought, "need not destroy individuality."[65] Mott's aversion to formal organizations extended to the women's rights movement as well. After the Civil War, she lamented that "it was a great mistake to . . . organize a Soc[iet]y For Wom[en's] Rig[hts]" because the "several Conventions held were far more effective."[66] To encourage reform on specific issues such as women's rights, Mott preferred the relatively informal, decentralized, non-hierarchical nature of the conventions over the more rigid and bureaucratic organizations and societies that emerged from them.[67] Thus Mott's alternative understanding of power is fundamentally egalitarian and voluntarist. Moreover, for Mott unity should never be secured by suppressing dissent within a group: Harmony will never be "absolute." Instead, true pluralism requires the sort of constructive conflict that arises when individuals confront injustice and oppression by questioning traditional beliefs and practices and translate true equality, freedom, and justice into action. Mott's rejection of coercion is unconditional, and she believes that she and other women's rights activists should "wish to avoid all angry opposition or ridicule." But she nevertheless maintains that women "must at the same time enter the ranks, prepared to 'endure hardness as good soldiers';—and not disclaim the needful antagonism which a faithful presentation of Womans wrongs imposes upon us."[68]

Mott is a pacifist, but she does not abandon the very notion of political power. Her non-resistance should not be mistaken for inaction. She wants to fundamentally transform American political life so that every individual can engage in self-rule, lead reflective and morally upright lives through her own devising, and encourage others to do the same. This transformation requires relentless self-reflection and scrutiny of dogma and can be attained only through the concerted action of self-governing individuals working together. On this view, power will not be wielded "arbitrarily" or coercively among unequal parties, but neither must it be completely abandoned. Rather, power will be shared deliberately and voluntarily among equals, laws will be founded on informed consent, and authentic representation of universal human concerns will replace narrow-minded political factions.[69]

## Mott's Legacy Revisited

Mott's antidogmatic approach offers a powerful critique of the society in which she lived and foreshadows several developments in feminist and democratic theory. Her lifelong conviction that racial and gender equality are inseparable is a precursor to intersectionality, a concept by which oppression is understood in terms of gender, race, and ethnicity as well as class. Like Wright and the Grimkés, Mott adopts a systemic view of oppression that is deeply rooted in the American project. Under the guise of legitimacy, male elites perpetuate oppressive doctrines regarding slavery, gender roles, and economic inequality. Unreflective individuals passively accept these dogmas, absolving themselves of any responsibility for the injustices that result. Individual power is transferred to the elites, autonomy disappears, and true accountability is lost. Mott's unreflective citizen is not asked to take personal responsibility for political decisions or work with others to rid her community of inequality and injustice. Oppression is allowed to flourish beneath a veneer of legitimacy imposed by patriarchal authorities. The absence of a vibrant political community in which citizens can develop their capacities and work together to solve problems for Mott deprives individuals—men and women alike—of the opportunity to become fully human, that is, moral beings.

The sort of radically egalitarian conception of political power elaborated by Mott, along with her understanding of non-violent resistance, offer important yet neglected early contributions to American democratic and deliberative theory. Mott encourages the direct, active engagement of all citizens to create a more just society. She proposes a highly participatory and egalitarian view of common life that holds individuals accountable to themselves and to one another. For Mott, there is "no power delegated upon one portion of the people over another."[70] Rather, power is shared among equals and exercised in many ways, whether it be through voting, petitioning, speaking in public or private to single-sex or "mixed" audiences, participating in segregated or integrated reform societies, or any other such activities. Citizens continually scrutinize dogmas and received doctrine, Christian and otherwise, for embedded justifications of oppression, and they voluntarily accept only those teachings that encourage true equality and freedom.

As Mott continually reminds her audience, the task of challenging assumptions about the nature of political power and oppression, the meaning of autonomy, and the requirements of justice is never complete. By advocating a more active, participatory society, Mott urges current and future generations to continue the struggle for greater equality and freedom and a more just political order.

## 6

# Elizabeth Cady Stanton's Rhetoric of Ridicule and Reform

No book on political theory and the founding of American feminism would be complete without an examination of Elizabeth Cady Stanton, often referred to as the "philosopher" of the early women's rights movement. Our theoretical understanding of Stanton's work has been advanced by a number of studies that trace elements of liberal Enlightenment rationalism and their legalistic applications. An influential volume of selected readings by Stanton and Susan B. Anthony begins with a series of essays that situate Stanton within "nineteenth century liberal political theory" based on her understanding of "female self-sovereignty" and "Anglo-American feminism" as well as aspects of "revolutionary republicanism."[1] Stanton's devastating critique of Christian misogyny in her later work *The Woman's Bible* has been characterized as an extension of the separation of church and state characteristic of liberal Enlightenment theory.[2] Stanton's pioneering efforts to collectivize women as a "gender class" transformed American law, and her use of a kind of "experiential" or pragmatic philosophizing that is based on "shared values rather than essentialist truths" and relies on "experiential narratives" foreshadows second-wave consciousness-raising.[3] To demonstrate Stanton's theoretical complexity, her ideas have been systematically classified according to Rogers Smith's "multiple traditions" of political theory, which include "liberalism," "civic republicanism," racial, ethnic, and socioeconomic "ascriptivism," and a new category, "radicalism."[4] And a recently published expansive historical biography of Stanton further contributes to our understanding of the richness and complexity of her controversial life and work.[5]

Stanton's work has also been widely criticized for the polarizing elitism and racism that compromised its overall effectiveness.[6] She was notorious for elevating the concerns of educated white women by disparaging uneducated men of various races and ethnicities and by failing to explicitly advocate for black women. Stanton mocked the hypocrisy of the white male American ruling elite who vociferously opposed the enfranchisement of educated white women while allowing white, immigrant, and freed black men to vote, regardless of educational attainment. Stanton's deployment of commonplace elitist and racist vocabulary intensified after the Civil War when faced with the prospect that constitutional amendments would grant suffrage to uneducated freed black men before extending it to elite white women like herself. The alliance Stanton forged with the wealthy yet eccentric racist George Francis Train further deepens the suspicions surrounding her worldview.[7] Stanton's comments were likely designed to appeal to her privileged white male audience by expressing shared values, but for critics, she effectively "reified the social hierarchy her speech was intended to undermine." Through "her attempt to establish a sense of sameness between white women and the white men in her audience, Cady Stanton subtly (and probably inadvertently) casts black people as the Other against which all white people might define their interests." As a result of her characterization, "the not-so-subtle message to her auditors is that white men are more like white women than they are like black men." By implicitly supporting the elitism she sought to challenge, Stanton "asked not for revolution so much as for help in redistributing class privilege."[8]

Others have sought to reframe Stanton's contributions while acknowledging the tensions within them. Stanton was determined "to establish that the rights of the Jeffersonian individual, or the rights of a citizen of the United States, belonged equally to women and men," even though "she committed herself to a particular battle over the rights of women . . . that set her apart from, and sometimes at odds with, her putative allies."[9] After the Civil War, Congress directed arguments "for limited suffrage at women but ultimately used them too against black men." Thus "Stanton faced a political community in which popular opposition to woman suffrage provided a socially acceptable and politically safe way to reject the importance of any suffrage." Under these extreme conditions, Stanton

established herself as a rare voice of resistance to the devaluation of voting rights and of commitment to an ideal of equal rights, guaranteed to American citizens. Without a doubt, Stanton can be heard to stray from an ideal of universal rights and lapse into the language of social and racial hierarchies, usually at moments when her vision of a genuine republic had lost public support. But at those same moments, her convictions about the importance of achieving equal citizenship in a republican government also shine through.[10]

The underlying principles from which Stanton never ultimately wavered are the "self-sovereignty of individuals" and "universal suffrage."[11]

A recent examination of Stanton's rhetorical deployment of sympathy also highlights the more constructive nature of her contributions. One of the most important reasons for the lack of support among men for expanding women's rights is their overreliance on abstract reasoning and legalistic argumentation, which fail to capture the complexity of women's experiences. To counter men's insensitivity, Stanton in her early career appealed directly to the emotions of her male audience through various anecdotes about the hardships suffered by women.[12] In so doing she tapped into an understanding of sympathy similar to that articulated by Scottish Enlightenment thinkers such as Adam Smith and other popularizers. When these appeals proved ineffective because men could not share the experiences of women directly, Stanton shifted to indirect description, a rhetorical technique described by Smith, which helps her avoid directly confronting and alienating her male audience. Like Smith's moral theory of rhetoric, Stanton's approach seeks to encourage her audience to engage in self-reflection and contemplate significant reform for women.[13]

I cannot hope to match the detail of Sue Davis's book-length study or Lori Ginzberg's authoritative biography of Stanton in this chapter. However, I do want to make a contribution to the ongoing debate regarding Stanton's elitism and racism. The well-documented controversies surrounding her views, though stemming from legitimate criticisms, run the risk of overshadowing Stanton's remarkable achievements in advancing women's rights. I expand on the view of Ann Gordon and others that Stanton's work should be understood in terms of an unwavering dedication to fundamental principles, such as individual citizenship, while acknowledging the contentious nature of her views on race and class. To do so, I adopt Sue Engbers's use of Adam Smith's theory of rhetoric as an interpretative frame to examine Stanton's rhetorical strategies in greater detail. Specifically, I argue that Stanton lays out a set of fundamental principles early on in her career from which she does not significantly waver. Included among these fundamental principles is a systematic attack on the hypocrisy of elite white men who refuse to extend the rights they enjoy as American citizens to women. It is in her early work that we find precursors of many of Stanton's most controversial arguments. Critics have linked her views to the rise of social Darwinism. Yet closer examination of the context in which these arguments arise reveals that many pre-date the emergence of social Darwinism and thus precede the controversial theories of racism and sexism that were based on evolutionary constructions and biological categories. If Stanton's early views were not motivated by social Darwinism, perhaps other influences were at work. I explore the possibility that Stanton's early comments are components of a broader rhetorical approach in which she frequently deploys ridicule, sarcasm, and other strategies to expose hypocrisy and advocate for reform, while consistently arguing for the equality of all people, male and female, poor and rich, black and white. I do not rule out the possibility that Stanton eventually accepted some of the tenets of social Darwinism and, in so doing, exhibited elitist, racist, and even sexist tendencies. However, it is equally plausible that Stanton was simply continuing her rhetorical strategy, appropriating popular concepts, ideas, and even prejudices, to suit her overall purposes. It is not necessarily the case, therefore, that throughout her lifetime Stanton simultaneously held ascriptive views along with her liberal, republican, and "radical" ideas, without ever reconciling them. Nor should we use Stanton as an exemplar to conclude that the early women's rights movement was inherently racist or elitist. Neither the overly positive portrayals that inadequately account for her significant flaws nor the bleak assessments of her harshest critics provide a complete picture of Stanton.

While relatively narrow in focus, my analysis raises important questions about the early women's rights movement and Stanton's role in it. I argue that the degree to which Stanton's views, and by extension, the movement itself, were endemically racist or elitist is less clear than suggested by critics. The perspectives of individual advocates varied widely, as my book has shown, some more prone to racism and elitism than others. Moreover, the movement itself changed considerably over time, in response to pivotal historical events such as the Civil War, and with the emergence of new theories and ideas, such as social Darwinism. If we overlook the nuance and complexity of the movement and its advocates, we miss important opportunities to appreciate their ongoing relevance in our own increasingly complex world.

To gain a greater understanding of Stanton's early views, I closely examine a relatively obscure work that nevertheless lays the groundwork for much of her later writings and speeches. This manuscript held considerable importance in Stanton's mind, for in a letter to her daughters, Stanton "called it her 'first speech,' one 'delivered several times immediately after the first Woman's Rights Convention'" at Seneca Falls, first at the Waterloo Quaker Meeting House and later to the Congregational Friends in Farmington. Equally important, from 1848 to 1850, Stanton relied on the address "as a source for short articles" in the *Lily* and for the introductory remarks of her 1850 "Address to the Women of the State of New York in Waterloo." The manuscript served as the basis for a well-known and widely circulated version later published in 1870, entitled "Address of Mrs. Elizabeth Cady Stanton, Delivered at Seneca Falls and Rochester, N.Y., July 19th and August 2nd, 1848." In fact, to emphasize the continuity between this manuscript and Stanton's later ideas, an editor of the 1870 version "carefully adjusted the text to eliminate the scene set in the opening paragraphs and convert to present tense all references to the conventions and their demands."[14] A careful reading of the manuscript reveals that Stanton's political theory is founded on several basic principles that remain more or less consistent over her lifetime. Stanton's controversial comments can also be seen as part of a broader rhetorical strategy that consistently argues for the equality of all people, male and female, poor and rich, black and white.

## Thematic Parallels between Stanton and Smith

Although there is no evidence that Stanton was directly influenced by Smith's theory of rhetoric, she was doubtless exposed to the popularized versions of Scottish Enlightenment theory that were commonplace in nineteenth-century American education. Moreover, independent of any direct influence, Smith's complex and insightful analysis of rhetorical techniques helps us to recognize and evaluate their use by Stanton. Indeed, many aspects of Stanton's approach reflect those of Smith's moral and rhetorical theory, including indirect description, sympathy, alienation, and the impartial spectator. Building on these parallels in the following section, we can more clearly see how Smith's rhetoric of ridicule helps reframe Stanton's contributions. After exploring Smith's and Stanton's moral rhetoric of ridicule, I show that Smith's description of historical rhetoric allows us to gain a better understanding of Stanton's rhetorical approach to biblical criticism and to see that her rhetoric is not simply emotional or rational but, rather, a complex amalgam of the two.[15]

For Smith, indirect description is necessary because "no action, however affecting in itself can be represented in such a manner as to be very interesting to those who had not been present at it, by a bare narration where it is described directly" (*LRBL*, ii.5). Indirect description captures the "situation that gives occasion to other passions which interest us" or "the effects it had on those who were either actors or spectators of the whole affair" (*TMS*, I.ii.2.2; *LRBL*, ii.5). And because emotions are "internall invisible objects," they, too, must be made perceptible through the context, circumstances, and situations in which they arise and the effects they cause (*LRBL*, i.161, i.182). There are numerous examples in which Stanton employs indirect description to discuss controversial topics that could alienate her male audience. Instead of criticizing men directly, Stanton repeatedly alludes to the "context, circumstances, and situations" in which women's oppression occurs and its corruptive effects on American society. Stanton also describes many instances in which the oppression of women corrodes the sympathetic bonds between men and women and weakens homosocial relationships, especially among women. As we will see, Stanton can be seen deploying a kind of impartial spectator as she ridicules elite white men for their hypocrisy and implicitly contrasts their behavior with an ideal vision of an American citizen, who consistently applies the fundamental principles of the Declaration of Independence to others regardless of their sex, race, or class.

At the very beginning of the manuscript, Stanton provides an example of the failure of sympathy as a moral force. Stanton declares that she is compelled to enter the public realm and speak because "woman alone can understand the height and the depth, the length and the breadth of her own degradation and woe." According to the idea of female "exceptionalism," for which Stanton is well known, women and men differ fundamentally by nature and, as such, adopt different social and cultural roles. Women could also be considered "exceptional" in their higher moral capacities, as Stanton suggests when she claims that women have a superior level of understanding of their circumstances when compared with men. Yet Stanton clarifies that the differences between the sexes are not natural; they are culturally and socially determined: "Man cannot speak for us—because he has been educated to believe that we differ from him so materially, that he cannot judge of our thoughts, feelings and opinions by his own." Thus men are prevented from engaging in sympathy with the Other, namely, women, not because of their nature, but rather because of their "false education." The lack of sympathy also thwarts men's ability to function as complete human beings because it prevents them from making moral judgments. For "moral beings can only judge of others by themselves," Stanton explains, and "the moment they give a different nature to any of their own kind they utterly fail." The challenge, therefore, is to establish sympathetic bonds between the sexes by educating men to view women as "their own kind," and presumably vice versa.[16]

One of Stanton's most memorable examples of the failure of sympathy between men and women appears in her 1854 "Address to the New York Legislature." She vividly describes the "frenzied mother, who, to save herself and child from exposure and disgrace," presumably due to out-of-wedlock conception, "ended the life that had but just begun" and is "dragged before" a "tribunal" of "grim-visaged judges, lawyers, and jurors" to be "grossly questioned in public" about the most intimate of matters. Stanton seems to reassert an exceptionalist argument by lamenting, "Shall laws which come from the logical brain of man take cognizance of violence done to the moral and affectional nature which predominates, *as is said*, in woman?"[17] And she implies that only women can judge other women when she asks her audience of male legislators to imagine their own daughters in the same predicament and consider: "Would it not, in that hour, be some consolation to see that she was surrounded by the wise and virtuous of her own sex; by those who had known the depth of a mother's love and the misery of a lover's falsehood?" However, the qualification "as is said" is notable, and Stanton is merely asking for the right to "an impartial jury" of "one's peers" to be extended to women. It is not men's rational superiority over women that makes such a judgment impossible. Rather, it is "the present undeveloped state" of the relations between the sexes in which "the one in power fails to apply the immutable principles of right to any grade but his own"—a relation that exists even between the "nobleman" and the "peasant" and the "slaveholder" and the "slave." Indeed, Stanton seems to go out of her way to undermine the notion that women are by nature morally superior to men in the sentence that follows her question:

> Statesmen of New York, whose daughters, guarded by your affection, and lapped amidst luxuries which your indulgence spreads, care more for their nodding plumes and velvet trains than for the statute laws by which their persons and properties are held—who, blinded by custom and prejudice to the degraded position which they and their sisters occupy in the civil scale, haughtily claim that they already have all the rights they want.[18]

Even women of the most noble families are corrupted by the unjust social forces at work.

Thus for Stanton, the oppression of women arises from strong social and cultural forces that effectively teach men a false lesson in superiority, which in turn prevents sympathetic engagements with women and deeper understanding of their condition. The false education that instructs individuals to believe that moral differences equal moral inequality harms men and women alike. The "tyranny" men exercise over women has caused the "degraded and inferior position occupied by women all over the world."[19] Presumably, if such an education is "false," Stanton's proposed reforms provide a more "true" alternative based on true equality.[20]

Adam Smith describes the same problem of the failure of sympathy resulting from a false sense of superiority (*TMS*, I.iii.3; see also *LRBL*, i.107 and ii.90). As the "grand" men place themselves above others, their self-absorption prevents them from gathering adequate information in order to make informed moral judgments. For Stanton, the "selfishness" that arises from man's "false education" has made his own moral nature "an almost total shipwreck."[21] For both thinkers, the results are essentially the same. Just as for Smith the "grand" men are rendered incapable of pursuing "what is noble and honorable," so, too, for Stanton man's selfishness "has destroyed the nobleness, the gentleness that should belong to his character, the beauty and transparency of soul."[22] Although he sometimes rises above his self-centeredness to "get a glimpse of the narrowness of his soul, as compared with women," Stanton explains, man quickly dismisses his own insight and therewith the possibility of reform. He excuses his alleged inferiority in a hypocritical way, namely, by elevating women to the level of martyrdom and celebrating their moral superiority while systematically depriving them of the opportunity to show their true moral nature. For Smith, hypocrisy reigns supreme among corrupted men as well, who rely on "fraud and falsehood" to secure their reputation at all costs (*TMS*, I.iii.3–8).

For Smith's selfish, corrupted man, true moral insight is achieved only when, through sympathy, he realizes that "he is but one of the multitude in no respect better than any other in it" (*TMS*, II.ii.2.1). Smith describes the selfish man's realization in terms of the "impartial spectator." We have clear echoes of this kind of moral transformation in Stanton's vivid example of the drunkard who "was hopelessly lost until it was discovered that he was governed by the same laws of mind as the sober man." Stanton describes the drunkard's process of realization as a kind of "magic power" connected to "kindness and love," through which he somehow removes himself and at the same time sees himself both as a drunkard and as a sober man. The "magical" creation of a kind of impartial spectator allows him to see himself in all the manifestations in which he is seen by others. Both Smith's selfish man and Stanton's drunkard are ashamed when they view themselves from the perspective of others. In their desire for the approbation of others, the process of moral education begins.[23]

Striking parallels can also be seen between the destructive effects of male domination on women's spirit in Stanton's depiction, on the one hand, and the alienating effects of specialized labor on the human soul as Smith describes it in the *Wealth of Nations*, on the other (*WN*, V.i.f.50).[24] As the rich and noble in commercial society become desensitized to the less privileged in Smith's theory, so, too, do men become oblivious to the sufferings of women in Stanton's. Women, like common laborers in Smith's commercial society, are literally devalued. Both women and laborers are incapable of flourishing fully as human beings, not because they are naturally inferior to men or to the wealthy, respectively, but rather because they are deprived of education and intellectual stimulation. Stanton's woman leaves her books and studies just at the time a young man is entering thoroughly into his—then comes the cares and perplexities of married life. Her sphere being confined to her house and children, the burden generally being very unequally divided, she knows nothing beside and whatever yearning her spirit may have felt for a higher existence, whatever may have been the capacity she well knew she possessed for more elevated enjoyments—enjoyments which would not conflict with these but add new lustre to them—it is all buried beneath the weight that presses upon her.[25]

Smith declares that the deprivation experienced by laborers is not only deeply corrupting but also renders them incapable of being good citizens. "Of the great and extensive interests of his country, he is altogether incapable of judging" (WN, V.i.f.50). Likewise for Stanton, the hypocrisy and moral shortcomings among privileged American men compromise their ability to function as good citizens: "The disgraceful riots at our polls where man in performing so important a duty of a citizen ought surely to be sober minded. The perfect rowdyism that now characterizes the debates in our national congress—all these are great facts which rise up against man's claim to moral superiority."[26]

For Stanton and Smith, the key to combating excessive inequality and injustice is education. Smith calls for public education "to prevent the almost entire corruption and degeneracy of the great body of the people" (WN, V.i.f.49). For Stanton, it is only because women are deprived of the same opportunities to demonstrate their true abilities that men believe themselves intellectually superior to women. "Man's superiority," she writes, "cannot be a question until we have had a fair trial. When we shall have had our colleges, our professions, our trades, for a century a comparison may then be justly instituted."[27]

Smith diverges from Stanton, however, in supporting the separate education of women by parents or guardians rather than through formal schooling. He notes that, for women,

every part of their education tends evidently to some useful purpose; either to improve the natural attractions of their person, or to form their mind to reserve, to modesty, to chastity, and to oeconomy: to render them both likely to become the mistresses of a family, and to behave properly when they have become such (WN, V.i.f.47).

And although Smith's proposed education promotes moral develop-ment for those of "rank and fortune" as well as "common people," it also supports different levels of instruction according to class. Thus laborers should learn to "read, write, and account" at an early age and be exposed to basic principles of "geometry and mechanicks" as an "introduction to the most sublime as well as to the most useful sciences" (*WN*, V.i.f.55). Instruction for the elite will be more comprehensive, presumably offer-ing more detailed knowledge of reading, writing, mathematics, and the sciences, the practical application of which rests in its ability to improve moral judgment. By contrast, Stanton insists that everyone—women included—be given the opportunity to develop whatever talents and abili-ties they have in "colleges," "professions," "trades," or wherever they wish.

And yet both Stanton and Smith deplore the sort of intellectual edu-cation men receive that fails to make them better moral beings. Thus, for example, Stanton observes that divinity students utterly lack that which they are supposed to have been taught, namely, "perfect moral recti-tude . . . a devoted spirit of sacrifice . . . [and] a perfect union in thought opinion and feeling among those who profess to worship the one God." Instead, for Stanton, there is "much bitterness, envy, hatred and malice between these contending sects" of these highly educated men.[28] Law-yers and physicians display the same sort of hypocrisy. Along similar lines, Smith criticizes the abstract, useless education received by "gentle-men," especially in the intricate moral systems of philosophy that fail to improve their character so that they might be truly worthy of "publick esteem" (*WN*, V.i.f.46, 52).

Like Smith, who argues that people benefit more from practical ex-perience than any abstract theory or moral system, so, too, does Stan-ton believe that men who falsely "believe in the[ir] natural inborn, inbred superiority both in body and mind" should devote themselves not only "to the attentive perusal of their Bibles" but also "to historical research, to foreign travel—to a closer observation of the manifestations of mind about them and to an humble comparison of themselves with such women as Catherine of Russia" and other female writers and po-litical figures.[29] Stanton explains that "we seldom find this class of ob-jectors among liberally educated persons, who have had the advantage of observing their race in different countries, climes, and under different phases."[30] For Smith and Stanton, abstract moral speculations will not secure equality and justice. Rather, moral improvement will arise through commonsense observations and experiences of the plurality of the human condition, for these alone foster the openness to diversity and capacity for self-reflection that are essential for moral judgment.

In spite of their harsh critiques of the societies in which they live, both Smith and Stanton believe that their respective worlds contain the tools of reform. For Stanton social progress has inadvertently benefited women, in spite of lingering inequalities. "As the nations of earth emerge from a state of barbarism," she writes, "the sphere of woman gradually becomes wider" even though her situation is still inferior to that of men.[31] Although in the "United States of America woman has no right either to hold office, nor to the elective franchise," suffrage and political opportunities have been expanded to a broader swath of men than in any other society. The founding principles of democracy and equality having thus been established in one of the most advanced societies, all that is required is to follow through with those principles to their logical end by extending them to all members of society. Similarly, for Smith, commercial society has exacerbated the inequalities between rich and poor, but it has also brought benefits. As if guided by a kind of "invisible hand," the poor "derive" from the "luxury and caprice" of the rich "that share of the necessaries of life, which they would in vain have expected from his humanity or his justice" (*TMS*, IV.I.10). Conditions are ripe for a fuller development of the moral sentiments of all human beings, rich and poor alike.

Upon closer inspection, Stanton and Smith share similar perspectives on several key points. Stanton implements the concept of indirect description to great effect, as she conjures various scenarios that expose the plight of women to an otherwise oblivious audience. She traces the corrosive effects of women's oppression on the sympathetic relations between all Americans, male and female. Stanton understands the alienation of American women who are deprived of opportunities to expand their talents and increase their knowledge, and she emphasizes the importance of public education in addressing the inequities of American society. Having established these parallels between the two thinkers, we can now look at the role of ridicule in their respective moral theories of rhetoric.

## Stanton's Moral Politics of Ridicule

In her biography of Stanton, Lori Ginzberg observes that in the 1848 manuscript of her "maiden speech" Stanton

> offered many of the arguments she would elaborate, the prejudices she would attack, and those she would hold, for decades to come. Funny, ironic, condescending, rambling, and overblown, the speech is classic Stanton. Later addresses would be more polished, as Stanton learned to combine sharp criticism with wit and charm, but many of the ideas seem to have been born whole.

"The organization of the speech," Ginzberg notes, "would become Stanton's signature style." As she systematically undermined virtually every argument used to oppress women, "Stanton was in her element— she had had a lot of practice proving that she could beat men on their own terms. She employed irony and sarcasm, facts and anecdotes, to great effect, poking at men's vanities and laughing at their pretensions."[32]

In his *Lectures on Rhetoric and Belles Lettres* and *Theory of Moral Sentiments* the staid and sober Smith spends a considerable amount of time discussing an equally flamboyant figure, Jonathan Swift, who is infamous for his deployment of ridicule in critiquing the corruption of his society. In spite of the fact that Swift was not regarded as a serious thinker, Smith declares the writer "remarkable for his propriety and his precision"—crucial traits of the moral rhetorician (*LRBL*, i.100).[33] Indeed, Swift is "the most proper and precise of all the English writers," Smith claims, because he has "a complete knowledge of his Subjects, . . . arrange[s] all the parts of his Subject in their proper order, . . . [and] paint[s] <or> describe[s] the Ideas he has of these in the most proper and expressive manner" (*LRBL*, i.104–105). Highlighting the social and political significance of Swift's rhetoric, Smith also emphasizes the gravity of his critique of "tyranny either religious or civill" and his refusal to pander to his audience (*LRBL*, i.101). Instead of flattering his readers with edifying celebrations of its virtues or subjecting it to moral harangues, Swift performs the more difficult and unpopular task of exposing the tyrannies of his society and resisting complacency at all costs.[34] For "all of his writings," Smith claims, "are adapted to the present time either in ridiculing some prevailing vice or folly or exposing some particular character" (*LRBL*, i.102).

Stanton's work clearly reflects a style strikingly similar to Smith's version of Swift. Stanton revels in her nonconformity as she refuses to accept the circumscribed role carved out for her in nineteenth-century America. Disappointed by the lack of opportunities provided to her, Stanton sets her sights on the "grand" men of America, especially those who have political power, and seeks to bring them down to earth by revealing the inherent contradictions in their own thinking.[35] In the process, she aims to elevate women who have underestimated their own abilities and failed to demand full equality for themselves. She is clearly disdainful of what she sees as the shocking hypocrisy of American men who refuse to live up to their own standards and the founding principles they celebrate. She speaks with a bluntness that many doubtless found excessively harsh—and still do today, given the controversy that continues to surround her. Like Swift, Stanton is supremely confident in her own good judgment.[36] Both are clearly preoccupied with the pressing issues of their day and ultimately prefer concrete solutions over abstract ruminations (*LRBL*, i.102).[37] Both are clearly skeptical about religious and political institutions, ever mindful of their tendencies toward tyranny.[38]

Smith declares that "it is [Swift's] talent for ridicule that is most commonly and I believe most justly admired" (*LRBL*, i.107). According to Smith, ridicule is "either when what is in most respects Grand or pretends to be so or is expected to be so, has something mean or little in it or when we find something that is realy mean with some pretensions and marks of grandeur" (*LRBL*, i.108). Ridicule utilizes the "different combinations" of admiration or excitement over what is "grand" and of contempt over what is "mean" or "any great contradiction" generally that thwarts the expectations of the audience (*LRBL*, i.108–109). And when the target of ridicule elicits contempt, the audience does not merely laugh as it would in response to a simply humorous depiction, but its laughter is "mixt with somewhat of anger" (*LRBL*, i.111). Indeed, ridicule taps into the audience's sense of moral indignation. "What chiefly enrages us against the man who injures or insults us," in this case, the ridiculous hypocrite, "is the little account which he seems to make of us, the unreasonable preference which he gives to himself above us, and that absurd self-love, by which he seems to imagine, that other people may be sacrificed at any time, to his conveniency or his humour" (*TMS*, II.iii.1.5). For Smith, one of the main causes of political and social ills is that people often fail to sympathize with others because they wrongly believe themselves to be superior (or inferior). As a result, these individuals are incapable of making sound moral decisions and functioning as full human beings (*TMS*, III.3.5). By sympathetically speaking through a character who pretends to be superior or wrongly perceives himself inferior, or a character who says but does not do what he should, Swift uses ridicule to tap into the audience's sense of moral indignation.

Ridicule initially turns the seemingly natural desire for approbation and the avoidance of blame on its head by depicting for the audience characters who are utterly oblivious to these very desires. Members of the audience are encouraged to reflect on their own desire for approbation and avoidance of blame and the implications for self-forgetting. However, the audience does not turn immediately to itself and reflect on its own behavior. Smith adds an intermediary stage by which the audience conjures its own impartial spectator as a lens through which to examine its own behavior (*TMS*, III.2.3). Without the added step of imagining an impartial spectator, we would risk fooling ourselves into thinking that we deserve praise when in fact we do not. Simply because we believe we deserve praise does not mean that we truly deserve it. Smith claims that a human being naturally acts, "not only with a desire of being approved of, but with a desire of being what ought to be approved of; or of being what he himself approves of in other men" (*TMS*, III.2.6–7). It is in this regard that human beings are motivated by "the real love of virtue, and with the real abhorrence of vice," and not mere flattery. As a result of the conjuring of the impartial spectator by self-reflection or by "sympathizing with the hatred and abhorrence which other men must entertain for him," the individual "becomes in some measure the object of his own hatred and abhorrence." Not only is the agent affected. "The situation of the person, who suffered by his injustice, now calls upon his pity" (*TMS*, II.ii.2.3). Of course, self-delusion always remains a possibility, but it is less likely to occur for Smith if the impartial spectator is added to the process of self-reflection.

Ridicule is one of the most powerful forces for equality as well. Ideally, the "great" are humbled, the "low" are elevated to their rightful position, and the rhetorician and the audience are brought to the same level of understanding. For Smith, when an individual "views himself in the light in which he is conscious that others will view him, he sees that to them he is but one of the multitude in no respect better than any other in it." And when people observe injustices committed against others, especially through ridiculous portrayals, they remember that "this man is to them, in every respect, as good as he" and "they readily, therefore, sympathize with the natural resentment of the injured, and the offender becomes the object of their hatred and indignation" (*TMS*, II.ii.2.1).

Thus a number of interrelated priorities in Smith's moral theory are brought together through the rhetoric of ridicule, including the suitability of approbation or disapprobation of the object portrayed, the appropriate rhetorical style that must capture the "incongruity" between the subject matter and the "portrayal of it," and finally, the propriety of the speaker's character and emotions and his desire to "do good or harm to another."[39] Ridicule draws from Smith's theories of sympathy, indirect description, and the impartial spectator as audiences reflect on those who are ridiculed and ultimately on their own behavior. As such, ridicule is a potentially powerful tool for political critique and moral reform.

Swift's moral rhetoric of ridicule earns additional credibility because, for Smith, his keen sense of observation allows him to gain essential knowledge about people, especially those who are most unlike himself. Smith admires Swift because, for instance, "his rules for behavior and his directions for a Servant shews a knowledge of . . . characters that could not have been attained but by the closest attention continued for many years." Swift's insight into the human condition extends to his "political works" as well (*LRBL*, i.105). As a result, Swift is able to make appropriate and useful moral determinations by projecting himself into different "characters," such as servants, and portraying them accurately. "When he speaks in an other character," Swift does so in an authentic and credible way. His purpose is to make his characters "express their admiration and esteem for those things he would [he] expose." Swift's use of ridicule inspires the contrasting emotions of admiration and contempt among his audience, thus beginning the process of moral instruction (*LRBL*, i.120–121). By poking fun at religious and political hypocrites and those who occupy positions of power and prestige undeservedly, Swift helps his audience begin the process of moral education by giving them the opportunity to see that which is otherwise taken for granted and by relating the ridiculous portrayal to themselves.[40]

To emphasize the value of Swift's rhetoric in conveying moral teachings, Smith claims that the satirist, like the Roman writer Lucian, provides "a System of morality from whence more sound and just rules of life for all the various characters of men may be drawn than from most set systems of Morality" (*LRBL*, i.125). Both men exercise the art of ridicule in a "gentlemanly" way because "Real foibles and blemishes in the Characters or behaviour of men are exposed to our view in a ridiculous light." As a result, ridicule "tends to the reformation of manners and the benefit of mankind" (*LRBL*, i.v.116).

I argue that, like Smith's Swift, Stanton deploys a rhetoric of ridicule for the sake of educating her audience in moral philosophy. Tapping into the human desire for approbation and aversion to blame, she encourages her audience to overcome their avoidance of self-criticism so they can better understand the natural equality and sense of justice that is shared by all human beings. Stanton's rhetoric most closely approaches Smith's theory as she confronts the members of her audience, ridicules their hypocrisy, and provides an opening for them to realize that only through reform can they avoid shame or the disapprobation of sensible-minded people.[41]

It is in the context of exposing the fundamental hypocrisy of elitist men through ridicule that Stanton makes the kind of stock racist and elitist remarks for which she has been criticized. Lamenting the fact that, in violation of the founding principles, women are not permitted to exercise consent to their government by voting, Stanton proclaims that "we need not prove ourselves equal to Daniel Webster to enjoy this privilege for the most ignorant Irishman in the ditch has all the civil rights he has, we need not prove our muscular power equal to this same Irishman to enjoy this privilege for the most tiny, weak, ill shaped, imbecile stripling of 21 has all the civil rights of the Irishman." She continues:

> We should not feel so sorely grieved if no man who had not attained the full stature of a Webster, Van Buren, Clay or Gerrit Smith could claim the right of the elective franchise, but to have the rights of drunkards, idiots, horse-racing rowdies, ignorant foreigners, and silly boys fully recognized, whilst we ourselves are thrust out from all the rights that belong to

citizens—it is too grossly insulting to the dignity of woman to be longer quietly submitted to.[42]

She bases her analysis on the founding principle that "all men in this country have the same rights however they may differ in mind, body, or estate."[43]

Commentators assume that Stanton is speaking from her own perspective of a highly intelligent elite woman embittered by her own lack of opportunity. Although there is a clear element of classism in Stanton's comments, it is important to note that she is voicing the opinions held by the elite men she targets as well, addressing them in a language they would understand. Perhaps Stanton, like Swift, is temporarily and rhetorically adopting the persona of a man to expose the hypocrisy surrounding the founding principle of government by consent. She, like Swift, "speaks in an other character" to make her audience "express their admiration and esteem for those things" she would "expose." In other words, Stanton "exposes" the fact that elite men rely on the assumption that all men are equal while simultaneously upholding profound social and cultural inequalities among them. It does not necessarily follow, however, that Stanton agrees with these elite men and views the ditch diggers with similar disdain. Using Smith's description of ridicule as a frame of analysis, we see that Stanton highlights the fact that the "great" or elite men view themselves as superior and look down on their male inferiors when in reality the latter enjoy the same—or at least comparable—rights they themselves enjoy. Moreover, elite men view themselves superior in spite of the fact that there are others among them—the Websters and Van Burens—who surpass them. When it comes to political rights, elite men are in reality no better than their social inferiors or worse than their superiors. All men and women are truly created equal in Stanton's universe, as in Smith's.

Through the lens of Smith's moral theory and, by extension, Swift's rhetoric of ridicule, we see that Stanton also uses indirect description to conjure a kind of impartial spectator and provide her audience an opportunity to broaden their moral education, thereby laying the groundwork for reform. Rehearsing virtually every argument made to deny equality to women, Stanton effectively adopts the persona of a man. In doing so, she indirectly displays male critics' misunderstanding of the founding principles—and, in particular, their failure to live up to their own standards—in order to induce shame. Stanton, too, is tapping into the audience's desire for approbation and aversion to blame by exposing the contradictions between the opinions and assumptions held by elite American men, on the one hand, and the logical extensions of their arguments as they would apply to women, on the other. The impartial spectator who emerges between Stanton's male persona and her audience is the authentic American citizen who, unlike the elite man she mimics or the elite men she addresses, consistently upholds the founding principles of the Declaration and extends those rights and privileges to all. The audience draws from this impartial spectator as it realizes the error of its ways and contemplates reform.

Stanton continues to compound the irony of patriarchal oppression, observing ruefully that there is one kind of equality that all men, "great" and "mean," share. Men of all classes use their perceived privilege to oppress women: "From the man of highest mental cultivation, to the most degraded wretch who staggers in the streets do we hear ridicule and coarse jests, freely bestowed upon those who dare assert that woman stands by the side of man."[44] Presumably this is not the sort of equality Stanton's elite male audience would want to share.

Stanton must expose the hypocrisy surrounding equality among men through ridicule in order to proceed to her key point, namely, that elite men deprive all women, "great" and "mean," of whatever class or intellect, of the same rights they extend to other men, "great" and "mean" alike. Otherwise, her target audience would remain untroubled by the denial of those same privileges to women. The whole situation is exposed by Stanton to be utterly ridiculous: Elite men preach the gospel of equality but fail to live by it; they wrongly believe themselves superior to men of lower social status and behave as if they are equal to or better than the truly "great men"—the Websters and Clays—who are in fact their moral superiors. As Smith predicts, Stanton's audience should also indulge in laughter that is "mixt with somewhat of anger" at the injustice and hypocrisy of it all (*LRBL*, i.111). Stanton, like Smith's Swift, is offering the audience an opportunity for moral education. Although elite men could conceivably pride themselves in extending equal rights to inferior men as an act of benevolence, they must also realize that they are no better than their inferiors when it comes to rights. Equally important, through Stanton's rhetoric of ridicule, elite men should realize that they in fact stand on equal footing with the women they systematically deprive of the same rights. American men and women are "but one of the multitude in no respect better than any other in it" (*TMS*, II.ii.2.1). Although the extent of Stanton's populism is ambiguous, given the dearth of evidence, it is possible that if the "mean" or lower-class men happened to hear Stanton's mockery, they, too, would realize that, in spite of their perceived lack of privilege when compared to the "great" elite men, they nevertheless enjoy the same rights as their "superiors." And as they share the cultural and social status of women, so, too, should they want to extend those rights to their "equals."

It is now clear that as early as 1848 Stanton was offering versions of the controversial arguments that reappear in various forms throughout her career. For example, in the 1854 "Address to the Legislature of New York," she proclaims:

> We have every qualification required by the constitution, necessary to the legal voter, but the one of sex. We are moral, virtuous, and intelligent, and in all respects quite equal to the proud white man himself, and yet by your laws we are classed with idiots, lunatics, and negroes; and though we do not feel honored by the place assigned us, yet, in fact, our legal position is lower than that of either; for the negro can be raised to the dignity of a voter if he possess himself of $250; the lunatic can vote in his moments of sanity, and the idiot, too, if he be a male one, and not more than nine-tenths a fool.[45]

In her impassioned 1865 letter to the *National Anti-Slavery Standard* entitled, "This Is the Negro's Hour," Stanton responds to longtime women's rights advocate Wendell Phillips, who originally used the phrase to indicate his sudden shift in priorities at the 1865 American Anti-Slavery Society anniversary. Phillips explained that he hoped "some day to be bold enough to add 'sex'" to his ideal version of the proposed constitutional amendment for suffrage. "However, my friends," he continued, "we must take up but one question at a time, and this hour belongs exclusively to the negro."[46] Stung by his apparent betrayal, Stanton raises the "serious question whether we [women] had better stand aside and see 'Sambo' walk into the kingdom first." She points out that the enfranchisement of freed black men before women of either race affects black women directly, explaining that, "if the two millions of Southern black women are not to be secured in their rights of person, property, wages, and children, their emancipation is another form of slavery."[47]

Although she continues with the dubious line of argument that for black women "it is better to be the slave of an educated white man, than of a degraded, ignorant black one," Stanton is clearly not endorsing slavery or necessarily attacking all black men directly, as critics contend. Nor did she necessarily feel compelled to make such deliberatively provocative arguments in response to the threat of immediate enfranchisement for freed black men at the expense of woman suffrage that emerged after the Civil War, as defenders imply.[48] It is equally plausible that Stanton is simply continuing—however callously—the style of argument from the moral rhetoric of ridicule she established early in her career. Moreover, this letter contains one of the few instances in which Stanton appeals explicitly to freed black women who, in spite of their emancipation, would still lack any legal rights in marriage to black men if they, like all women, were denied the vote. As another counterweight to the charge of racism, Stanton makes clear that she advocates equality for all men and women, black and white, by declaring unequivocally that, "in changing the status of the four millions of Africans, the women as well as the men should be secured in all the rights, privileges, and immunities of citizens," and that suffrage should be extended to men and women of all races.[49]

An excellent example of Stanton's use of an impartial spectator appears in her discussion of elite and lower class men in her 1860 address "A Slave's Appeal." Whereas other speeches and writings appeal to an impartial spectator through indirect description, as the audience imagines a kind of neutral third party between the ridiculing rhetorician and the object of her ridicule, Stanton presents a vivid, unforgettable image directly to her audience:

> Just imagine an inhabitant of another planet entertaining himself some pleasant evening in searching over our Declaration of Independence, our Constitution, or some of our Statute-books; what would he think of those "women and negroes" that must be so fenced in, so guarded against? Why, he would certainly suppose we were monsters, like those fabulous giants or Brobdignagians of olden times, so dangerous to civilized man,

from our size, ferocity and power. Then let him take up our poets, from Pope down to Dana; let him listen to our Fourth of July toasts, and some of the sentimental adulations of social life, and no logic could convince him that this creature of the law, and this angel of the family altar, could be one and the same being.[50]

By creating a third man, or impartial spectator—in this case, a "Martian"— Stanton drives her point home. Comparing the founding principles with the oppressive conditions of American society, the space visitor would notice the profound disjunction between theory and practice. The alien's findings would be reinforced by a perusal of Anglo-American literature, which provides an idealized view of women that does not comport with reality. As the Martian would be confounded, so, too, should American society—and especially the members of Stanton's audience who aid and abet the oppression. Note as well Stanton's reference to Swift's "Brobdignagians" from his well-known satirical novel *Gulliver's Travels*. If "women and negroes" are perceived to be giant Brobdignagians, by implication elite men who oppress them must be adopting the perspective of the much smaller Gulliver or even the Lilliputians. Although these men seem to be in charge and rule with confidence, they are actually vulnerable and insecure. Again we see Stanton employing the moral rhetoric of ridicule to expose the hypocrisy of corrupt elites and advocate for reform.[51]

Returning to the 1848 manuscript, we see Stanton offering a comprehensive account of virtually every argument given in American society to deny women the right to vote. In so doing, Stanton is not simply describing the facts of women's plight or conveying her observations. Instead, she is using indirect description by conjuring the complex circumstances, conventions, and context of American society in order to evoke a sympathetic response and begin the process of moral education. As she describes women's situation and rehearses the typical arguments against women's suffrage and equal rights, Stanton juxtaposes them with a view of the founding principles properly understood, as arising from the Declaration of Independence and the Constitution—arising, that is, from American society itself in its truest expression.

The impartial spectator would be equally appalled by the public mischaracterizations of the women's rights conventions in Rochester and

Seneca Falls. Men accused women of meeting merely to gossip or "go into the detail of social life alone," to "petition the legislature to make our Husbands just, generous and courteous, [or] to seat every man at the head of a cradle and to clothe every woman in male attire."[52] In response, Stanton argues that, like the patriots of the American Revolution—model citizens who here serve as impartial spectators of American society—women

> assemble[d] to protest against a form of government existing without the consent of the governed, to declare our rights to be free as man is free—to be represented in the government which we are taxed to support—to have such disgraceful laws as give to man the right to chastise and imprison his wife—to take the wages which she earns,—the property which she inherits and in the case of separation the children of her love—laws which make her the mere dependent on his bounty—it was to protest against such unjust laws as these and to have them if possible forever erased from our statute books, deeming them a standing shame and disgrace to a professedly republican, christian people in the nineteenth century.

As the men of the Revolutionary era fought for the freedom of their country, so, too, did these women declare their "right to vote according to the Declaration of the government under which we live."[53]

Stanton also repeats the argument that women should not vote because they are too frail and delicate and, by implication, morally superior to withstand the tumult and rowdiness of the political sphere, especially at polling places. The corollary, of course, is that men are morally inferior because they cause the trouble and yet they are (physically) stronger than women and thus better able to endure it. But Stanton lucidly argues that because men are prone to conflict, they misunderstand moral courage by characterizing it purely in martial terms. Even young men are sufficiently prepared somehow to survive the onslaught of corruption. Stanton implicitly juxtaposes these assumptions with what should be the logical conclusion of the argument, namely, that the morally superior should and must vote in order to purify political life. She also shifts the definition of moral courage away from the martial understanding and toward wisdom and patriotism associated with Christian pacifism. And yet an impartial observer would notice immediately that those who best fit the given description of the ideal voter and moral role model are precisely those who are excluded. For it is women, not men, who occupy the moral high ground and demonstrate the highest Christian moral strength of courage and nonviolence, yet it is they who are denied the vote. To continue the moral education, Stanton explains that, if the premise of women's moral superiority were true, they should be at the polls to protect their young sons from corruption and to purify the political realm. This is precisely the understanding that would be reached by the impartial observer. The audience, informed by the perspective conjured by Stanton as a kind of impartial spectator, would realize that their own actions and views regarding the role of women cannot be praised according to the true principles of American society. Men would realize that, in assuming their ideas and actions to be correct, they have failed to truly uphold the founding principles of the society they claim to revere. In their vanity and selfishness, men have blinded themselves to their own hypocrisy. It is important to emphasize that Stanton is not creating an abstract ideal of the liberal individual, as critics contend, but rather deploying the very same sort of practical morality outlined by Smith that takes for its starting point the given situation in a particular society—in this case, American society as expressed in its founding principles—and shapes moral reform accordingly.

Stanton criticizes another related claim made by American men, namely, that if women were to vote, they would misuse their privilege by advocating for objectionable goals that "so entirely violate every principle of right and justice." Stanton points out that men value the vote so much that they are "tenacious" in maintaining that right for themselves, using it to advocate interests of "right and justice" such as the 1848 "[F]ree [S]oil" antislavery party and codifying their legal interests in the "statute books" through their representatives. Women, she argues, are no less capable of exercising that right responsibly, and given the vote, they would be equally committed to the interests of "right and justice," including "woman's rights."[54] The impartial observer would see that the logical conclusion of the prevailing wisdom is again thwarted by the denial of woman suffrage—in this particular case because there is no logical reason to assume that women, unlike men, would misuse the vote for nefarious or selfish purposes.

## Beyond Reason and Emotion: Smith's Historical Rhetoric and Stanton's Biblical Critique

Subsequent passages in Stanton's manuscript can be framed in terms of another aspect of Smith's theory of rhetoric, namely the rhetoric used by historians, which is in turn thematically connected to his views on sympathy, indirect description, and the impartial spectator. Smith defines historians broadly to include a wide variety of writers whose purpose is not simply to relate the facts in a detached, objective fashion or "merely to entertain" with their tales but, rather, to have "in view the instruction of the reader" (*LRBL*, ii.16–17). Historians provide a moral education through their depictions of "the more interesting and important events of human life" because the ultimate purpose of the account "points out to us by what manner and method we may produce similar good effects or avoid similar bad ones" (*LRBL*, ii.17). Historians make extensive use of indirect description, according to Smith. A history is "interesting" when it includes details that "expose the causes of every thing only in proportion to the impression it makes" (*LRBL*, ii.v.19). Just as Shakespeare's writings are rhetorically successful because the dialogues they contain "make the persons of the Dialogue relate the effects any object had upon them," rather than simply relating the "objects" themselves, so, too, can historians invent speeches to convey "observations" that are "not so properly made in the person of the writer" but instead indirectly, through the imagined observations of a historical character (*LRBL*, i.160; ii.43). Like Shakespeare, historians who create speeches to convey the ultimate causes of historical events heighten interest without sacrificing credibility because the characters are expressing the authors' own views, albeit indirectly.

In a broader discussion of the use and abuse of history in his own time, Smith explains that, although the historian appeals to the moral sensibilities and impressions of the audience, he uses neither an "oratorical" style relying on emotional appeals nor a "didactick" style requiring "labored and formal demonstrations" to prove the truth of the historical event or "fact" in question (*LRBL*, ii.39–40). This is relevant because many historians have been charged by "several sects in Religion and politicall disputes" with the responsibility to demonstrate the truth of "those facts on which the claims of the parties they favoured depended."

This has led many to use the "didactick" style, thereby detracting from the true purpose of their work. To avoid a tedious "dissertation about the Truth of a Fact," the historian, "barely mentioning the authorities on both sides," is "to shew for what reason he had chosen to be of the one opinion rather than the other" (*LRBL*, ii.40). Smith explains how the process would work:

> A Historian might first relate the Event according to the most likely opinion and when he had done so give the others by saying that such or such a Circumstance had occasiond such or such a mistake or that such a misrepresentation had been propagated by such a person for such Ends. This would be making a fact of it. (*LRBL*, ii.v.39)

By giving the Devil his due, so to speak, and as he maintains audience interest and engagement, Smith's historian leads the audience through particularly contentious religious and political matters and toward the truth. He does so by juxtaposing the "most likely opinion" with the alternative "mistake" or "misrepresentation" and thereby conjures an "impartial spectator" as the audience distances itself from both perspectives in order to weigh each of them. The truth of the "fact" in question is not simply "made" or asserted by the historian. Instead, the historian conducts a kind of "proof" or "demonstration" through the use of indirect description and by appealing to the impartial observer, who reflects the ultimate opinion held by the audience. Only after the juxtaposition is the audience most likely to arrive at the same conclusion that the "fact" offered by the historian is "true."

Although we might expect Stanton to fall into either the category of a deeply affected orator, given her often visceral language, or a "didactick" logician, given the tendencies to interpret her work in a legalistic way, several aspects of her discussion of the biblical justifications for women's subordination fall into Smith's historical style of rhetoric and the use of juxtaposition and indirect description. As Smith stops short of arguing that the historian can prove the truth of his assertions with certainty, so, too, does Stanton realize that she cannot "prove" the "truth" of her interpretation of the Bible based only on the asserted "falsehood" of alternative views. Like Smith's historian, and like other early women's rights activists and abolitionists who held progressive views on Christianity, Stanton can only make the strongest case possible. In the 1848 manuscript, she focuses on one of the most frequently cited biblical passages used to justify women's inferiority, namely, Paul's command that women should obey their husbands (Colossians 3:18).[55] The command, "Wives obey your Husbands in the Lord," is "exceedingly limited" for Stanton because women, as the recipients of the order, are also given the responsibility for determining "what is in the Lord." As a result, according to Stanton, "There can be no subordination where the one to whom the command is given," namely, the wife, "is allowed to sit in judgement on the character of the command" as directed by God.[56] "That best of Books," she concludes, "is ever on the side of freedom and we shrink not from pleading our cause on its principles of universal justice and love."[57] In Smithean terms, Stanton attempts "to shew for what reason" she believes her view of the Bible is the "most likely opinion" by juxtaposing it with the commonly held yet "mistaken" view and encouraging her audience to arrive at similar conclusions.

In an earlier passage of the manuscript Stanton takes a similar approach to interpreting the biblical account of the Fall. She begins by relating the account most often used to justify the rational superiority of men over women.[58] Adam and Eve were placed in the garden and lived peacefully and harmoniously. "The Evil One saw their happiness and it troubled him," however, so "He set his wits to work to know how he should destroy it." Yet Stanton proceeds to retell the story in a way that is consistent with her worldview and in juxtaposition with the traditional account. In her version, it is Adam, not Eve, who "could be easily conquered through *his affection for the woman*." And it is Eve, not Adam, who "could be reached only through her intellectual nature." She, not Adam, is offered "the knowledge of good and evil" by Satan who "promised to gratify the desire she felt for intellectual improvement." Although Stanton does not deny the Fall occurs, she attributes Adam's haste to eat the apple to "his love for Eve" in spite of the fact that "he knew he was doing wrong." In Stanton's version Eve's sin is more justifiable than Adam's because her desire for knowledge arises from the unjust intellectual deprivation of women, whereas Adam's emotional nature and vulnerability have been obscured by male hypocrisy. Stanton concludes her revisionist biblical interpretation with the question: "Which I ask you was the 'creature of the affections?'"[59] As the audience follows Stanton's account, it is continually invited to recall the traditional version in which Eve is the primary cause of the downfall because she is the first to give in to temptation. Adam, in Stanton's retelling, is equally, if not more, culpable, yet he continues his undeserved and unjustified dominion over all other beings, including Eve.

Although Stanton is known for offering a more secularized view of women's rights than her radical abolitionist predecessors and for delivering one of the most consistent attacks on established religion in American political thought, she does not advocate atheism or abandon Christianity altogether. She would certainly agree with Smith's contention that "science is the great antidote to the poison of enthusiasm and superstition; and where all the superior ranks of people were secured from it, the inferior ranks could not be much exposed to it" (WN, V.i.g.14). For Smith, religious fanaticism thwarts the proper exercise of sympathy because it hypocritically requires the silencing of all dissent and unquestioning support by civil authorities (WN, V.i.g.7). Swift was equally critical of religious and political "tyrannies" and sought to expose them through ridicule. Stanton, too, deplores the hypocrisy with which religious men degrade women and engage in theological squabbles instead of aiming at genuine virtue. Smith's preference is to "reduce the doctrine" of competing religions "to that pure and rational religion, free from every mixture of absurdity, imposture, or fanaticism, such as wise men have in all ages of the world wished to see established" (WN, V.i.g.8). This sort of "pure and rational religion" is complementary to the "general rules" of "civility and hospitality" and the "habitual reverence" for the "duties of politeness" that emerge well before established religions appear. In the past, religious believers would ascribe to their deities "sentiments and qualities which are the great ornaments of humanity, and which seem to raise it to a resemblance of divine perfection, the love of virtue, and beneficence, and the abhorrence of vice and justice" (TMS, III.5.2, 4). Smith emphasizes that the "natural sense of duty" upon which primitive religions are based emerged "long before the age of artificial reasoning and philosophy" (TMS, III.5.4).

Stanton can be seen to offer her own version of a "pure and rational" religion that offers the same moral code for men and women. She writes:

> I believe in Christ—I believe that command Resist not evil to be divine. . . . Let frail man, who cannot foresee the consequences of an action to walk humbly with his God—loving his enemies, blessing those who curse him and always returning good for evil.[60]

Stanton deploys some of her most powerful and eloquent language to describe the proper role of Christianity in women's lives:

> Let woman live as she should, let her feel her accountability to her Maker—Let her know that her spirit is fitted for as high a sphere as man's and that her soul requires food as pure and refreshing as his—let her live *first* for God and she will not make imperfect man an object of reverence and idolatry—Teach her her responsibility as a being of conscience and of reason—that she will find any earthly support unstable and weak, that her only safe dependence is on the arm of omnipotence. Teach her there is no sex in mind, that true happiness springs from duty accomplished. . . . She will become conscious that each human being is morally accountable for himself that no one can throw upon another his burden of responsibility, that neither Father, Husband, Brother nor son, however willing they may be, can relieve woman from this weight, can stand in her stead when called into the presence of the searcher of spirits.[61]

Many years later, in her introduction to *The Woman's Bible*, Stanton would reiterate the importance of the "general principles" of Christianity and other religions "that teach love, charity, liberty, justice and equality for all the human family," that rely on "the golden rule," and that provide "lofty examples of good and true men and women, all worthy of our acceptance and imitation."[62]

## Stanton's Rhetoric of Ridicule: A Cautionary Tale

In spite of Stanton's unwavering commitments to women's rights and universal suffrage, she seems, at the very least, to have suffered from the same sort of misunderstanding that afflicts rhetoricians who employ ridicule to critique political, religious, and moral injustice. Smith's cautions here are instructive. For Smith, Swift's approach is vulnerable to misunderstanding and misuse by those who are less perceptive and talented. Like Voltaire, Swift is admired for his "most improper and insolent contempt of all the ordinary decorums of life and conversation," yet both "have thereby set the most pernicious example to those who wish to resemble them, and who too often content themselves with imitating their follies, without even attempting to attain their perfections" (*TMS*, VI.i.10). One might imagine Swift's audience dwelling on the anger and contempt they experience at the spectacle he conjures without reflecting on their own absurdities and shortcomings. Like Swift and Voltaire, Stanton's rhetoric risks misunderstanding because her audience may interpret her comments at face value and fail to reflect on their own racism, sexism, and elitism. In all her brashness, Stanton perhaps sets a "most pernicious example" for her audience without leading them to the next steps toward reform.

Smith's warning proves prescient. Whether intentional or no, the racism and elitism in Stanton's rhetoric has for many obscured her lifelong struggle for reform. In this regard, Stanton has failed the most important requirement of Smith's moral theory of rhetoric, namely, the "propriety" test. At such a tumultuous time in American history, Stanton's language was not "correct and Proper," nor did she always "write but in a manner most suitable to the Nature of the Subject" (*LRBL*, i.119). A clear indication of the problem is reflected by the sentiments of Frederick Douglass, whose decision to prioritize immediate suffrage for freedmen over that of women in the face of imminent threats to black voting rights in the North and South was met with fierce opposition by Stanton. Unlike staunch women's rights advocates such as Lucy Stone, Henry Blackwell, and others, who reluctantly and with great difficulty ultimately chose to support the immediate enfranchisement of freed black men, Stanton refused to back down. In her now-infamous 1869 "Address to the National Woman Suffrage Convention," Stanton warns:

> If American women find it hard to bear the oppressions of their own Saxon fathers, the best orders of manhood, what may they not be called to endure when all the lower orders of manhood, what may they not be called to endure when all the lower orders of foreigners now crowding our shores legislate for them and their daughters. Think of Patrick and Sambo and Hans and Yung Tung, who do not know the difference between a monarchy and a republic, who can not read the Declaration of

Independence or Webster's spelling-book, making laws for Lucretia Mott, Ernestine L. Rose, and Anna E. Dickinson.

In spite of the fact that debates over women's suffrage were taking place throughout Europe, Stanton wonders,

> Shall American statesmen, claiming to be liberal, so amend their constitutions as to make their wives and mothers the political inferiors of unlettered and unwashed ditch-diggers, boot-blacks, butchers, and barbers, fresh from the slave plantations of the South, and the effete civilizations of the Old World?[63]

Following Stanton's tirades, Douglass responds that "there is no name greater than that of Elizabeth Cady Stanton in the matter of woman's rights and equal rights." However, he continues, "My sentiments are tinged a little against *The Revolution*," Stanton's paper, because "there was in the address to which I allude the employment of certain names, such as 'Sambo,' and the gardener, and the bootblack, and the daughters of Jefferson and Washington, and all the rest that I can not coincide with." And although "there were few houses in which the black man could have put his head, this wooly head of mine found a refuge in the house of Elizabeth Cady Stanton," Douglass clarifies his ultimate position thus:

> I must say that I do not see how any one can pretend that there is the same urgency in giving the ballot to woman as to the negro. With us, the matter is a question of life and death, at least, in fifteen States of the Union. When women, because they are women, are hunted down through the cities of New York and New Orleans; when they are dragged from their houses and hung upon lamp-posts; when their children are torn from their arms, and their brains dashed out upon the pavement; when they are objects of insult and outrage at every turn; when they are in danger of having their homes burnt down over their heads; when their children are not allowed to enter schools; then they will have an urgency to obtain the ballot equal to men.[64]

Douglass's tempered yet principled response, balancing magnanimity in recognition of Stanton's lifelong dedication to equality for women and African Americans with unflinching criticism of her shortcomings, can perhaps guide us in our own assessment of Stanton's complex and controversial legacy. And although Stanton clearly fails to uphold one of the elements of propriety advanced by Smith—namely, the suitability of rhetoric to the particular context and circumstances in which it emerges—she undoubtedly fulfills another of his key requirements. For Smith, Swift's rhetoric is "severe," "harsh," and "unpleasant," but "this stile suits well enough with the morose humour of that author" (*LRBL*, i.53). The proper rhetorician, Smith tells us, "never seems to act out of character." It may similarly be said of Stanton that, although she does not always speak "in a manner . . . suitable to the Subject," her lifelong use of ridicule to shame her opponents into accepting women's equality—a weapon she deploys more often than not to great effect—reflects a rhetorical style that is true to "the character [s]he naturally inclines to" (*LRBL*, i.136).

# The Shadow and the Substance of Sojourner Truth

It seems fitting to conclude this book with a brief examination of one of the most elusive and complex figures in the early women's rights and abolitionist movements. This title, "The Shadow and the Substance of Sojourner Truth," is taken from a message printed on a *carte de visite*, a small collectible photograph, bearing Truth's image. Truth publicly emerged among abolitionist and early women's rights circles on the heels of Elizabeth Cady Stanton with the publication of her autobiography, *The Narrative of Sojourner Truth*, in 1850, and with her appearance a year later at the Women's Rights Convention in Akron, Ohio, where she delivered her famous "Ain't I a Woman" speech.

The analysis of several early women's rights advocates and abolitionists that I have presented in this book provides a rich framework with which to examine Truth's important yet neglected contribution to American political thought. The emergence of ridicule in Stanton's work as a powerful rhetorical tool for reform helps us better understand Truth's frequent deployment of the tactic in her own speeches and writings. The central role of Quaker faith in shaping the theoretical contributions of Angelina and Sarah Grimké and Lucretia Mott prepares us to appreciate the influence of Truth's religious convictions on her arguments to end slavery and the oppression of women. Indeed, Truth was aided early on by Quakers, who helped her wage a successful lawsuit to free her illegally enslaved son and continued their support throughout her career, even inspiring her mode of dress.[1] In the *Book of Life*, a collection of newspaper articles, letters, autographs, statements, and other works written for and about Truth, Lucretia Mott signed herself as Truth's "co-laborer in the cause of our race."[2] The performative elements of Wright's and Mott's theorizing are fully realized in Truth's own activities, as she compels her audience through her very presence to confront the systematic oppression in the society in which they live and their own unwitting contribution to that oppression and offers them a mode of inquiry and self-reflection that provides the foundation for reform. Truth's very identity as a freed black woman embodies the concept of intersectionality, and her participation in the abolitionist and early women's rights movements compelled audiences to confront the effects of race, gender, and class oppression. As someone who actually experiences all of the effects of intersectionality, Truth is immune to many of the criticisms waged against white counterparts who sought to establish sympathetic connections with enslaved peoples but who were hampered by their own race, gender, and class privilege.

There are significant challenges, however, in undertaking a theoretical analysis of Truth's contributions. Like her contemporary Harriet Tubman, Truth was illiterate and left behind no record written in her own hand.[3] Truth's *Narrative* was written by a Northern white abolitionist, Olive Gilbert, so careful reading is needed to discern her own ideas among Gilbert's embellishments. Later editions of the *Narrative* were edited by another Northern white abolitionist, Frances Titus, who added *The Book of Life*, which reveals additional fragments of Truth's identity from multiple sources. Even the most famous speech Truth delivered, popularly known as "Ain't I a Woman," was transcribed years later, in 1863, by Frances Dana Barker Gage, a white Northern abolitionist whose recollection differs markedly from an eyewitness account recorded by Marius Robinson and published soon after the speech was delivered in the abolitionist newspaper *Anti-Slavery Bugle*. Accounts of some of Truth's speeches are included in the *History of Woman Suffrage*, which, as we already know, was often subject to the editorial discretion of its authors.[4]

The lack of a written record might lead us to doubt that Truth's theoretical contributions can be analyzed in a substantive way. Indeed, "Truth is seen not as the author of her words and experiences but as a repository for them." Much like Tubman, who was mythologized as a "Black Moses," Truth has been interpreted by subsequent writers "more as a spectacle or emblem than as a thinker and speaker."[5] Other black female abolitionists and women's rights advocates who did leave more extensive writings behind, such as Harriet Jacobs, who wrote her own *Narrative*, and Frances Ellen Watkins Harper, who authored several books of poetry and novels, might seem more appropriate subjects for theoretical analysis.[6]

An important goal of this book has been to demonstrate the relevance of alternative means of theorizing beyond the conventional written treatise, including speeches and letters as well as public activities and performances. Truth's life and work can offer vital sources of information that help illuminate some of the key theoretical underpinnings of the early women's rights and abolitionist movements. However, to bring these ideas to light, we must first attempt to recover Truth as a unique individual with her own perspective, a fact that has been obscured by interpreters who have mythologized and idealized Truth and appropriated her for their own purposes. We must also try to find Truth's own thoughts and ideas among the innumerable narratives that have been developed by others and imposed upon her. By uncovering the reality of Truth's life and work to the best of our ability, we see that Truth is no less important simply because we lack the sort of extensive source material left behind by her counterparts. Indeed, Truth is an integral part of the ongoing conversation among the early women's rights advocates and abolitionists I have examined in this book.

## A Quixotic Sojourn to the Truth

To say that Truth represents the ideal perspective of the freed black woman would vastly devalue her individuality. Moreover, to idealize Truth would gloss over the paradoxes surrounding her life and work that merit further consideration because they reflect many of the tensions and ambiguities of the abolitionist and early women's rights movements themselves.[7] Truth's experience as a slave seems unique in part because slavery in the North is not documented as extensively as Southern slavery, which has shaped popular perception. Truth was born into slavery in a Dutch community in upstate New York, lived under a different name—Isabella van Wagenen—and probably spoke Dutch as her first language. It would take until 1827 for New York to officially abolish slavery, but the process developed gradually during the period of Truth's enslavement, beginning around 1799. New York legally recognized slave marriages in 1809, a right no Southern state granted. Slave-owning households in New York were far smaller and more widely dispersed than those in the South. Truth did not live on a large plantation with a large community of slaves. Instead, she was essentially a member of a small family, albeit one that regularly abused her.

Truth's environment differs from the "metaphorical slave South" depicted so memorably in Harriet Beecher Stowe's *Uncle Tom's Cabin*. To be sure, there are elements of Truth's life and work that are consistent with Stowe's portrayal, with its "stock of characters" such as "the long-suffering, Christian slave, the cruel master with his whip and his mulatto concubine, the outraged slave mother, the slave trader, even the kind master and the jealous mistress."[8] Yet other elements defy the stereotype of slavery that has been handed down to us by Stowe and others. Truth's first masters did treat her harshly and separated her from her parents at a young age. Yet John Dumont, the man who owned Truth for most of her early life, was less physically cruel. Although Truth was forbidden to marry her first love, Dumont arranged for Truth to marry another slave he owned, with whom she bore five children and remained until she gained her freedom. Truth was never forcibly separated from her children, yet to convey her anguish at being unable to provide a normal family life, she would repeatedly compare herself to the "outraged slave mother" whose children were torn away from her and sold. Dumont praises Truth as an incredibly productive worker, both in the fields and within the household, a biographical element to which Truth frequently alludes. Yet Truth suffered long-term emotional, physical, and sexual abuse in the Dumont household.[9] In an act of betrayal, Dumont reneged on his promise to release her in advance of the emancipation law, forcing Truth to escape, but only after she felt released from any legal or financial obligations to him. We might have assumed that Truth would have abandoned the Dumonts permanently after 1827, but she maintained a complicated relationship with them. Even after she secured freedom for herself, Truth was powerless over the fates of the rest of her children, who were legally emancipated but still indentured to Dumont. In another act of betrayal, Dumont had even sold one of her sons illegally to a Southern slave owner, forcing Truth to file a lawsuit against him. In spite of Dumont's repeated treachery, Truth wanted to return to him because, as the *Narrative* describes, she missed the camaraderie of her fellow slaves, especially during holidays. According to Truth, however, her frivolity brought on a direct encounter with God and exposed the error of her ways. Yet, even after her conversion experience, Truth was present at Dumont's wife's deathbed in 1846, and she maintained contact with Dumont until 1849, when he left New York and was never heard from again.

Truth struggled constantly to define herself in a world that sought to define her. Thus, even as she renamed herself Sojourner Truth, a bold act of self-reclaiming, supporters and detractors alike continually tried to shape her identity. Truth was persuaded to wear traditional Quaker dress, and at one point, as if to protect her at an appearance before a hostile audience in Indiana, she was effectively swaddled in clothing, which made her feel as if she were armed and "going to battle."[10] Truth posed patiently for numerous *carte de visite* photographs, dressed in attire chosen for and by whites, but she personally controlled their distribution and used the profits to support herself.[11] She allowed a white Northern woman to write the story of her life, and yet she eventually gained the publishing rights to her autobiography and marketed it aggressively. The *Book of Life* was based on Truth's personal scrapbook, but was edited by Titus. Among the most extreme acts of appropriation, however, is Gage's decision to include the refrain "A'n't I a woman" in Truth's most famous speech and to translate Truth's words into a stereotypical Southern slave dialect, while Robinson's contemporaneous account of the speech noted no such refrain or accent.[12] Indeed, if Truth had any accent at all, it would likely be Dutch.[13] Gage was herself influenced by Harriet Beecher Stowe's 1863 article about Truth, "The Libyan Sibyl," which was published in the *Atlantic Monthly*. As the title suggests, Stowe's article drew from a variety of racial stereotypes in depicting Truth, including, of course, a Southern slave dialect.[14]

Even Truth's physical appearance confounded easy categorization. At six feet tall, a powerful, dark-skinned woman dressed in modest attire, Truth simultaneously reflected masculinity and femininity. In one of the most infamous events recounted in her *Narrative*, when Truth was confronted at a meeting by proslavery hecklers who accused her of being a man, she exposed her breasts, explaining that she had nursed many white children while a slave but not her own. What initially seemed to be an act of submission was transformed into an act of defiance. Truth simultaneously shamed the white men who taunted her, mocked the hypocrisy of white women who prided themselves on their maternal roles while depriving black women of the same privilege, and reclaimed the right of motherhood for herself and other black women.[15] The incident illustrates the unique ground Truth occupied within the women's rights and abolitionist movements, "sometimes aligning herself with women against the sexism of men and sometimes aligning herself with blacks against the racism of whites."[16]

Frederick Douglass further adds to the complexity of Truth's identity. In his often-quoted description of Truth, Douglass writes:

I met here for the first time that strange compound of wit and wisdom, of wild enthusiasm and flint-like common sense, who seemed to feel it her duty to trip me up in my speeches and to ridicule my efforts to speak and act like a person of cultivation and refinement. I allude to Sojourner Truth. She was a genuine specimen of the uncultured negro. She cared very little for elegance of speech or refinement of manners. She seemed to please herself and others best when she put her ideas in the oddest forms. She was much respected at Florence, [Massachusetts,] for she was honest, industrious, and amiable. Her quaint speeches easily gave her an audience, and she was one of the most useful members of the Community in its day of small things.[17]

Assiduously cultivating an image of sophistication and erudition to align himself and gain credibility with his white audience, Douglass grudgingly admires Truth's ability to "ridicule my efforts to speak and act like a person of cultivation and refinement" in spite of the fact that she "cared very little for elegance of speech." And yet Douglass also disparages Truth as "a genuine specimen of the uncultured negro" who gives "quaint" speeches and cares only about "small things" pertaining to her community.[18] Douglass simultaneously elevates her status and reinforces the "pastoral" stereotype of the black woman, which was used to neutralize whatever destabilizing influence these women might have on white supremacy.[19]

Although Douglass, like many others, noted Truth's rapier wit and wry sense of humor, their power as critical tools could also be "undercut by the hegemonic norms of white femininity and masculinity" she sought to challenge, and her simple style could be "easily dismissed as quaint and comic."[20] Truth clearly provoked her white audience, but they could also "laugh at her antics without having to acknowledge her challenge to their dominance."[21] Truth clearly challenged Douglass as well, but his portrayal, much like that of his white audience, traps her among the intersectional forces of oppression because of her race, sex, and socioeconomic status.[22]

In describing Truth's speaking style as the "oddest" combination of "wit and wisdom" and of "wild enthusiasm and flint-like common sense," Douglass raises questions about Truth's intellect. Truth's reliance on simple speech and her "folksy" practical reasoning seem for Douglass to be signs of her intellectual inferiority. Yet they might instead be interpreted as rhetorical tools that allowed her to navigate a public realm dominated by cultivated speech and the written word. By offering up her own ideas in her own style, Truth could avoid being challenged by those seeking to corroborate her views through written sources. For example, her claim not to be familiar with the written Scriptures paradoxically gave Truth more latitude to interpret the Bible as she saw fit.[23]

Characterizing Truth's practical wisdom merely as a rhetorical device that was shaped in response to white hegemony, while entirely plausible, might also serve to undermine her power of individual agency. For there are indications that Truth chose to communicate her "truth" orally rather than in writing, not simply reactively or out of necessity, but deliberately. Like Adam Smith and many of the women's rights advocates I have discussed, Truth held a critical view of excessive intellectualism and favored practical reasoning with a moral purpose. Thus she ridiculed "'Greek-crammed' preachers who focused on the remote past instead of on the teeming present," and admonished college students for "writing down notes on what she said, advising them instead to take notes as she did in her head."[24] Truth could speak authentically and spontaneously because her ideas were not filtered through elite opinion, while still freely associating with those who could read and write and held views similar to her own. Perhaps, then, these elites did not silence Truth or appropriate her for their own purposes; perhaps instead the alliance Truth forged with her supporters was one of cooperation rather than exploitation.[25]

In the *Narrative*, Gilbert writes that when Truth was "examining the Scriptures, she wished to hear them without comment; but if she employed adult persons to read them to her . . . they invariably commenced to explain, by giving her their version of it; and in this way, they tried her feelings exceedingly."[26] Like Mott and the Grimkés, Truth profoundly distrusts elites who have sought to maintain their positions of power by imposing their scriptural interpretations on their unwitting audiences. Indeed, Truth takes on the clergy directly in her encounters with "Second Adventist" believers in Connecticut and New York. She observes that the preachers "appeared . . . to be doing their utmost to agitate and excite the people, who were already too much excited," by telling them that Jesus would immediately appear before them. Proclaiming their doctrine to be "absurd" because it contained so many contradictions, Truth held fast even when the preachers "commenced a discussion with her, by asking her questions, and quoting scripture to her."[27] Whereas Mott and the Grimkés urged their readers to return to the Bible itself and devise their own interpretations of the Scriptures, Truth could not do that because of her illiteracy. Instead, Truth asked children to read the Scriptures to her because "they could read distinctly . . . without comment." As a result, Truth "was enabled to see what her own mind could make out of the record, and that, she said was what she wanted, and not what others thought it to mean."[28]

Much like the inner light that provided the basis for the progressive Quaker worldview held by Mott and the Grimkés, Truth often referred to the voice of God that directed her thoughts and actions. Thus Truth "wished to compare the teachings of the Bible with the witness within her." Applying practical reasoning, Truth "came to the conclusion, that the spirit of truth spoke in those records, but that the recorders of those truths had intermingled with them ideas and suppositions of their own." Gilbert then interjects her own conclusion, claiming that "this is one among the many proofs of [Truth's] energy and independence of character."[29]

## Truth as a Woman in Speech and Deed

A comparison between Robinson's eyewitness account of Truth's speech in Akron and Gage's much later recollection in the *History of Woman Suffrage* reveals several consistencies that we can infer are what she actually said and did. These consistencies are important to examine carefully because they allow us to see Truth as more than simply a "vehicle" for Gage's agenda. It is likely that Gage used Truth to urge her own readers to link the issues of women's rights and abolitionism for "political expediency" and at the same time to "assuage white privilege" and mitigate potential conflict.[30] However, instead of robbing Truth of individual agency by denying the possibility that she ever overcame the appropriation of Gage and others, or diminishing the significance of her words by characterizing them simply as rhetorical devices that emerge under white supremacy, we should try to allow Truth to speak on her own behalf to the greatest extent possible. There is, of course, always the risk of (re)appropriating Truth for the purposes of this study. However, I think it is possible to fully acknowledge the impact of racism and sexism on Truth's life and work while allowing her original contributions to emerge.

It is evident in both accounts that Truth's physical presence and speaking voice left an indelible impression on her audience. By drawing parallels between her own physical strength and that of men, she suggests that there is no basis for unequal treatment of herself or other women like her. Truth's initial concession to male opponents, namely, that women have an intellectual capacity of a "pint" whereas men have a "quart," is qualified by her subsequent request that men allow women's "pints" to fill with knowledge in spite of their fear of the consequences. That men have likely neglected to fill their own "quart"-sized minds is implied, moreover, when Truth alludes to their "fear and confusion," in spite of their presumed superiority, at the prospect of women fulfilling their potential. Her turn in both accounts to the biblical story of Eve is reminiscent of earlier reinterpretations by women's rights advocates that question her responsibility for the Fall. Interestingly, although Gage is confounded by Truth's "pointed, witty, and solemn" revision, claiming that she "couldn't follow" Truth "through it all," Robinson's straightforward account of her remarks indicates no such confusion.[31] Both accounts then record Truth's emphasis on the prevalence of the female disciples of Christ—especially Mary, who bore the savior—as evidence against the notion that inequality between men and women is justified by biblical teachings.

There are, however, important differences between the two accounts. Gage's use of a stereotypical Southern slave dialect to portray Truth's words, along with her embellishment of the dramatic details surrounding the speech, clearly indicate Gage's desire to exaggerate her own position in the movement and to exercise her own authority over the narrative, thereby contributing to Truth's objectification. Yet Gage's editorializing can also be seen as an attempt, however misguided, to present an account reflecting the perspective of the audience. Thus, for example, although Robinson noted no hostility among the crowd, Gage heightens the tension between Truth and her audience, not just for her immediate purposes, but perhaps also to allude to the underlying racism and sexism within the movement itself and to highlight the importance of Truth's presence in exposing the hypocrisy of those who held bigoted views. Gage portrays Truth as waiting patiently for two days before speaking, listening to various religious leaders who opposed women's equality and presented arguments based on patriarchal biblical interpretations. Perhaps Gage wanted to establish Truth's credibility by showing that Truth knew and understood the positions she would proceed to attack. Even if Truth had spoken without any noticeable accent whatever, the bigots in the audience would likely only hear what they expected to hear, namely, the stereotypical voice of the uneducated slave.

Gage uses various rhetorical strategies to emphasize the power of Truth's presence and the impact of her message on the audience. By highlighting Truth's physicality, for instance, she lends physical, visual weight to her words. Gage's depiction of Truth directly confronting her audience perhaps reflects the conflict that lies beneath the surface of the movement. Even the refrain "Ain't I a woman" is a statement of the obvious point Truth is trying to make but that is merely implied in Robinson's account.

Returning to the elements that are consistent in both accounts, we see Truth's extended deployment of the rhetoric of ridicule I discussed in the previous chapter. Its probable aim was to shame her audience, encourage self-reflection, and open opportunities for change. In Robinson's account, Truth begins with a seemingly odd phrase, "I am a woman's rights." One possible explanation for the statement is that Truth's physical strength, courage, and self-confidence demonstrate that she quite literally "is" an exemplar of equality, a living embodiment of the ideals of the movement. By defining herself according to masculine standards, claiming that she has "as much muscle as any man, and can do as much work as any man," Truth mocks men who use physiological differences between men and women to justify their superiority and exposes their hypocrisy in refusing to extend the equality they enjoy to women like herself. As if to acknowledge that her physical justification for equality would not extend to the vast majority of her audience, composed of white women who never developed physical stamina and strength through manual labor, Truth turns to the intellectual justifications for male domination that are used more frequently against such women.[32]

In her irony-tinged comparison between women's "pint" capacity for knowledge and men's "quart" capacity, she belittles men who are "afraid" of allowing women to educate themselves. If men are correct in believing that women naturally possess less capacity for intelligence, she suggests, they have nothing to fear. The very men who pride themselves on having a "quart" capacity for wisdom are "all in confusion, and don't know what to do." Rather than acting like "children," men should allow women to fulfill their true potential so that the men may "feel better." As if comforting a male child reluctantly sharing a toy with a female playmate, Truth explains, "you will have your own rights, and [women] won't be so much trouble."[33]

In both accounts, Truth's references to the biblical justifications for women's oppression are similar to those made by other women's rights advocates, but she introduces several innovations, each employing ridicule to drive her argument home. Whereas Frances Wright and others defend Eve by pointing out Adam's own failures, Truth observes that, if Eve were sufficiently powerful to cause the downfall of mankind, men should "give her a chance to set it right side up again." She again mocks men for contradicting themselves, perhaps out of fear, by endowing Eve with the formidable power to thwart the future of humanity while at the same time using her as a justification to deny women the power to control their own lives. Like other women's rights advocates, Truth offers a list of the biblical women who never abandon their faith in Christ. But she goes further in undermining the commonly held notion that women's inherent sinfulness justifies their oppression by observing that Jesus "never spurned a woman from him" and by challenging religious men to follow his example. Truth adds another devastating point, namely, that God, along with a woman, brought Christ into the world, thereby elevating the status of women. By asking her male audience, "Man, where is your part?" Truth highlights woman's unique relationship to God while rhetorically belittling men.[34]

But after criticizing men for not demonstrating their faith as clearly as Mary and other female followers of Christ, Truth then qualifies her attack. Proclaiming that "the women are coming up" and demanding their rights, Truth acknowledges that "a few of the men are coming up with them" and supporting women's rights as well. And she concedes that "man is in a tight place," perched precariously among simultaneous demands for emancipation, suffrage, and equal rights. Truth concludes her speech with a vivid image of the besieged man: "The poor slave is on him, woman is coming on him, he is surely between a hawk and a buzzard." In the comparison between the slave and the woman, on the one hand, and a hawk and a buzzard, on the other, it is not clear who is the hawk and who is the buzzard. One thing, however, is clear: Men are the equivalent of the helpless carrion and, as such, are far more vulnerable than they realize.[35]

Truth echoes many of these sentiments in her 1867 speech to the first annual meeting of the American Equal Rights Association. She admonishes men for failing to advocate for women's rights. Again she points out that, despite being the equal of men in strength, stamina, and the capacity for strenuous labor, she is nevertheless treated unequally. This time aligning herself with "the German women," who also "work in the field and do as much work" as men "but do not get the pay," Truth explains that "what we want is a little money." Wryly pointing out that men would actually free themselves from women "when we get our rights" because "we shall not have to come to you for money," Truth turns the tables by adding that it "may be you [who] will ask us for money."[36]

In this later speech, however, Truth acknowledges the controversial nature of her efforts. "I am rejoiced that you are glad," she begins, "but I don't know how you will feel when I get through." Although slaves have been freed and will be enfranchised, the failure of black men to advocate for the enfranchisement of black women means that slavery has not been "root and branch destroyed." In a bold, even shocking demonstration of intersectionality, Truth compares black men to white slave owners. Without universal suffrage, she asserts, "colored men will be masters over the women, and it will be just as bad as it was before." Describing her activity with determination as "keeping the thing going while things are stirring" because "the ice is cracked," Truth reinforces her comparison between freed black men and white slave owners by conceding, "I know that it is hard for one who has held the reins for so long to give up" his position of dominance. Black men have been liberated, yet they remain oppressors, while black women have been freed, yet remain slaves. Although relinquishing power over women "cuts like a knife," Truth provides a measure of comfort to black men: "It will feel all the better when it closes up again."[37] Ironically, Truth here echoes

Stanton's much-criticized comments in "This Is the Negro's Hour" concerning the prospect of granting suffrage exclusively to freed black men who would then subjugate black women.[38] Here we see a vivid example of how Truth's unique embodiment of intersectionality frees her to address conflicts between race, gender, and class in ways that her white counterparts could not.

Truth again draws on the rhetorical trope by which she ridicules the idea of unequal intellect between men and women so as to discredit stereotypes and advocate for equality. She explains that "white women are a great deal smarter, and know more than colored women," who "do not know scarcely anything" except "washing, which is about as high as a colored woman gets." As these women toil, they are also exploited by black men who "go about idle, strutting up and down," and who "ask for their money and take it all, and then scold because there is no food." Truth mocks black men for their hypocrisy and stereotypical behavior, as they are freed from oppression only to oppress others of their own race. And in spite of their strength and capacity for hard work, black women allow themselves to be taken advantage of by men. Even if black women are deprived of equal opportunities for education, they can be made aware of their exploitation and reclaim their independence from men—as Truth's own example attests. As lingering educational and economic inequalities between black and white women persist, Truth declares that legal protections should be extended to all women, black and white, for "in the courts women have no right, no voice." She goes on to ridicule men who deny women legal standing on the grounds that the court "is not a fit place for women." Even though the court is corrupt, women should "have their voice there among the pettifoggers" as well. Truth archly alludes to the hypocrisy of men who covet access to legal protections and yet allow the integrity of the courts to be debased: "If it is not a fit place for women, it is unfit for men to be there" as well.[39]

## "A Strange Compound of Wit and Wisdom": Truth's Theoretical Contribution

In spite of the mixed messages he conveyed, Douglass aptly described the contradictions and complexities surrounding Truth's life and work. By combining "wit and wisdom" as well as "wild enthusiasm and flint-like common sense," Truth matched Douglass's authority and credibility with her own. Truth humbled Douglass, not by actively mocking or scorning him, but rather simply by being herself, speaking plainly and acting honestly. Truth's unique experience as a Northern slave defies the caricature created, however unwittingly, by Stowe and other abolitionists. By revealing a more multifaceted view of slavery, in which her relations with her owners were simultaneously adversarial and cooperative, Truth effectively humanizes slaves and owners alike, thereby providing opportunities for further exploration of the complexities of racism. Truth's physical appearance and mode of speech provide, to use Seyla Benhabib's terms, a "concrete" other that supplants the "generalized" other, namely, the stereotypical slave.[40] By dressing in white women's attire, Truth confounds her audience's expectations while forging an alliance with her white counterparts. And by emphasizing her physical strength, she aligns herself with black men in a common cause while also showing white women the kind of power they could possess, literally or figuratively. Confidently asserting her presence, Truth challenges preconceptions and assumptions simply by being herself. Finally, by systematically exposing the hypocrisy of those in power, whether white men, white women, or even black men, Truth encourages her audience to reconsider established norms and entertain the possibility of a more egalitarian America that includes universal enfranchisement, equal pay for equal work, and equal representation under the law. Given that reformers continue to argue for these basic rights even today, Truth's appreciation of their fundamental importance is indeed prescient.

# Conclusion

## *America's Founding Feminists*

In 1828, a brash young Scotswoman burst onto the American stage to offer one of the first critiques of American society exposing the systemic oppression of ordinary citizens at the hands of the ruling white male elite. As an alternative, she offered a model of inquiry that encouraged individuals to scrutinize the mechanisms of power in order to ensure the legitimacy of political authority as the authentic reflection of the popular will. Years before Karl Marx would publish the *Communist Manifesto*, Frances Wright traced the political, economic, and social corruption of commercial society. But whereas Marx saw no political solution to the problem of capitalism, Wright presented an early version of American socialism as the young republic contemplated the potential enfranchisement of marginalized peoples in the Jacksonian era. And well before Alexis de Tocqueville arrived in America, Wright would lay out the foundation for a comprehensive plan of reform that emphasized the importance of civil society and dealt directly with slavery and the oppression of women.

Soon after Wright's arrival, another female traveler, from England, argued forcefully and directly that the gravest ills of American society were slavery and the oppression of women. Refashioning Adam Smith's moral theory of sympathy, Harriet Martineau offered a cure for these ills that sought to reestablish sympathetic bonds between all people—black and white, male and female, rich and poor—while maintaining the integrity of each individual. By bridging the gap between people of different sexes, races, and socioeconomic status, her dialectical understanding of sympathy provided a pathway to abolishing slavery and ending the oppression of women.

Three progressive Quaker women were often dismissed as "no-government" Garrisonians or labeled "quietists" or "withdrawers." Yet

Angelina Grimké, Sarah Grimké, and Lucretia Mott actually provided the foundations for a Quaker political theory that offered a third way between the constitutional doctrines of secular Whiggism and secularized Puritanism that predominated in Jacksonian America. Contained within their religious worldview is a set of ideas that form a comprehensive and coherent political theory on issues of equality, freedom, citizenship, representation, deliberation, and constitutional reform. Although their faith in God is unwavering, for these women the application of human reason in discerning his will is equally crucial. Human beings therefore have the moral and spiritual imperative not to rest easy in their faith or defer to elite interpreters of Scripture. Rather, they must develop their powers of reason to the best of their ability and apply those powers to building "a more perfect union," one that is more equal, free, and just.

Balancing reason and emotion, Angelina Grimké's theory of sympathy and its role in rhetoric conveys a moral and political teaching that lays the foundation for meaningful political change by allowing closer connections between the enfranchised and the marginalized. Specifically, Grimké redefines human rights in an inclusive way that applies to free and enslaved peoples, male and female alike, thereby advancing the twin goals of abolitionism and women's rights. Sarah Grimké shows the political implications of this progressive strand of Quakerism. The word of God, as ascertained by each individual through synteresis, or the inner voice, and interpreted through reason, provides the basis for an eternal "fundamental constitution," the first principles of which inform our understanding of the American Constitution and the political institutions derived from it, and can be used to shape and reshape American political, cultural, and social practices. Quaker deliberation, a mode of collective discernment that aims at consensus while allowing for individual dissent in a respectful, mutually supportive environment, offers a unique approach to political decision making, representation, and reform. Lucretia Mott provides a model of democratic citizenship based on this interplay of independent thinking and collective deliberation. By exposing the hidden sources of inequality, oppression, and injustice, Mott's antidogmatic approach empowers human beings to shape an egalitarian, voluntarist political system that is based on authentic consent born of philosophic reflection. As embodied in the thought of the Grimkés and Mott, "Quaker constitutionalism" thus provides a model for peaceful reform and political change.

Two other women who seem to have little in common—one wealthy, highly educated, and white, the other poor, illiterate, and black—were united not only by their commitment to women's rights but also by the rhetorical strategies they used to argue for change. By deploying a rhetoric of ridicule, Elizabeth Cady Stanton exposed the hypocrisy that lay at the root of women's oppression and began a process of moral instruction that relied on its own versions of sympathy, the impartial spectator, and other aspects of Adam Smith's moral theory. Sojourner Truth emerges as a master of the art of ridicule as she criticizes men and women of all races and provokes them into reexamining their double standards and hypocrisies. Using her unique status as a free black woman of modest means to destabilize stereotypes and biases through her speech and actions, Truth continually provoked her audience to consider reform in ways that her more privileged white counterparts could not. By inducing shame among their audiences and exposing the systemic nature of oppression, both Stanton and Truth encouraged the self-reflection that is a prerequisite for social change.

Although Kimberlé Crenshaw notes that intersectionality, a term she coined in the 1980s, is not a recent discovery in feminist theory, it is often treated as such.[1] Yet, as my study shows, each of these women called attention to the importance of intersectionality from the start of the women's rights movement and struggled continuously with its crosscurrents. Wright, for example, characterized the ills of American society in terms of intersectional forces. She understood that racial identities are social constructions, not fixed biological categories; revealed the complex dynamics of power by which elites, through race, gender, and class privilege, strive to maintain their influence; and was keenly aware of the dangers of backlash and the importance of co-opting elites to enact reform. As slave owners turned abolitionists who regularly associated with freedmen and women, the Grimkés' personal experience of intersectionality shaped their respective worldviews. Even Stanton, though criticized for her employment of racist language, characterized the oppression of women in terms of gender, race, and economic inequality. And, of course, Truth personified and projected her own unique experience of intersectionality and sought throughout her life to address the problems that arose from its inner tensions. Indeed, Wright, Martineau, the Grimkés, Mott, Stanton, and Truth all understood how racism and sexism were created and perpetuated in the political and legal fabric of America by elites who sought to maintain their power and privilege, how ordinary Americans were unwittingly corrupted by slavery and the oppression of women, and how the American project itself was diminished by racial, gender, and economic inequality.

To be sure, these early women's rights and abolitionist advocates worked within the confines of the social, political, and cultural norms in which they lived, and yet they also tried to expand and reform those same norms to accommodate a changing society. In this regard, their contributions represented "constituent moments," "historical accidents," and "countercurrents" where "difference emerges."[2] By "disrupting" the canon, these women created new opportunities for alternative political theories and modes of theorizing. They also served as "civic founders" who expanded the fundamental principles of the American project to address the needs of the disenfranchised, thereby laying the groundwork not simply for women's suffrage but also for the broader expansion of civil, political, and human rights that would characterize much of the twentieth century and continues to unfold today.[3]

The fiery speeches of Wright, the deceptively quaint travel narrative of Martineau, the passionate rhetoric of Angelina Grimké, the astutely provocative public writings of Sarah Grimké and Stanton, the antidogmatic inquiries of Mott, and the "flint-like common sense" of Truth: These diverse examples of public discourse have long been excluded from the canon of "legitimate" political theory, too often dismissed as mere advocacy or activism. It is my hope that this study has helped make clear that American political thought in fact emerges in unexpected places and is heard in many different voices. If we are to keep American political theory relevant in an increasingly diverse world, now more than ever we must remain open to new voices and to methodologies that enable us to hear them.

# NOTES

## INTRODUCTION

1 Obama, "Inaugural Address."

2 Ibid. On June 24, 2016, Obama designated the Stonewall National Monument at the historic site of the Stonewall Uprising in New York City. And on April 12, 2016, the Sewall-Belmont House in Washington, DC, headquarters of the National Woman's Party led by the suffragist Alice Paul, was designated by Obama as the Belmont-Paul Women's Equality National Monument.

3 Ibid.

4 In the same speech Obama forges the following connections as well: American immigrants with "Holocaust survivors, Soviet defectors, the Lost Boys of Sudan," and "strivers who cross the Rio Grande" from Mexico to the United States; "slaves who built the White House and the economy of the South" with "countless laborers who laid rail, and raised skyscrapers"; and "fresh-faced GIs who fought to liberate a continent" in World War II with "the Tuskegee Airmen, . . . Navajo code-talkers, and the Japanese Americans who fought for this country even as their own liberty had been denied." See Obama, "Remarks Commemorating the 50th Anniversary."

5 Ibid.

6 Ibid.

7 Although Obama's presidency only recently ended, there have been examinations of his political philosophy. Kloppenberg, *Reading Obama*, traces the influence of American pragmatism and major thinkers such as John Rawls and Reinhold Niebuhr on Obama's worldview. Leeman, *Teleological Discourse*, examines the teleological elements in Obama's speeches and writings. Schultz, "Obama's Political Philosophy," reviews the influence of the "Chicago School" on Obama's ideas. Frank and McFail, "Barack Obama's Address," analyze the advantages and disadvantages of Obama's "rhetoric of consilience" that unites disparate strands of American history. Although Edmund Fong praises Obama because he has "tried to pluralize and widen the terms by which we might memorialize the American exceptionalist canon" by "injecting hints of dissonance" through the juxtaposition of "unconventional" Americans in his speeches, he has nevertheless fostered "a sense of resignation and an uncritical embrace of exceptionalism." See Fong, *American Exceptionalism*, 173–174.

8 I do not by any means claim that the early women's rights movement and abolitionism were essentially the same phenomenon, and I do not wish to conflate

them. Many advocates for women's rights were not abolitionists, and many abolitionists did not support the enfranchisement of women. However, the women examined here did participate in both movements in various ways.

9 Buccola, *Political Thought of Frederick Douglass*; Steven Smith et al., *Writings of Abraham Lincoln*; Kateb, *Lincoln's Political Thought*; and Morel, *Lincoln's Sacred Effort*.

10 Whereas I agree with commentators who ultimately see ambivalence in Tocqueville's reflections on slavery, others are more critical of his views. See Rogers Smith, "Beyond Tocqueville, Myrdal, and Hartz"; and Janara, *Democracy Growing Up*.

11 Beaumont, *Civic Constitution*, 165.

12 Ibid., 186–194.

13 Ibid., 197.

14 Ibid., 165.

15 Jason Frank, *Constituent Moments*, 8.

16 Jason Frank, "Besides Our Selves," 390.

17 Not only did Tocqueville compose several extended theoretical works, but he actively engaged in political life as well. Recent efforts situate Tocqueville's contributions within a larger context of visitors and critics to America from Britain and France, including Frances Trollope, many of whom were abolitionists and supporters of women's rights. See Craiutu and Isaac, *America through European Eyes*. However, intense preoccupation with the Frenchman's theories continues, extending his reach to such improbable places as Asia and even the Middle East. See Boyd and Atanassow, *Tocqueville and the Frontiers of Democracy*.

18 For example, see Sheldon, *Political Philosophy of Thomas Jefferson*; Fruchtman, *Political Philosophy of Thomas Paine*; Sheldon, *Political Philosophy of James Madison*; Pangle, *Political Philosophy of Benjamin Franklin*; Murphy, "Limits and Promise" and "Trial Transcript"; Steven Smith et al., *Writings of Abraham Lincoln*; Fornieri, *Abraham Lincoln's Political Faith* and *Abraham Lincoln: Philosopher Statesman*; and Kateb, *Lincoln's Political Thought*.

19 Examples include Deneen and Romance, *Democracy's Literature*; Zuckert, *Natural Right*; Seery, *Political Companion to Walt Whitman*; Turner, *Political Companion to Henry David Thoreau*; Jason Frank, *Political Companion to Herman Melville*; and Henderson, *Seers and Judges*.

20 Murphy, *Conscience and Community* and "Limits and Promise"; and Hall, "Beyond Self-Interest."

21 Davis, *Political Thought of Elizabeth Cady Stanton*; and Buccola, *Political Thought of Frederick Douglass*.

22 Bartlett, *Liberty, Equality, Sorority*.

23 Sapiro, *Vindication of Political Virtue*; Gunther-Canada, *Rebel Writer*; Taylor, *Rights of Woman as Chimera*; and Botting, *Family Feuds*.

24 Botting, "Wollstonecraft in Europe"; and Botting and Matthews, "Overthrowing the Floresta-Wollstonecraft Myth."

25  Flexner and Fitzpatrick, *Century of Struggle*; Melder, *Beginnings of Sisterhood*; DuBois, *Feminism and Suffrage*; and Wellman, *Road to Seneca Falls*.

26  Hewitt, "From Seneca Falls to Suffrage?"; Faulkner, *Lucretia Mott's Heresy*; Isenberg, *Sex and Citizenship*; and Ginzberg, *Untidy Origins*.

27  Lerner, *Grimké Sisters from South Carolina*, 2004 ed.; Faulkner, *Lucretia Mott's Heresy*; and Ginzberg, *Elizabeth Cady Stanton*.

28  Anderson, *Joyous Greetings*; Sklar and Stewart, *Women's Rights and Transatlantic Antislavery*; and Sklar, Schüler, and Strasser, *Social Justice Feminists*.

29  Hewitt, "Seeking a Larger Liberty"; and Parker, *Articulating Rights*.

30  Cima, *Performing Anti-slavery*.

31  Hersh, *Slavery of Sex*.

32  The cause of the schism is still debated. Other possibilities include tension between supporters of moral suasion and political action and the rejection of Garrisonian "no-government" or anarchic sentiments. See Ginzberg, *Women and the Work of Benevolence*; and Laurie, "Putting Politics Back In."

33  Matthews, "Race, Sex"; Bennett, *Democratic Discourses*; and Quanquin, "There Are Two Great Oceans." Examinations of localized movements reveal that a number of female antislavery activists did not consistently support women's rights and pursued a variety of goals. See Hewitt, *Women's Activism*; and Ginzberg, *Women and the Work of Benevolence*. By contrast, studies that focus on Stanton and the movement in the mid- and late nineteenth century tend to emphasize the racial antagonisms between the groups. See Newman, *White Women's Rights*; and Caraway, *Segregated Sisterhood*.

34  Isenberg, *Sex and Citizenship*.

35  Zaeske, *Signatures of Citizenship*; and Ginzberg, *Untidy Origins*.

36  Marilley, *Woman Suffrage*.

37  Hewitt, *Women's Activism*; Judith Wellman, "The Seneca Falls Women's Rights Convention"; and Isenberg, *Sex and Citizenship*.

38  Bartlett, *Liberty, Equality, Sorority*; and Hoffert, *When Hens Crow*, 1995 ed.

39  Strong, *Perfectionist Politics*, 40–41.

40  Lerner, *Feminist Thought of Sarah Grimké*; Hersh, *Slavery of Sex*; and DuBois, *Feminism and Suffrage*. Although Sklar initially includes Sarah Grimké's earlier work as among those that contributed to the secularism of the movement, in a later essay she acknowledges the importance of religion in her thought. See Sklar, "Women as Good Citizens."

41  Hardesty, *Women Called to Witness*.

42  Pagliaro, "Uncommon Education of Lucretia Mott"; Michaelson, *Speaking Volumes*; and Zink-Sawyer, "From Preachers to Suffragists."

43  Speicher, *Religious World of Antislavery Women*.

44  Isenberg, *Sex and Citizenship*, xvii.

45  Calvert, "Quaker Theory."

46  Katherine Henry, *Liberalism and the Culture of Security*.

47  Tompkins, *Sensational Designs*.

48 Howard, "What Is Sentimentality?," 63–64.

49 Abruzzo, *Polemical Pain*; Bennett, *Democratic Discourses*; Berlant, *Queen of America*; Douglas, *Feminization of American Culture*; and Bacon, *The Humblest May Stand Forth*, 120–140.

50 Bacon, *The Humblest May Stand Forth*, 121.

51 Ibid., 126.

52 Ibid., 137.

53 Howard, "What Is Sentimentality?," 64.

54 Kimberly Smith, *Dominion of Voice*, 201–202.

55 Ibid., 203.

56 Howard, "What Is Sentimentality?," 70.

57 Branson, "James Madison and the Scottish Enlightenment"; Kloppenberg, "Virtues of Liberalism"; Corrigan, "Habits from the Heart"; Fleischacker, "Adam Smith's Reception"; O'Neill, "John Adams versus Mary Wollstonecraft"; and Segrest, *America and the Political Philosophy of Common Sense*.

58 Johnson, *Nineteenth-Century Rhetoric*, 14.

59 Zagarri, "Morals, Manners."

60 Bartlett, *Liberty, Equality, Sorority*; Hoffert, *When Hens Crow*, 1995 ed.; and Abruzzo, *Polemical Pain*.

61 Bacon and McClish, "Reinventing the Master's Tools," 41n12. The manuscript that has since been published as *Lectures on Rhetoric and Belles Lettres* is a two-volume collection of notes written by one of Smith's students that was discovered in 1958. The original lectures, along with Smith's personal notes, no longer exist. The credibility of the manuscript has been demonstrated in a number of ways, including historical accounts of the lectures, the recurrence of ideas and concepts in Smith's other works, the accounts of John Millar, one of Smith's students, and the testimonial of Hugh Blair, who attended the original lectures. See Bevilacqua, "Adam Smith and Some Philosophical Origins."

62 Camfield, "Moral Aesthetics of Sentimentality."

63 Greiner, *Sympathetic Realism*.

64 Abruzzo, *Polemical Pain*.

65 Kelly, *Propriety of Liberty*, chap. 3; and Abruzzo, *Polemical Pain*.

66 Kerber, "Separate Spheres"; Welter, "Cult of True Womanhood"; and Campbell, "Femininity and Feminism." In the second edition of her book, Nancy Cott refines her "universalizing," or homogenizing, understanding of the discourse of domesticity to better accommodate the diversity of experiences of early American women. See Cott, *Bonds of Womanhood*.

67 Isenberg, *Sex and Citizenship*; and Sutton, *House of My Sojourn*.

68 Howard, "What Is Sentimentality?," 73.

69 Ryan, *Women in Public*.

70 Campbell, "Femininity and Feminism"; and Browne, "Encountering Angelina Grimke" and *Angelina Grimké*.

71 Habermas, Lennox, and Lennox, "Public Sphere," 49.

72  Fanuzzi, *Abolition's Public Sphere*, xiii; Hendler, *Public Sentiments*, 214; and Elbert, *Separate Spheres No More*, 3.

73  Isenberg, *Sex and Citizenship*, 43.

74  Bacon, *The Humblest May Stand Forth*. Habermas is not the only theorist who has been used as a frame of reference for examinations of early women's rights, abolitionism, and the public realm. Others include Hannah Arendt and Jacques Ranciere. See Isenberg, *Sex and Citizenship*; and Jason Frank, *Constituent Moments*.

75  Jason Frank, "Besides Our Selves," 390.

76  Jason Frank, "Publius and Political Imagination," 91. Cooke, *The Federalist*, 594, cited in ibid.

77  Fraser, "Rethinking the Public Sphere," 123.

78  Fanuzzi, *Abolition's Public Sphere*; Tyler, *Freedom's Ferment*; and Bennett, *Democratic Discourses*.

79  Jason Frank, *Constituent Moments*.

80  Beaumont, *Civic Constitution*.

81  Jason Frank, *Constituent Moments*, 8.

82  Beaumont, *Civic Constitution*, 2; emphasis in original.

83  Bartlett, *Liberty, Equality, Sorority*; and Gardner, *Empowerment and Interconnectivity*.

84  Davis, *Political Thought of Elizabeth Cady Stanton*.

85  The emergence of civic republicanism and liberalism as categories of analysis can be traced primarily to the works of J. G. A. Pocock and various communitarian political theorists. For an extensive critique of the portrayal of liberal and republican ideals as mutually exclusive, see Isaac, "Republicanism v. Liberalism?" For a critique of Rogers Smith's multiple traditions theory, which also relies on broad categories, see Stevens, "Beyond Tocqueville, Please!"

86  Jim Jose, "No More like Pallas Athena," 2.

87  Ibid., 4.

88  Jason Frank, *Constituent Moments*, 212–213.

89  Zerilli, "Feminist Theory," 107, 110.

90  Based on this argument, early women's rights advocate Frances Wright and other female thinkers can be situated within the larger context of utilitarianism, a school of thought that has been defined primarily by the contributions of male writers such as Jeremy Bentham. See Gardner, *Empowerment and Interconnectivity*.

91  Penny Weiss further emphasizes that "the men are not the standards here—positive or negative—by which to measure the women, but ways to make the latter visible and comprehensible in their similarities and differences." See Weiss, *Canon Fodder*, xxiii–xxiv.

92  There is, of course, a measure of hypocrisy in the characterization of the intellectual inheritances of women thinkers as derivative, whereas the interchange of ideas among professional male philosophers is considered a perfectly legitimate

"set of battles over timeless positions." Not only is philosophy seen as "the tracing of a male line (patrilineal), the notion of patrimony is also one of male inheritance, legacy, and heritage. . . . Notions of entitlement and dominance . . . are passed down from philosophical 'fathers.' . . . Their right to philosophy itself and their right to be called philosophers is not questioned. . . . Historical feminist philosophers, on the other hand, have had to justify their position as philosophers, the legitimacy of their subject matter, and even the legitimacy of their audience if their target audience is women." See Gardner, *Empowerment and Interconnectivity*, 13–14.

93 Zerilli, "Machiavelli's Sisters," 252.

94 A comprehensive list of examples would be vast. However, notable studies include an examination of Wollstonecraft from the perspective of Aristotle's political theory on the basis of an "affinity" between their ideas, in spite of the fact that Wollstonecraft does not engage Aristotle's theories directly; nor does she "explicitly adopt elements" of his philosophy. See Taylor, *Rights of Woman as Chimera*, 139. In order "to present and assess [Walt] Whitman as a political thinker," his work is compared "with what Alexis de Tocqueville says in his great *Democracy in America* . . . mainly in search for points of agreement" that demonstrate that "Whitman shared the concerns of the best of the political thinkers." See Lawler, "Walt Whitman as Political Thinker," 245. Plato and Aristotle have been used to elucidate aspects of Abraham Lincoln's political thought. See Jaffa, *Crisis of the House Divided*. Saint Thomas Aquinas and Aristotle frame other examinations of Lincoln's contributions. See Fornieri, *Abraham Lincoln: Philosopher Statesman*. And, of course, scholars have long traced the influence of theorists such as John Locke, Montesquieu, David Hume, and Adam Smith on the Founders.

95 Branson, "James Madison and the Scottish Enlightenment"; Kloppenberg, "Virtues of Liberalism; Corrigan, "Habits from the Heart"; Fleischacker, "Adam Smith's Reception"; O'Neill, "John Adams versus Mary Wollstonecraft"; and Segrest, *America and the Political Philosophy of Common Sense*.

96 For example, "Although Stanton most certainly did not draw directly from Smith," a study notes, "given that during her lifetime his lectures on rhetoric were thought to have been destroyed, the relationship between rhetoric and sympathy that we can see in Smith helps in discerning a relationship between the two in Stanton's work as well and in appreciating the extent to which this 'masterful logician' used sophisticated emotional appeals as well." See Engbers, "With Great Sympathy," 318. A number of additional studies of nineteenth-century rhetoric refer to Smith's theories in particular. See Howard, "What Is Sentimentality?"; Johnson, *Nineteenth-Century Rhetoric*; Zagarri, "Morals, Manners"; Bartlett, *Liberty, Equality, Sorority*; Hoffert, *When Hens Crow*, 1995 ed.; Abruzzo, *Polemical Pain*; Greiner, *Sympathetic Realism*; Kelly, *Propriety of Liberty*; Kimberly Smith, "Storytelling, Sympathy"; Camfield, "Moral Aesthetics of Sentimentality"; and Cima, *Performing Anti-slavery*.

97 There are a few exceptions. See Hanley, *Adam Smith*; McKenna, *Adam Smith*; Hanley, "Style and Sentiment"; and Kapust and Schwarze, "Rhetoric of Sincerity."

98  I discuss Tocqueville's apparent refusal to acknowledge other narratives on American women and slavery in my analysis of Frances Wright and Harriet Martineau.

99  Recent efforts have devised a methodology with which to establish a causal relationship between early women's rights advocates by analyzing "philosophical/textual evidence (direct references" between writings "or striking parallels in philosophical terms and arguments between the two thinkers)," combined with "autobiographical evidence . . . biographical evidence . . . and contextual evidence." See Botting and Carey, "Wollstonecraft's Philosophical Impact," 709–710. However, as I argue in chapter 5, this methodology also runs the risk of oversimplifying or mischaracterizing the intellectual heritage of these advocates. A particular example of the difficulty in forging causal connections between the advocates is reflected by Sarah and Angelina Grimké who, "had they read the writings of Frances Wright or heard her speeches, might have been spared many years of agonized intellectual struggle, for the ideas the young Englishwoman projected so boldly and prematurely were those they themselves would later advocate to a similar chorus of defamation. But as yet their religion kept them from the very possibility of free intellectual inquiry." See Lerner, *Grimké Sisters from South Carolina*, 1967 ed., 95.

100  Kimberly Smith, *Dominion of Voice*, 5.

101  Zerilli, "Feminist Theory," 110–113.

102  Berlant, *Female Complaint*, 35.

103  Ibid., 6.

104  Zerilli, "Feminist Theory," 117.

105  Ibid., 112, 120.

106  Beaumont, *Civic Constitution*, 2.

107  Holland, "After Antigone," 1129.

108  Zerilli, "Feminist Theory," 107.

109  Kimberly Smith, *Dominion of Voice*, 203–204.

110  Lerner, *Feminist Thought of Sarah Grimké*, 5.

111  Durso, *Power of Woman*; and Hall, "Beyond Self-Interest."

112  Davis, *Political Thought of Elizabeth Cady Stanton*.

113  Caraway, *Segregated Sisterhood*; Newman, *White Women's Rights*; Stansell, "Missed Connections"; and Mitchell, "Lower Orders."

114  Faye Dudden's in-depth examination of the contentious post–Civil War debates over the extension of suffrage to women as well as to African American men sheds important light on the complexity of Stanton and Anthony's activities and motivations. For Dudden, it was not simply racism that motivated Stanton and Anthony to challenge those who wished to secure suffrage first for freed black men and later for women, nor was it the inherently radical nature of their goals that led to their defeat. Rather, it was their absolute conviction that women's suffrage had a "fighting chance" at a crucial moment in history that drove these reformers to use whatever means necessary for success. See Dudden, *Fighting Chance*. For Lisa Tetrault, an essential component of Stanton and Anthony's

activism at this time was the deliberate fashioning of what would become known as the conventional narrative of the early women's rights movement, the *History of Woman Suffrage*. Stanton and Anthony provided an "alternative [suffragist] memory of the Civil War" in which women's rights was among the fundamental causes over which the battle was fought and, as such, had to be seen as a unified effort toward an inevitable goal. See Tetrault, *Myth of Seneca Falls*, 17.

## CHAPTER 1. LIFTING THE "CLAUD-LORRAINE TINT" OVER THE REPUBLIC

1 Bentham, *Works of Jeremy Bentham*, 551.

2 Quoted in Morris, *Fanny Wright*, 1.

3 Quoted in ibid., 66.

4 Ibid., 88–89.

5 Kissel, *In Common Cause*.

6 Whitman traveled freely among some of the most influential early women's rights activists of the nineteenth century. He was close friends with Abby Hills Price and became acquainted with her reformist colleagues Paulina Wright Davis and Ernestine Rose as well. Among many things, Rose and Whitman shared a mutual interest in keeping the memory of Wright alive and seeking to rehabilitate her reputation as one of the earliest women's rights reformers. The composition of Whitman's *Leaves of Grass* coincides with one of the most active periods in the early women's rights movement, the 1850s, in which annual national conventions and numerous local meetings were regularly held before they were sidelined by the Civil War. Many of Whitman's works bear the stamp of the writings and speeches given by these women, with whom he regularly corresponded and visited. See Ceniza, *Walt Whitman and 19th-Century Women Reformers*.

7 The historian Ellen Carol DuBois credits Wright with being "the first public figure in United States history to advocate women's rights" and to promote a radical republicanism that, "with its hostility to the family and its emphasis on women's economic independence, provided an alternative to the ideology of separate spheres that dominated thinking about women's place by 1830." See DuBois, "Outgrowing the Compact," 837–838. Wright's unconventional approach to women's rights, which rejected the "cult of domesticity" and the notion of natural differences between the sexes, has been noted by other commentators as well. See Travis, "Frances Wright."

8 Morris, *Fanny Wright*, 216–217.

9 Wright's difficulties have been characterized not merely in terms of challenging gender norms but in upending rhetorical traditions as well. As a practitioner of neoclassical rhetoric, whose origins can be traced back to the Scottish Enlightenment, Wright fell victim to the "tension between the concept of public speech as a tool of influence to motivate political action and the ideals of political rationality, equality, and order that a politics of public debate was supposed to realize." See

Kimberly Smith, *Dominion of Voice*. For an account of the mixed reception of Wright's speeches, see Eastman, *A Nation of Speechifiers*.

10  There is no evidence that Tocqueville read Wright's work as he prepared his own observations on America. Wright would send copies of her 1848 historical treatise *England the Civilizer* to Richard Rush, the American ambassador to France, and asked him to provide one to Tocqueville, but there is no evidence that Tocqueville received a copy or read it. See Morris, *Fanny Wright*, 278.

11  Fortunately, recent scholarship has broadened the scope of nineteenth-century American political thought beyond Tocqueville to include additional thinkers whose contributions have been hitherto neglected. See Craiutu and Isaac, *America through European Eyes*; and Vetter, "Sympathy, Equality."

12  Although Wright also required a return on her initial investment, she did not personally profit from the exchange. Instead, she insisted that the funds would be applied to purchasing additional slaves and covering various expenses for emancipation and colonization.

13  Wright, *Reason, Religion*, 30. Named after the seventeenth-century French painter Claude Lorrain, a Claude glass was a mirror or lens used primarily by landscape painters to blur details and soften colors, thereby helping artists achieve a more "painterly" or aesthetically pleasing work.

14  Quoted in Morris, *Fanny Wright*, 290.

15  Gardner, *Empowerment and Interconnectivity*, 118. I am adding Owen to Gardner's list of influences on Wright's philosophy.

16  Tillery, "Tocqueville as Critical Race Theorist," 640, 648.

17  Wright should also be counted as a contributor of "intersectionality's intellectual roots" along with Maria Stewart, a freed slave and the first black woman to speak in public. Wright explores the interrelation between race and gender as socially constructed categories that are often masked by a "neutral legal system," which creates and reinforces racial and gender inequalities as it simultaneously avoids explicit racism and sexism. See Faulkner and Parker, *Interconnections*, 2–3.

18  Wright began to deliver her first lectures in 1828 and published them in a collected volume, *Course of Popular Lectures*, in 1829. In 1831, she added a *Supplement* that included the final four lectures she delivered in America before leaving in 1830. In 1836, Wright returned to America and began another lecture tour. Three of these lectures were printed in volume 2 of *Course of Popular Lectures*, which she self-published in Philadelphia in 1836. The speeches focused more narrowly on political controversies of the time, such as the creation of the Second Bank of the United States. Of the final lectures Wright delivered in 1838, only one was prepared for publication. See Morris, *Fanny Wright*, 325n59; and Wright, *Reason, Religion*. By then, Wright found herself largely alienated, discredited, and mired in domestic disputes. My analysis is based largely on the first lecture tour because her speeches were more widely available and thus more likely to influence contemporaries such as Tocqueville.

19 Gardner helpfully situates Wright's work within a larger examination of the development of a feminist utilitarian philosophy in which knowledge is pursued not just for its own sake but, rather, for the sake of empowering those who are marginalized and oppressed and bringing about social and political reform. Other feminist utilitarians include Anna Doyle Wheeler, William Thompson, Catherine Beecher, and John Stuart Mill. My study differs from Gardner's in several ways. First, I emphasize the political implications for Wright's theorizing specifically in terms of citizenship. Second, I analyze in more detail the similarities and differences between Wright's theorizing and Bentham's to highlight the originality of her thought. Third, I characterize Wright as a precursor to American pragmatism, not just utilitarianism.

20 Gardner, *Empowerment and Interconnectivity*, 151.

21 Morris, *Fanny Wright*, 14.

22 From Robina Millar "Wright also imbibed an anachronistic, 1790s version of Anglo-American republicanism . . . [that] reinforced the idealistic literary depictions of the US that Wright devoured in the Glasgow University Library," which were written by Botta and others. "Combined, they confirmed Wright's belief that the US was a progressive republican utopia." See Bederman, "Revisiting Nashoba," 440.

23 Claeys, "Utopianism, Property," cited in Rendall, "Prospects of the American Republic," 145–146.

24 Rendall, "Prospects of the American Republic," 146–147.

25 Ibid., 156.

26 Owen, *Observations on the Effect*, 10. Along similar lines, although Millar approved of the progress that accompanied commerce and manufacture, he was also critical of the harmful effects of economic specialization and the division of labor on the individual, writing that "the pursuit of riches becomes a scramble in which the hand of every man is against every other." Quoted in Morris, *Fanny Wright*, 14.

27 Wright, *Reason, Religion*, 30.

28 Ibid., 211.

29 Claeys, *Citizens and Saints*, 10.

30 Ibid., 14.

31 Ibid., 14–15.

32 Wright, *Reason, Religion*, 254–255.

33 Ibid., 219.

34 Claeys, *Citizens and Saints*, 12.

35 Indeed, years before Karl Marx and Friedrich Engels would offer a dialectical account of human history that for many critics did not sufficiently address the concerns of women, Wright was hard at work on a history of civilization, *England the Civilizer*, which observed a tension between corrupt "male" imperialism and virtuous "female" humanism. For Wright, this tension must be resolved not by violent revolution but, rather, by focusing on "self-sufficient communities" that

would provide "unity without restraint and independence with security." See Morris, *Fanny Wright*, 279–280.

36  Claeys, *Citizens and Saints*, 13. Critics have characterized Wright essentially as a retrograde republican who "rejected the role of the central government in making change and hoped that government as an oppressive entity would somehow be abolished or disappear." Because "Wright believed that through moral suasion and personal action she, as an individual, could profoundly shape the direction and the character of the nation," she "represents an earlier era of reformers' suspicion toward the federal government and reliance on moral suasion that was gradually replaced" by more progressive activists such as Sarah and Angelina Grimké, who "accepted a role for the federal government in enacting legislation and passing constitutional amendments that could promote the changes they sought." See Parker, *Articulating Rights*, 61, 65. My alternative understanding of Wright as a politically oriented socialist challenges the idea that Wright's failure to articulate an anachronistically expansive view of the federal government indicates that she did not adequately understand the nature of progressive political reform. Although Wright supported many aspects of Jacksonian politics, it was not because she was critical of the federal government as an institution but rather because she saw Jackson's democratic populism as a means—however flawed—to address the systemic inequalities of American society. See Morris, *Fanny Wright*, 246. To use an anachronistic understanding of "big government" to criticize Wright and to praise others such as the Grimkés risks mischaracterizing the rich contributions they make to our understanding of political power and influence.

37  Crook, "The United States in Bentham's Thought," 283–284.

38  Wright, *Reason, Religion*, 246; emphasis in original.

39  Ibid.; emphasis in original.

40  Ibid., 49.

41  Ibid., 227–228.

42  Ibid., 233; emphasis in original.

43  Ibid., 233.

44  Ibid., 250; emphasis in original.

45  Ibid., 201; emphasis in original.

46  Owen, *Observations on the Effect*. The historian David Ramsay, author of *History of the American Revolution* (1789), also describes American slavery in conditional terms and avoids moral condemnation of Southern slave owners. Wright admits having read Ramsay as a young women before deciding to embark to America. See Kornfeld, "From Republicanism to Liberalism."

47  Although Owen's influence has been emphasized by commentators, Bederman claims that the first version of Nashoba is actually more indebted to George Rapp, who had established a number of thriving religious communities throughout America. "Wright proposed to open a pilot project—a large model farm populated by at least 100 slaves who would work the fields according to George Rapp's superproductive 'united labor' system. Within five years, Wright calculated,

the average slave working under this system would produce enough . . . to pay his owner a fair price for his purchase, to cover the project's overhead, and to transport him and his family, with all necessary farming implements, to a foreign colony such as Liberia or Haiti." The "superproductive labor system would allow each slave to earn enough to pay for the purchase of an additional slave to replace him" as well. See Bederman, "Revisiting Nashoba," 447–448. Subsequent manifestations of Nashoba would more closely resemble Owen's community.

48  Fleischacker, "Adam Smith and Cultural Relativism," 28.

49  Tillery, "Tocqueville as Critical Race Theorist," 640.

50  Ibid., 641.

51  Wright, *Views of Society*, 39.

52  Ibid., 38.

53  Tocqueville, *Democracy in America*, 352–353.

54  According to one of her harshest critics, Wright "did not believe that recently freed 'negroes' or their immediate descendants were capable of being good republican citizens—an opinion she would retain when she planned Nashoba" because "generations of enforced slavery . . . had rendered American negroes inferior to whites in both character and appearance." However, even this critic concedes that for Wright "their inferiority—however difficult to stamp out—stemmed not from *intrinsic* racial character but from the lasting degradation caused by slavery." See Bederman, "Revisiting Nashoba," 443; emphasis added.

55  Wright, *Views of Society*, 41, 44.

56  Tocqueville, *Democracy in America*, 342.

57  Wright, *Views of Society*, 41–42, 268.

58  Tocqueville, *Democracy in America*, 343.

59  Wright, *Views of Society*, 41.

60  Tocqueville, *Democracy in America*, 343, 342; and Wright, *Views of Society*, 43.

61  Wright, *Views of Society*, 44.

62  Tocqueville, *Democracy in America*, 350.

63  Tillery, "Tocqueville as Critical Race Theorist," 641.

64  Critics observe that Wright issued an attack on the institution of marriage that supported "free love" among blacks and whites and emphasized the need for co-education in unifying the races only after the salacious revelations were publicized. "Unable to admit failure," a critic speculates, Wright simply "chose to change tacks." She "decided that her efforts had begun at the wrong end" and so would instead "engage in a lecture campaign to reform the collective body politic." See Travis, "Frances Wright," 391.

65  The facts surrounding the sex scandal at Nashoba are not in dispute, and Wright would speak out forcefully against the institution of marriage. However, it is not clear that Wright actually endorsed "free love" or that she advocated reproductive control, another important source of controversy. "Historians have assumed that Wright's lectures must have included discussions of reproductive control, but there is little in the available record to bear this out." Although Wright was

"not unfamiliar with the subject," she "said nothing publicly" about it. By contrast, Wright's co-editor Robert Dale Owen published a book, *Moral Physiology*, between 1830 and 1831 under the imprint "Wright & Owen," which did contain a "concise, careful, logical argument about the need for fertility control." See Janet Brodie, *Contraception and Abortion*, 89, 120–121. Perhaps Wright had been tarred with the same brush used against her male counterpart as well.

66  Tillery, "Tocqueville as Critical Race Theorist," 648.

67  Wright, *Views of Society*, 268–269. Wright makes similar observations about Native Americans who would eventually benefit from education in spite of the meager numbers of successful students at that time. Ibid., 111.

68  Ibid., 268. Moreover, "If prevailing opinion [against race mixing] accounts for the approach to emancipation Wright chose in 1825, it surely does not account for the intrepidity that led her to act publicly against slavery at great personal and financial risk, nearly a decade before either the formation of a radical abolitionist movement, committed to 'immediate emancipation' rather than colonization, or the rise of women antislavery writers and speakers." See Karcher, "Frances Wright of the *Free Enquirer*," 83.

69  Wright, *Views of Society*, 110.

70  Tocqueville, *Democracy in America*, 356. These beliefs, combined with Tocqueville's contention "that blacks have the potential to 'change' their condition and 'induce the whites to abandon the opinion they have conceived of the intellectual and moral inferiority' of the race," suggest that he in fact rejected the notion "that blacks were congenitally incapable of democratic citizenship." See Tillery, "Tocqueville as Critical Race Theorist," 643. Wright's support for miscegenation and universal education indicates that she, too, rejected the idea that blacks could never become full citizens and challenges claims of persistent racism in her theories.

71  Tocqueville's and Wright's hope that "assimilation would lead eventually to full racial equality" opens them to the accusation that "they did not see assimilation as a form of racism, for they were convinced, as were many [elites] of this period, that assimilation was vastly preferable to racist notions of fixed biological difference. In their minds, assimilation denoted a social vision that encompassed both a melding of peoples *and* a firm sense of hierarchy—an invitation to Others to participate (as almost-but-not-quite Anglos) in the body politic." This understanding of assimilation is racist because it relies on "evolutionary constructions of racial progress and sexual difference" and on an understanding of the roles of reformers "as civilizers of racially inferior peoples," a direct outgrowth of imperialism and colonization. See Newman, *White Women's Rights*, 20–21. Given that social Darwinism emerged years after Wright's and Tocqueville's works were written and that their support for imperialism and colonization is ambiguous, however, the charge of racism on these particular grounds would be questionable and, at the very least, anachronistic.

72  Gardner, *Empowerment and Interconnectivity*, 146–147.

73 Quoted in Rendall, "Prospects of the American Republic," 147. John Millar was ultimately indebted to Smith's four-stage theory of history, which was itself consistent with the social constructionist view that human behavior was determined largely by cultural, political, and economic circumstances, not by any fixed principles or natural law.

74 Wright, *Views of Society*, 23.

75 Ibid., 218.

76 Tocqueville, *Democracy in America*, 590.

77 Wright, *Views of Society*, 22.

78 Tocqueville, *Democracy in America*, 591.

79 Ibid., 592.

80 Ibid., 593. A plausible account of this phenomenon claims that "Tocqueville constructs a very different trajectory for the democratic woman's life" than for democratic man, "a narrative that owes more to a particular cultural disquiet than to observation of American practice or clear-eyed analysis of democratic tendencies." See Welch, *De Tocqueville*, 196. This contradiction in Tocqueville's thought is explained not only in terms of the "classical republican political theory" of his time, which insisted on "the strict confinement of women to the household and the enforcement of female chastity," but also in terms of a visceral reaction on his part against the "excesses of the Old Regime and those of the Revolution," which propelled him to embrace a reformed aristocratic Catholicism that "waved domesticity as a flag to symbolize the reformed and purified status of the class as a whole." See ibid., 197, 199, 202. Welch even speculates that Tocqueville projects "his own existential experience of moral choice in a democracy" onto the image of the American woman, in which he "resolutely turned his back on his ancestral past" and gained no "compensating sense of righteousness, or new fellowship, or any lasting joyfulness." See ibid., 204. My study offers an additional explanation of this contradiction in terms of Tocqueville's own problematic theory of sympathy and his lingering republicanism, in addition to the needs of the particular society he addresses in his work.

81 Tocqueville, *Democracy in America*, 602.

82 Ibid., 593.

83 Ibid., 603.

84 Ibid.

85 Ibid., 601.

86 Wright, *Views of Society*, 218.

87 Ibid.

88 Ibid., 22–23.

89 Ibid., 22.

90 Ibid., 218.

91 Throughout his career Bentham corresponded with several influential Americans such as Ben Franklin, John Quincy Adams, James Madison, and Richard Rush. Frequently he would offer to codify state laws to eliminate the destabilizing influ-

ence of English common law, which lingered in post-revolutionary America. See Williamson, "Bentham Looks at America," 287–293. Bentham had advised the French to examine the American model of government as early as 1788.

92  Only one volume of Bentham's *Constitutional Code* was published in his lifetime, itself the result of many years of work and multiple edited versions. Given that Wright's visits with Bentham coincided with the time spent formulating his constitutional principles, it would be reasonable to assume that the two exchanged ideas. Although Bentham and Wright have been grouped together in a broader category of "codifiers" who are criticized for prematurely abandoning English common law as a guide for expanding women's rights in America, there are important differences between the two thinkers, as I will show, and among the others included in this group. See Sullivan, *Constitutional Context*.

93  Crook, "The United States in Bentham's Thought," 280–281.

94  Wright, *Reason, Religion*, 52; emphasis in original.

95  Ibid., 63; emphasis in original.

96  Ibid., 65.

97  Ibid., 31.

98  Ibid., 32.

99  Ibid., 68–69.

100  Ibid., 69–70.

101  Ibid., 70; emphasis in original.

102  Tillery, "Tocqueville as Critical Race Theorist," 645.

103  Wright, *Reason, Religion*, 70–71.

104  Ibid., 76–77.

105  Ibid., 89–90.

106  Tillery, "Tocqueville as Critical Race Theorist," 643.

107  Wright, *Reason, Religion*, 62–63.

108  Quoted in Morris, *Fanny Wright*, 3.

109  Quoted in ibid.

110  Beecher, *A Treatise on Domestic Economy*.

111  Tillery, "Tocqueville as Critical Race Theorist," 646.

112  Wright, *Reason, Religion*, 279–280.

113  Ibid., 31.

114  Ibid., 45.

115  Ibid., 54.

116  Ibid., 54, 60.

117  Ibid., 105.

118  Rosen, Introduction, xxxiv–xxxv.

119  Crook, "The United States in Bentham's Thought," 281.

120  Wright, *Reason, Religion*, 174.

121  Ibid., 104.

122  Ibid., 105.

123  Ibid., 56.

124 Ibid., 69–70.

125 Ibid., 64.

126 Ibid., 65; emphasis in original.

127 Ibid., 116; emphasis added.

128 Ibid., 159; emphasis added.

129 Ibid., 164.

130 Wright's plan for education includes several controversial elements, such as the requirement that parents be kept at arm's length from their children so they would not "interfere with or interrupt the rules of the institution." However, they play an important role by reinforcing the experiential method of inquiry and in the process educate themselves as well. The parent "is to encourage in his child, a spirit of inquiry and equally to encourage it in himself. He is never to advance an opinion without showing the facts upon which it is grounded; he is never to assert a fact, without proving it to be a fact. He is not to teach a code of morals, any more than a creed of doctrines; but he is to direct his young charge to observe the consequences of actions on himself and on others; and to judge of the propriety of those actions by their ascertained consequences." See ibid., 217, 85.

131 By bringing together an experiential view of knowledge with a commitment to social reform, Wright anticipates additional elements of critical feminist theory such as its "reliance on experiential analysis" and "pragmatic philosophical traditions" in which a "standard practice is to begin with concrete experiences, integrate these experiences into theory, and rely on theory for a deeper understanding of the experiences." These methodological approaches are designed to counter the "post-modern paradox" that occurs when critical feminist theorists attempt to document the systematic oppression of women, on the one hand, while denying, on the other, "the possibility of any universal foundations for critique," an inevitable byproduct of asserting the social construction of knowledge and the impossibility of universal truth. See Rhode, "Feminist Critical Theories," 620–621.

132 Wright, *Reason, Religion*, 46–47; emphasis added.

133 Ibid., 270.

134 Wright's power as a path-breaking role model is further reinforced by the fact that "she expressed her views through multiple channels: her lectures and speeches, which she published in the *Free Enquirer*, alongside the commentaries they elicited in the press, and her responses to those commentaries; items written before and after her tenure as editor—including poems, a play, a manifesto attacking the marriage institution and defending race-mixing, economic essays, and reportage on the European scene—all of which enhanced Wright's visibility even in her absence; a series of fables she composed specifically for the *Free Enquirer*, and above all, her editorials." By studying her work, we "recover an alternative model of nineteenth-century women's authorship and editorship that broadens our understanding of the options available to those who sought to influence the public through the press." See Karcher, "Frances Wright of the *Free Enquirer*," 81–82.

135 Traubel, *With Walt Whitman in Camden*, 1:80, 2:204, 205, 500.

136 Jason Frank, "Promiscuous Citizenship," 158.

137 Buhle and Buhle, *The Concise History of Woman Suffrage, 162.*

## CHAPTER 2. HARRIET MARTINEAU ON THE THEORY AND PRACTICE OF DEMOCRACY IN AMERICA

1 Lipset, *Harriet Martineau*, 7. And "in emphasizing the value system as a causal agent, Martineau was an early precursor of one of the major sociological orientations, an approach that attempts to analyze the effect of values on structure and change" that is emblematic of the later works of Max Weber, Talcott Parsons, and Gunnar Myrdal. See ibid., 10.

2 Hoecker-Drysdale, *Harriet Martineau*, 51. Another critic has described *How to Observe* as "a primitive sociological methodology" without explaining why it lacks sophistication. See Pichanick, *Harriet Martineau*, 75. An indication of Martineau's lack of originality is that her "career is defined by her auxiliary usefulness to a male-dominated culture." See David, *Intellectual Women*, 31; see also 54–57. Although R. K. Webb's detailed biography of Martineau marshaled a resurgence of interest in her works, he fails to challenge persistent characterizations of her behavior in terms of "hysteria" and sexual frustration. See Webb, *Harriet Martineau*.

3 Freedgood, "Banishing Panic."

4 Hoecker-Drysdale, *Harriet Martineau*, 57. Building on the characterization of Martineau as the "first woman sociologist," commentators observe that "before Karl Marx, and decades before Emile Durkheim and Max Weber, Martineau sociologically examined social class, forms of religion, types of suicide, national character, domestic relations and the status of women, delinquency and criminology, and the intricate interrelationships between repressive social institutions and the individual." See Hill and Hoecker-Drysdale, "Taking Harriet Martineau Seriously," 9.

5 Prochaska, *Eminent Victorians*, 20–21.

6 Others have noted the unique combination of breadth and depth in her works. "The image that emerges out of such a patchwork reveals Martineau to be the literary grandmother par excellence whose obscurity in literary history stems from the impossibility of pigeonholing her contributions." See Logan, *The Hour and the Woman*, 260. Martineau "gained public recognition as a populariser of political economy, a sociological traveller, a contemporary historian, a domestic novelist, a philosophical invalid, a defender of mesmerism and an author of children's stories." As a result, Martineau became "a living embodiment of interdisciplinarity and its possibilities . . . and an expert in each of the disciplines in its own right." See Sanders and Weiner, "Introduction," 1.

7 Linda Peterson, "From French Revolution to English Reform," 430.

8 Roberts, *The Woman and the Hour*, 15.

9 Easley, "Gendered Observations," 83. Along similar lines, although translation was a way in which female writers such as Martineau gained credibility in a male-

dominated literary world, it was also used to subvert conventional gender roles by allowing women to convey their own ideas indirectly, thereby avoiding undue notoriety. See Scholl, *Translation, Authorship*.

10 Linda Peterson, *Becoming a Woman of Letters*, 30.

11 Linda Peterson, "From French Revolution to English Reform," 448–449, emphasis in original.

12 Barbara Caine, *English Feminism*, 70–71.

13 Easley, "Gendered Observations," 80.

14 "Although Martineau, like Malthus, never supported voluntary family limitation and advocated only delay of marriage," critics asserted otherwise. See Huzel, *Popularization of Malthus*, 75.

15 Ibid., 8. Martineau allied herself closely with Malthus's theories, and when she expressed support for the New Poor Laws, many assumed that Malthus supported these changes as well, in spite of the fact that he never spoke out in favor of them. A controversial set of reforms that shifted responsibility for aid to the poor from local communities to the national government, the New Poor Laws were also associated with population control, the establishment of workhouses that, among other things, would create abysmal conditions for and separate families by segregating their inhabitants, all of which were seen to contradict the "feminine" principle of benevolence. Martineau's apparent zeal for "the classic Malthusian preventive check of moral restraint, that is, delay of marriage, while practicing strict chastity, until individuals are in a position to support their offspring," far surpassed Malthus's enthusiasm and further added to the controversy. See ibid., 62.

16 Vargo, "Contested Authority." Martineau's vivid depictions of the poor and the difficulties involved in applying the law can be seen as implicit criticisms as well. Others observe that Martineau's project is "riddled with a series of contradictions," and yet it "exposes logical flaws within the economic theory she intends to promote, making visible disjunctions hidden" by theoretical abstractions. See Klaver, *A/Moral Economics*, 58–59.

17 The publishers Saunders & Otley decided to shorten the title to *Society in America* for marketing purposes, namely, to appeal to readers of the burgeoning travel literature genre. The title of this chapter borrows from the original title proposed by Martineau as well. Although Martineau later expressed misgivings about *Society*, claiming that it was "too abstract" to be useful and instead turning to more concrete works such as *Retrospect of Western Travel* (1838), she wrote, "I have never regretted its boldness of speech. I felt a relief in having opened my mind which I would at no time have exchanged for any gain of reputation or fortune." See Martineau, *Harriet Martineau's Autobiography*, 401.

18 See Pichanick, *Harriet Martineau*, 49, 51; Thomson, *Adam Smith's Daughters*, 37; Logan, *Harriet Martineau*, 32–34; and Hunter, *Harriet Martineau*, 55–56.

19 Martineau, *How to Observe*, 30, 34, 40.

20 Ibid., 33.

21 Ibid., 34.

22 Ibid., 35.

23 Haakonssen, *Adam Smith*, xii. Samuel Fleischacker concurs: "Adam Smith is one of the most respectful of 18th century writers towards other societies," and given that "that morality might vary in accordance with culture was not widely accepted in Smith's time . . . the mere fact that he devotes a major division of his book to the subject is remarkable." Thus "we might say that Smith is a cultural pluralist, but not a relativist. He makes room for cultural variation within his picture of the good human life, but that picture, with its room for cultural variation, is supposed to hold for all human beings everywhere." See Fleischacker, "Adam Smith and Cultural Relativism," 26–27.

24 Martineau, *How to Observe*, 25.

25 Ibid.

26 Ibid., 26.

27 Ibid., 52. The importance of the concept of sympathy in Martineau's thought is reinforced by an essay written before her journey to America titled "On Moral Independence," which declares, "Man is made for sympathy. It is the deepest want and the highest privilege of his nature; a want by which in his most apathetic state he never ceases to be stimulated; a privilege of which, in his most degraded condition, he can never be wholly divested." See Martineau, *Miscellanies*, 179.

28 Charles Griswold observes a similar circularity in Smith's theory of moral sentiments. "Contrary to the agent's perspective," Griswold explains, "moral terms ultimately do not correspond to external, mind-independent reality but express our sentiments and judgment." Thus "moral 'reality' and the objective 'fabric of the world' are best understood, for Smith . . . as decisively formed by the self, and, in particular, by the imagination." See Griswold, *Adam Smith*, 362. See also Alexander Broadie, "Sympathy and the Impartial Spectator," 181.

29 Specifically, "although much in Smith's theory depends on the priority of the spectator's standpoint in the sympathetic process, with a slight shift of epistemic emphasis one could (mistakenly) also make veridical—as many have—the standpoint of the actor," which "destroys the notion of the impartial spectator" and "the argument against selfishness." Such a "shift in perspective would be encouraged by the thought that moral judgments are founded not on the impartial spectator's superior grasp of truth and reality but on the expression of self." See Griswold, *Adam Smith*, 371. Griswold concludes that, although Smith's theory allows individuals to see, among other things, "fraudulent claims to authority" in their own societies, it does not clearly help them "evaluate the social or political system as a whole" and thereby transcend the limits of their particular communities. See ibid., 369.

30 Martineau, *How to Observe*, 54. See also Fleischacker, "Adam Smith and Cultural Relativism," 28–31.

31 Martineau, *How to Observe*, 223.

32 Ibid., 54, 225; emphasis added.

33  Ibid., 226.

34  Ibid., 228.

35  Ibid., 229.

36  Ibid., 234.

37  Ibid., 239.

38  Griswold, *Adam Smith*, 372, 369. For Griswold, "genuinely Socratic dialogue," which consists of "direct questions" about "decency, civility, common humanity, and reason," is "systematically avoided" in *Moral Sentiments*. See ibid., 368.

39  Others find a less solipsistic Smith. In his discussions of infanticide, polygamy, and natural jurisprudence, Smith advocates a position of "openness" and "humility" when observing other cultures that does not preclude the ability to render judgment, albeit indirectly. In this regard, the observer who confronts cultures radically different from his own is forced to reconsider his own customs. See Pitts, *A Turn to Empire*, 44–47. Even if this were true, it is still the case that Martineau is more overtly dialectical, open, and "humble" in her understanding of sympathy than Smith, as this study shall demonstrate.

40  Another way of describing this aspect of Martineau's approach uses the metaphor of a "translator": "In Harriet Martineau's travel writing about America there are strong political and philosophical ideas. . . . She is trying to translate and make accessible, both to her home culture and the source culture, both being her target audience. . . . As for the American audience, they are forced to view themselves from the outside, and inspect themselves in a new—and often uncomfortable— way. In this manner, Martineau takes on the authoritative role of the translator, mediating between two cultural constructs to open both sets of eyes to their own failings and new possibilities." See Scholl, "Mediation and Expansion," 831.

41  Among these commentators should be included Tocqueville, who apparently spent a considerable amount of time reviewing Jean-Baptiste Say's *Cours d'Économie Politique* (1823), a well-known popularization of Smith's economic theories, while en route to and from America. See Welch, *De Tocqueville*, 16, 68.

42  Martineau, *Society in America*, 1:viii.

43  Ibid., 1:2.

44  Ibid., 1:3.

45  Ibid., 1:4–5.

46  This requires that the actual experiences of observation be properly interpreted. To this end, *How to Observe* outlines in great detail how travelers can make certain that their characterizations of societies are reasonably accurate. And *Society in America* begins with an extended discussion of the ways in which Martineau ensures that her observations of American society are as accurate as possible. See ibid., 1:v–xix.

47  Ibid., 1:x.

48  Ibid., 1:xii.

49  McCoy, *Last of the Fathers*, 1–7, 252, 261, 266, 308–309. Martineau was so deeply moved by her intensive conversations with the elder statesman that she devoted

an entire chapter to him in *Retrospect of Western Travel*. In spite of Martineau's fondness for Madison, she vehemently disagreed with his advocacy of colonization.

50 Martineau, *Society in America*, 1:8.

51 Martineau, *How to Observe*, 49.

52 Martineau, *Society in America*, 1:173–175.

53 Ibid., 1:163–164.

54 Martineau, *How to Observe*, 49–50.

55 Martineau, *Society in America*, 1:177–178.

56 Ibid., 1:178–179.

57 The first English and American editions of *Democracy in America* appeared in 1838. Much later in her career, Martineau astutely observes that Tocqueville's "logical treatment of an idealised theme" is "too plain" to accommodate the complexity of American society because "he saw few people," he "did not go southwards beyond Washington," and he "conversed very little." Martineau concludes, "The remark was that his book might have been written in his own library, without the trouble of voyage." See Harriet Martineau, "Representative Men: Alexis de Tocqueville," *Once a Week*, September 7, 1861, quoted in Martineau, *Writings on Slavery*, 6.

58 George W. Pierson claims that Tocqueville was alerted to Martineau's study by Beaumont but "was afraid . . . of having his thoughts jolted from the path of strict logic and rigorous deduction." In a letter to Beaumont, Tocqueville explains, "What you tell me about Miss Martineau's book makes me uncomfortable. . . . Every time I hear America spoken of, and well spoken of, I experience a veritable uneasiness." See Pierson, *Tocqueville and Beaumont*, 726.

59 Tocqueville, *Democracy in America*, 274.

60 Ibid., 308.

61 Ibid., 290.

62 Ibid., 291.

63 Ibid., 292.

64 Welch concludes, "Tocqueville's exaggerated racial scenarios are warnings about . . . situations . . . where one cannot count on internalized mores or outside pressure to restrain majorities from exceeding moral limits." See Welch, "Tocqueville on Democracy after Abolition," 239.

65 Tocqueville, *Democracy in America*, 341. For Smith's concurrence on this point, see *WN*, III.ii.12–13.

66 The result in Tocqueville's account is that the problems of racism and slavery "provoke sadness and resignation more than anger and action." See Reinhardt, *Art of Being Free*, 65. Barbara Allen emphasizes the point: "Not even Christianity, which Tocqueville consistently linked to republican principles, nor (remarkably) the evangelism he associated with the democratic revolution, nor even otherwise persuasive secular principles of moral equality seemed capable of eradicating racial antipathy in the New World. This final observation is particularly perplex-

ing, not only because we are used to thinking that Enlightenment ideals and evangelical belief inspired movements to end the slave trade and slavery (which Tocqueville does not deny) but also because Tocqueville consistently referred to the spirit of liberty and the spirit of religion as the source of most right-minded democratic progress in America." See Barbara Allen, *Tocqueville, Covenant*, 226.

67 Tocqueville, *Democracy in America*, 395–396.

68 Tillery, "Tocqueville as Critical Race Theorist," 640.

69 Martineau, *Society in America*, 2:115–116.

70 Martineau, *How to Observe*, 229.

71 Tocqueville, *Democracy in America*, 320.

72 Martineau, *Society in America*, 2:112–115.

73 Ibid., 2:128–129.

74 Ibid., 2:130–137.

75 Tocqueville's relatively brief account of the economic effects of slavery in *Democracy* would later be expanded in subsequent writings and speeches. See Barbara Allen, *Tocqueville, Covenant*, 225–259.

76 Another important aspect of Martineau's characterization of American slavery is her insistence on allowing slave characters to speak for themselves through accurate translation "instead of overwriting the language and manners of slaves." As a result, "Martineau narrows the gap between a pitying subject and an abused, objectified other." See Roberts, *The Woman and the Hour*, 45, 48.

77 Martineau's earlier tale of slavery, "Demerara," which was included in *Illustrations*, conveys the same message, as "members of this slave family, depicted above in such highly sympathetic terms, are also shown to be sullen, dishonest, vain, and stand offish. . . . In some passages 'Demerara' presents uncomfortable images of the nature and behavior of its characters. . . . Yet in the story Martineau clearly demonstrates that the negative behavior of the slaves results from the defects of the system more than from any inherent defect of character or race, a system equally damaging to those in power." See Hovet, "Harriet Martineau's Exceptional American Narratives," 66.

78 Martineau, *Society in America*, 2:291–292, 2:120. Martineau's historical novel *The Hour and the Man* (1841), a fictional biography of Toussaint L'Ouverture, operates in a similar fashion. The "arrangement of many scenes stages the process of interpretation for the reader," which is crucial in "understanding racial categories." By revealing the essentially ideological character of "positions coded as 'natural,'" thereby undermining their potency, Martineau "carries out her own particular project of discursive liberation." See Callanan, "Race and the Politics of Interpretative Disruption," 428–429.

79 Martineau, *Society in America*, 2:154.

80 Ibid., 2:157.

81 Martineau, *Society in America*, 1:310.

82 Martineau shows in several anecdotes how slaves could flourish with proper education and other opportunities. See ibid., 1:303–304. Although many British

female abolitionists regularly emphasized the importance of education in the process of emancipation, Martineau does so with vivid illustrations gleaned from her sympathetic interactions with slave owners and slaves that are designed to break through the hardened assumptions of her most skeptical readers.

83 Tocqueville's "treatment of subject peoples disturbs . . . precisely because his empathetic reconstruction of their plight leads to no corresponding sympathy for their right to a free way of life, and little compunction about dropping them out of the theoretical universe of democracy." See Welch, *De Tocqueville*, 64.

84 Martineau, *Society in America*, 2:118–119. Martineau's "brand of exceptionalism enacts familiar devices of destiny and redemption, but her vision is grounded by her sociological methodology, by an unusually long and deep engagement with the key figures in the abolitionist movement, and by her first-hand engagement with its attendant social and political pressures. Martineau, far from just an observer, took an active role in pushing America toward renewal and reform." See Hovet, "Harriet Martineau's Exceptional American Narratives," 74.

85 Because Martineau focuses on "the lack of willingness to effect change on the part of women themselves, preventing them from having political representation, . . . her association of women with slaves only goes so far: for her, women are not as disenfranchised as the slaves, and therefore must be held, at least in part, accountable for remaining in their bondage." See Scholl, "Mediation and Expansion," 830.

86 Martineau, *Society in America*, 1:199.

87 Ibid., 1:204.

88 Martineau, like Tocqueville, is impressed by the elevated position of women in American society when compared with their subjugated European counterparts. But the claim that Martineau concurs with Tocqueville that "familial power in America is, like political power, consensually acknowledged, freely elected, and checked" is rendered problematic by the analysis of consent presented here. See Goldstein, "Europe Looks at American Women," 539; emphasis in original.

89 Martineau, *Society in America*, 2:341.

90 Ibid., 3:110–113.

91 Ibid., 3:114–115.

92 Ibid., 3:114–117.

93 Ibid., 3:105–106.

94 Both Wollstonecraft and Martineau deplore the effects of social oppression on women's morality and intellect and insist that the deprivation of rights makes it impossible for women to be productive and morally upright citizens, wives, and mothers. Both call for increased educational and economic opportunities for, and greater political representation of, women. See Poston, *Mary Wollstonecraft*, 58–60. Martineau should be counted among early women's rights advocates who publicly disparaged the scandalous private behavior of Mary Wollstonecraft while surreptitiously appropriating many of Wollstonecraft's ideas. See Botting and Carey, "Wollstonecraft's Philosophical Impact," 709–710. It should also be

noted, however, that Martineau's critical remarks about Wollstonecraft in her *Autobiography* constitute an extension of her criticism of "literary lionism," which attacks the cult of celebrity—and often scandal—that surrounds powerful literary intellectuals. See Martineau, *Harriet Martineau's Autobiography*, 302–305. Rejecting literary lionism for herself, Martineau instead seeks to lead a respectable life and write accessible works that appeal to a broad variety of readers, including middle-class women who, like their male counterparts, are entering the labor force in increasing numbers and who are exhibiting greater desire for education and enlightenment.

95 Martineau, *Society in America*, 3:106.

96 Ibid., 3:119.

97 Martineau, *Society in America*, 2:337–338; emphasis added.

98 Beecher, "Peculiar Responsibilities."

99 Tocqueville, *Democracy in America*, 571.

100 Ibid., 577.

101 Ibid., 578.

102 Ibid., 587.

103 Ibid., 588.

104 Ibid., 589.

105 Welch, too, notes the "brotherhood" created among democratic men to the exclusion of women. See Welch, *De Tocqueville*, 194.

106 Tocqueville, *Democracy in America*, 590–591.

107 Ibid., 593.

108 Allen claims that Tocqueville is drawing from the covenant understanding of marriage, namely, "unions based on mutual promise and unreserved obligation and loyalty," rather than the contractual understanding of marriage advanced by John Stuart Mill and Harriet Taylor Mill. To Tocqueville, "the contract metaphor seemed . . . wholly inappropriate for these circumstances; intimate bonds of family and friendship depended on internal self-control, not the external constraint and enforcement of contracts." See Barbara Allen, *Tocqueville, Covenant*, 216–217. Although Martineau's account of women in America doubtless influenced the Mills, it seems that her account of consent is not simply synonymous with theirs. Instead of relying on the classical liberal logic of pure individualism, as do the Mills, Martineau enriches her understanding of contract and consent with her moral principle of sympathy. In this respect, she serves as a more formidable counterpart to Tocqueville than even Catharine Beecher would realize.

CHAPTER 3. FACING THE "SLEDGE HAMMER OF TRUTH"

1 Ceplair, *Public Years*, 166; emphasis in original.

2 Ibid., 25; emphasis in original.

3 Johnson, *Nineteenth-Century Rhetoric*. As I explain in the Introduction, these debates about sympathy found themselves popularized in various ways in America. George Campbell's *Philosophy of Rhetoric* (1776) was commonly used in American

education. Hugh Blair's *Lectures on Rhetoric and Belles Lettres* (1787), an adaptation of Adam Smith's same-named work, was widely available in mid-nineteenth-century America. The development of these discussions coincided with the emergence of commonsense philosophy, which furthered the popularization of complex moral theories by rendering them more accessible to the public. Frederick Douglass was influenced by commonsense philosophy through the works of James McCune Smith, a manumitted slave who studied at Glasgow University. See Lee, *Slavery, Philosophy*, 93–132. Commonsense philosophy is defined broadly, including thinkers invoked by Adam Smith such as "Locke, Malebranche, Berkeley, and Hume, as well as Scottish commonsense philosophers such as Dugald Stewart, Thomas Brown, . . . and Thomas Reid." Although commonsense philosophy holds out great appeal, by "positing a self-evident faculty whose explanatory power depends on the fact that it cannot by definition be argued," its response to debilitating skepticism "may not always pass logical muster, particularly if it is taken to be the diluted version taught to antebellum students." See ibid., 102, 130.

4 Zagarri, "Morals, Manners," 196.

5 Kimberly Smith, *Dominion of Voice*, 98–99.

6 See Hendler, *Public Sentiments*, 8–11, for a helpful overview.

7 Abruzzo, *Polemical Pain*, 132.

8 Ibid., 239.

9 Bacon, *The Humblest May Stand Forth*, 121; see also Sanchez-Eppler, "Bodily Bonds," 94–95.

10 Bacon, *The Humblest May Stand Forth*, 136, 137, 140. Grimké's claim to transparency and sincerity, which "was often conceived as entailing the exposure of a vulnerable self to potential injury," also allowed her to capitalize "on her status as an unprotected woman on the lecture circuit, turning her exposure and vulnerability to her rhetorical advantage." See Henry, *Liberalism and the Culture of Security*, 22. See also Brown, "A System of Complicated Crimes."

11 Parker, *Articulating Rights*, 63–65.

12 In another example, when Grimké was confronted by Weld, who claimed that her advocacy of women's rights was a distraction from the cause of ending slavery, she responded in ways that suggested that she ultimately desired "the questioning of all relations of authority in society." See Quanquin, "There Are Two Great Oceans," 85.

13 Beecher attacks Frances Wright and Harriet Martineau as well, as I discuss in chapters 1 and 2.

14 Lerner claims that the elders objected because the school was too "Presbyterian" and that, by leaving, Grimké would be neglecting her duties as a Quaker. Lerner, *Grimké Sisters from South Carolina*, 1998 ed., 74–76.

15 The British parliamentarian William Wilberforce led the successful effort to end the slave trade within the British Empire, culminating in passage of the Slave Trade Act in 1807.

16 Ceplair, *Public Years*, 202–203.

17  Ibid., 179.

18  Ibid., 200. Grimké's attack on Beecher's intellectualism is similar to Smith's condemnation of the moral philosophers of his time whose thoughts "have of late inclined to abstract and speculative reasonings which perhaps tend very little to the bettering of our practice" (*LRBL*, i.101–102). Also blameworthy are philosophers who formulate ethical theories working from a "vague and indeterminate idea" of morality at the expense of "particular examples" demonstrating the power of sympathy (*TMS*, IV.2.2).

19  Ibid., 37.

20  Beecher, *Essay on Slavery and Abolitionism*, 14.

21  Ibid., 9, 11.

22  Ibid., 24.

23  Ibid., 27.

24  Ibid., 44.

25  Ibid., 44–45.

26  Ibid., 41–42.

27  Ibid., 43.

28  Ibid., 34.

29  Ibid., 38.

30  Ceplair, *Public Years*, 64.

31  Ibid., 71; emphasis in original.

32  Ibid., 169.

33  Ibid., 54–56; emphasis in original.

34  Ibid., 191; emphasis in original.

35  Ibid., 195.

36  Ibid., 196–197, 194; emphasis in original.

37  Ibid., 55; emphasis in original.

38  Ibid., 57; emphasis in original.

39  Ibid., 67; emphasis in original.

40  Ibid., 171; emphasis in original.

41  Newman, *White Women's Rights*, 20–21.

42  Ceplair, *Public Years*, 58.

43  Ibid., 68–69; emphasis in original.

44  Ibid.

45  On this view, if Grimké is asking readers to sympathize with the suffering slave, it would only be because the slave is herself capable of sympathizing. For Smith, "moral judgment is an engine that drives identification" because "to the extent that we evaluate others morally we identify with them *per force*." Thus, if we view slavery through the lens of Smith's moral theory, whites "can't avoid identifying with" slaves if whites "seek to evaluate the justice" of their "conduct toward them." The slaves' "points of view will discipline" those of whites, "since judgments of justice aim for an impartiality with respect to" themselves and the slaves. See Darwall, "Sympathetic Liberalism," 161–162. For, Smith writes, when a "violator of

the more sacred laws of justice"—in this case, the Christian slave owner—"begins coolly to reflect on his past conduct . . . the motives which influenced it . . . appear now as detestable to him as they did always to other people." When people observe injustices committed against others—in this case, the slave—they remember that "this man is to them, in every respect, as good as he" and "they readily, therefore, sympathize with the natural resentment of the injured, and the offender becomes the object of their hatred and indignation" (*TMS*, II.ii.2.1). Although "the situation of the person, who suffered by his injustice, now calls upon his pity," the pity he feels is not necessarily disempowering to the sufferer, in this case the slave (*TMS*, II.ii.2.3). Smith's moral theory would also require of whites "not simply a sharing of their sense of having been wronged," but also "a recognition of their *authority* to *challenge* the wrong by resisting it, or, failing that, to demand some form of compensation or punishment." As a result, sympathy "empowers" those who suffer "to hold those who treat them unjustly *accountable* for their unjust injuries." Even if justice is not served, it must at some level include "all parties" involved. See Darwall, "Sympathetic Liberalism," 161–162. According to Smith, justice requires not only "shame," "grief," and "pity" but also "the dread and terror of punishment from the consciousness of the justly provoked resentment of all rational creatures," which would include slaves (*TMS*, II.ii.2.3). Grimké's allusion to the inevitability of slave revolts further reinforces the latter point. See Ceplair, *Public Years*, 64. On the potential for Smith's moral theory to grant a level of equality among those involved, see Debes, "Adam Smith."

46  Ceplair, *Public Years*, 60.

47  Ibid., 63.

48  Ibid., 64; emphasis in original.

49  Ibid., 50; emphases in original.

50  Ibid., 51; emphasis in original.

51  Ibid.; emphasis in original.

52  Quoting Hebrews 13:3; see ibid., 72; emphasis in original.

## CHAPTER 4. SARAH GRIMKÉ'S QUAKER LIBERALISM

1  Lerner, *Feminist Thought of Sarah Grimké*, 5. Grimké has been firmly placed in the broadly defined category of "Liberal Enlightenment Feminism," along with Mary Wollstonecraft, Frances Wright, Sojourner Truth, Elizabeth Cady Stanton, Susan B. Anthony, Harriet Taylor, and John Stuart Mill. See Donovan, *Feminist Theory*. See also Selvidge, *Notorious Voices*.

2  Calvert, *Quaker Constitutionalism*, 3.

3  Lerner, *Grimké Sisters from South Carolina*, 1967, 1998, and 2004 eds.; "Sarah M. Grimké's 'Sisters of Charity'"; and "Comment on Lerner's 'Sarah M. Grimké's "Sisters of Charity."'"

4  Lerner, *Creation of Feminist Consciousness*, 161.

5  Looking back on her earlier work on Grimké, Lerner acknowledges the difficulty: "Sarah's argument for the emancipation of women was almost entirely theologi-

cal; her language was biblical; her images were derived from Christian iconography. I was not trained in theology and had only cursory knowledge of Christian thought; thus I found it difficult to comprehend her arguments." Although Lerner claims to have immersed herself "in the intellectual context of which she was writing" by reading "only material she might have read," presumably including religious works, she concludes that "I have no desire to change my interpretation." See Lerner, *Feminist Thought of Sarah Grimké*, 4. Lerner reinforces her conclusion in the volume by emphasizing the importance of Grimké's later works, especially "The Education of Women," which "marks her farthest movement away from a largely moral and religious conceptual framework." See ibid., 31. Lerner "has attempted to understand Sarah's writings in the context of her Christian faith." However, "in writing as a non-believer about the faith basis of Sarah's reform, Lerner has failed to capture Sarah's faith as the driving force behind her reform work." See Durso, *Power of Woman*, 6.

6  Lerner, *Creation of Feminist Consciousness*, 163; emphasis added.

7  Parker, *Articulating Rights*, 72.

8  Ibid.

9  Ibid., 94.

10  Ibid., 65.

11  Ibid., 66.

12  Ibid., 78.

13  Ibid., 65.

14  Sullivan, *Constitutional Context*.

15  Ibid. Another recent study associates Grimké with the emergence of the "abstract woman" who is quite literally disembodied and hence contrary to the "situatedness" of contemporary standpoint feminism: "The subject, at least in its political existence, is perceived here as nothing but an anchor to which rights and liberties are attached (or, in the case of oppression, a locus from which specific sets of rights and liberties are negated)." See Kotef, "On Abstractness," 497. Measured in terms of the most jarring reminder of embodiment imaginable—namely, physical abuse—the upper-middle-class white woman is the most abstracted from the body; the working-class woman a bit less so; the slave the most embodied of all. However, to make Grimké fit into this analytical framework, the study focuses on a single letter, "The Legal Disabilities of Women," and proceeds, however reluctantly, to group Grimké among nineteenth-century reformers who show a similar tendency toward abstraction.

16  Sullivan, *Constitutional Context*, 7. Although Catharine Beecher's religious ideas, like those of other liberal feminists, "continued to be ignored or treated as something that had to be overcome in order for women to be free," she advocated "separate spheres" of influence for men and women, a view that is consistent with common law. Beecher is also notable for "her challenge to the excesses of liberalism and individualism that were beginning to dominate American political thought at the time, and her defense of the importance of the institutions of civil

society, which she considered to be absolutely essential for the health of a democratic nation." See Hall, "Beyond Self-Interest," 487.

17 Historians have faulted Sullivan's methodology, which relies on a handful of historical sources to represent entirety of the early women's rights movement, and the caricature she creates of the "liberal feminist" by conflating the diverse contributions of a variety of advocates. See Cott, "Kathleen S. Sullivan, *Constitutional Context*," 1534. Another suspects an underlying ideological agenda that propels Sullivan's work. See Isenberg, "Kathleen S. Sullivan, *Constitutional Context*," 447.

18 Grimké, her sister Angelina, and Lucretia Mott initially attended the Arch Street Meeting in Philadelphia. They felt alienated by the conservative orthodox tendencies of the meeting, which departed sharply from progressive Hicksite teachings. Mott decamped for the more progressive Cherry Street Meeting, but the Grimkés did not follow, nor did they rejoin another meeting.

19 Jane Calvert may object to grouping Grimké with Penn and Dickinson. On Calvert's view, the emergence of the Hicksite Quakers and especially the Garrisonian abolitionists—in particular, Lucretia Mott—signaled the abrupt end of Dickinsonian constitutionalism. For Mott and others, reason was simply synonymous with the light, or synteresis, not complementary to it, as it was for Dickinson. Garrisonians were "violently conflictual" in that they used incendiary rhetoric to shock audiences into ending slavery. As such, there was no persuasion based on unity, and the individual conscience was elevated over collective discernment. Garrison's famous burning of the Constitution signifies their desire to reject the document rather than reform it. However, it is unclear if Calvert's critique applies to the Grimkés as well. I argue that neither the Grimkés nor Mott should be automatically characterized as Garrisonians. And chapter 3 offers a limited defense of Angelina Grimké's rhetoric. See Calvert, *Quaker Constitutionalism*, 320–324.

20 Murphy, "Limits and Promise" and "Trial Transcript."

21 Calvert, "Quaker Theory," 590, and *Quaker Constitutionalism*, 11.

22 To apply Quaker constitutionalism to the Declaration would seem to contradict Dickinson's rejection of the document. However, Dickinson objected to the act of revolution itself, not to the principles of equality and liberty that are contained in the document, because those principles are consistent with the fundamental constitution. Indeed, Dickinson understood his political efforts in terms of a continuum with the first principles of the fundamental constitution, beginning with his work in the Stamp Act Congress, the First and Second Continental Congresses, the Confederation Congress, the Delaware, Pennsylvania, and Annapolis Conventions for Ratification, and the Constitutional Convention in Philadelphia. See Calvert, *Quaker Constitutionalism*, 14.

23 Ibid., 92.

24 See, more generally, Carlacio, "Ye Knew Your Duty, but Ye Did It Not"; and Bacon, *The Humblest May Stand Forth*.

25 Calvert, *Quaker Constitutionalism*, 66.

26 Ibid., 66–67.

27 Ibid., 86.

28 Ibid., 68–69.

29 In order that all might participate in the discernment process, all needed to be able to understand the issues at hand. Therefore one important Quaker testimony was plainness—clarity, simplicity, and honesty in all things, including speech. See ibid., 287–288.

30 Ibid., 80.

31 Ibid., 71.

32 Ibid., 92. Synteresis complementary with reason, not reason alone, is the "guide" to which Dickinson refers in a widely quoted statement at the Constitutional Convention: "Reason must be our only guide. Reason may mislead us. It was not Reason that discovered the singular & admirable mechanism of the English Constitution. It was not Reason that discovered or even could have discovered the odd & in the eye of those who are governed by reason, the absurd mode of trial by Jury. Accidents probably produced these discoveries, and experience has given sanction to them. This is then our guide." See ibid., 285.

33 Ibid., 77.

34 Ibid., 245.

35 Ibid., 94.

36 Ibid., 289.

37 Ibid., 34.

38 Ibid., 290.

39 Ibid., 38.

40 Ibid., 285.

41 Ibid., 285–286.

42 Lyon, *Deliberative Acts*, 23.

43 Calvert, *Quaker Constitutionalism*, 291.

44 Ibid., 293.

45 Ibid., 291.

46 Calvert, "Quaker Theory," 594.

47 Calvert, *Quaker Constitutionalism*, 72.

48 Ibid., 73.

49 Calvert, "Quaker Theory," 594.

50 Lyon, *Deliberative Acts*, 22.

51 Ibid., 23–24.

52 Cima, *Performing Anti-slavery*, 149.

53 Calvert, *Quaker Constitutionalism*, 38.

54 Ceplair, *Public Years*, 269. A secular interpretation characterizes Grimké's indirect approach as a rhetorical strategy by which she can "offer strong arguments while deflecting attention from her own authority." See Bacon, *The Humblest May Stand Forth*, 158. However, it is equally consistent with Quaker practice and principle.

55 Calvert, *Quaker Constitutionalism*, 137.

56 Ceplair, *Public Years*, 205.

57 Ibid., 204–205. For an account of male church leaders who supported women's rights in the face of resistance, see Zink-Sawyer, "From Preachers to Suffragists."

58 Ceplair, *Public Years*, 204.

59 Ibid., 258.

60 Lerner, *Creation of Feminist Consciousness*, 160–163. See also Hardesty, *Women Called to Witness*, 74–82.

61 Ceplair, *Public Years*, 207.

62 Ibid., 209.

63 Ibid.

64 Ibid., 213.

65 Ibid., 217.

66 Ibid., 242.

67 Ibid., 255.

68 Ibid., 244.

69 Ibid., 248.

70 Ibid., 206.

71 Ibid., 208; emphasis in original.

72 Although Lerner is correct in noting the importance of Grimké's work, it is not entirely accurate to claim that Grimké was the "first" woman to argue that gender is a culturally variable, arbitrary definition of behavior or to offer a systematic account of women's oppression. Although Grimké laments the fact that "my constant change of place has preventing me from having access to books, which might probably have assisted me in this part of my work," Grimké herself cites a number of sources, including Harriet Martineau's *Society in America*, which was published a year before Grimké's letters appeared. See Ceplair, *Public Years*, 219–220, 236. Grimké also relies on scriptural interpreters such as William Cave, Matthew Henry, Robert Mackenzie Beverley, and Adam Clarke. The letters pertaining to the history of women are largely derived from Lydia Maria Child's *Brief History of the Condition of Women, in Various Ages and Nations* (1835). In her speeches Frances Wright outlines a systematic view of oppression in which women and the disenfranchised suffer at the hands of elites who do anything to maintain their power and influence, and she calls for national universal education and other progressive reforms. Although she does not mention them by name, it is doubtful that Grimké would be unfamiliar with the progressive scriptural interpretations of George Fox and Margaret Fell, founders of Quakerism. And like virtually all early women's rights advocates, Grimké demonstrates familiarity with Mary Wollstonecraft's *Vindication of the Rights of Woman*.

73 Ceplair, *Public Years*, 212; emphasis in original.

74 Ibid., 213.

75 Ibid; emphasis in original.

76 Ibid., 215–216.

77 Ibid., 214. Grimké thus "linked the conversion of individuals, specifically women, to their response in faith to serve their neighbors in need." For it is a "faithful

Christian disciple's responsibility to appropriately steward one's gifts and the Christian woman's obligation to dismantle socially constructed barriers of class and race." See Warner, *Saving Women*, 97.

78 Ceplair, *Public Years*, 217.

79 Ibid., 221; emphasis in original.

80 Ibid.

81 Ibid., 223.

82 Grimké notes that women of the laboring class also suffer morally from their unequal status. "When their virtue is assailed, they yield to temptation with facility, under the idea that it rather exalts than debases them, to be connected with a superior being." See ibid.

83 Ibid.

84 Ibid., 225.

85 Ibid., 262.

86 Ibid., 231; emphasis in original.

87 Ibid., 232.

88 Ibid., 236.

89 Bacon, *The Humblest May Stand Forth*, 126.

90 Sanchez-Eppler, "Bodily Bonds," 95.

91 Ceplair, *Public Years*, 236.

92 Ibid., 237.

93 Ibid.; emphasis in original.

94 Ibid., 239; emphasis in original.

95 Ibid., 260; emphasis in original.

96 Jason Frank, *Constituent Moments*, 8.

97 Beaumont, *Civic Constitution*, xv.

98 Ibid., 10.

CHAPTER 5. "THE MOST BELLIGERENT NON-RESISTANT"

1 Greene, *Lucretia Mott*, 262.

2 Quoted in Palmer, *Selected Letters of Lucretia Coffin Mott*, xx.

3 Early religious progressives such as Mott and the Grimké envisioned women's rights in terms of a "true" Christianity, which relied on revised interpretations of the Bible to justify equality for women while deploring patriarchal clergies who misinterpreted Scripture. Although this message resonated strongly with the younger Stanton, she distinguished herself from Mott and other advocates such as Sarah Grimké by advocating a more humanistic view of Christianity, in response to Christianity's persistent repression of women. "Stanton's dream of a Religion of Humanity was continually interrupted by the real-life nightmare of women's religious fidelity to an oppressive system of Christianity. By the early 1880s Stanton saw the church and the Bible uncompromisingly, as looming obstacles to woman's liberty that needed to be leveled." See Kern, *Mrs. Stanton's Bible*, 96.

4  Well into her sixties, Mott also fought for equal access to streetcars in Philadelphia and forcefully advocated for better treatment of black soldiers after the Civil
War. See Faulkner, *Lucretia Mott's Heresy*, 4.

5  Ibid., 186.

6  Though she had limited understanding of their culture, Mott even supported
equality and freedom for Native Americans at a time when relatively few did so.
Subsequent women's rights advocates such as Matilda Jocelyn Gage would focus
greater attention on the plight of Native Americans.

7  Hewitt, "From Seneca Falls to Suffrage? Reimagining a 'Master' Narrative in
U.S. Women's History," 21. The *History of Woman Suffrage* has understated and
obscured other women's rights advocates such as Hannah Mather Crocker as well.
See Botting and Houser, "Drawing the Line of Equality," 266. The tensions within
the traditional narrative of the movement were not wholly lost on Stanton or
Anthony, however. Anthony lamented the tendency among younger advocates to
regard their predecessors such as Mott in terms of "something less than a 'usable
past.'" She was appalled, for example, when Carrie Chapman Catt's suffrage calen-
dar placed Mott at the bottom, calling it an "inversion of the 'natural order'" and
a violation of "the proper rank of old soldiers" within the movement. See Kern,
*Mrs. Stanton's Bible*, 94.

8  Davis, *Political Thought of Elizabeth Cady Stanton*, 44.

9  Ibid., 23.

10  Nancy Isenberg also notes the trend that continues to limit Mott's influence to
that of a mythic, prophetic figure whose role was "to initiate the movement"
rather than to lead it. On this view, Mott is "the voice of caution rather than
inspiration," a matriarchal, mystical, religious figure who had to be superseded
by more driven activists such as Stanton to allow true reform to emerge. Isenberg
wryly adds that "like [Saint] Peter, Stanton positioned herself . . . as the heir and
founder of the suffrage campaign." See Isenberg, *Sex and Citizenship*, 5, 3.

11  Faulkner, *Lucretia Mott's Heresy*, 216.

12  Hewitt, "From Seneca Falls to Suffrage?," 32–33.

13  Kraditor, *Means and Ends*, 59 and note 69. See also DuBois, *Feminism and Suffrage*, 35.

14  Greene, *Lucretia Mott*, 77–78.

15  Strong, *Perfectionist Politics*, 40.

16  Greene, *Lucretia Mott*, 34.

17  Strong, *Perfectionist Politics*, 41.

18  Ibid., 42.

19  Botting and Carey, "Wollstonecraft's Philosophical Impact," 713.

20  Botting and Carey qualify Wollstonecraft's influence on early women's rights
advocates with a number of disclaimers that she "should not be understood as
the sole inspiration," that "parallel terms and arguments do not independently
provide evidence of . . . direct influence," and that "the broader Christian, En-

lightenment, and Romantic traditions surely influenced" these women as well. Nevertheless, the authors contend that "a shared set of philosophical concerns, . . . combined with evidence of direct references . . . and/or autobiographical or biographical evidence of . . . engagement with Wollstonecraft's work" provides a preponderance of evidence that is "so strong" as to prove that the ideas arose from *A Vindication of the Rights of Woman.* An analysis of linguistic and theoretical convergences between the two women confirms for the authors that Mott not only "echo[es] Wollstonecraft's terms and arguments" but also "shares Wollstonecraft's view[s]" on education and "follows Wollstonecraft's arguments" about women's pursuits. See Botting and Carey, "Wollstonecraft's Philosophical Impact," 709, 710, 713.

21 An 1867 letter written by Mott claiming that she had read the book some "40 years ago" dates her encounter with the *Vindication* to the late 1820s. Palmer places the date even later, to the 1830s, based on her reading of a letter Mott wrote in 1858. See Palmer, *Selected Letters of Lucretia Coffin Mott,* 174n5, 392, cited in Botting and Carey, "Wollstonecraft's Philosophical Impact," 712. Further evidence is provided by Mott herself in an 1855 letter, in which she mentions that Wollstonecraft first made her "radical claim" for women's rights "60 or 70 years ago" but adds that Quakers made the same claim "still earlier 1660 & 70." See ibid., 234.

Mott had attended Nine Partners School, which provided a progressive Quaker education for girls and boys alike, similar to Wollstonecraft's vision, and she had taught there from 1808 until her marriage three years later. Nine Partners was one of the first schools to allow female teachers. See Faulkner, *Lucretia Mott's Heresy,* 33. The more "useful" model of coeducation Mott later calls for and that is attributed to Wollstonecraft is strikingly similar to that which she received at Nine Partners as well. See Greene, *Lucretia Mott,* 160, cited in Botting and Carey, "Wollstonecraft's Philosophical Impact," 713. Mott's recurring criticism of unequal pay for women, reminiscent of Wollstonecraft's views, is deeply rooted in her own experience as a young teacher. Mott saw her female mentor receive half the pay of fellow instructor and her future husband James, and as James's salary was raised, Mott herself received no pay at all. See Faulkner, *Lucretia Mott's Heresy,* 34, 37, 42.

22 Wollstonecraft, *A Vindication of the Rights of Men; with, a Vindication of the Rights of Woman, and Hints,* 238, 239, 264, 265, 286; and Botting, *Family Feuds,* 174–175.

23 Cima, *Performing Anti-slavery,* 147; emphasis in original.

24 Greene, *Lucretia Mott,* 25.

25 Ibid., 26.

26 Ibid., 27.

27 Ibid., 30.

28 Ibid., 91, 103.

29 Greene, *Lucretia Mott,* 28. Sarah Grimké offers a detailed critique of the notion of an organized priesthood but falls short of attacking dogmatism itself. Grimké

also laments the lack of independent thinking among women, but the idea of living without any kind of doctrinal inclination is, it seems, distinctively Mott's. See Ceplair, *Public Years*, 246–258.

30 Greene, *Lucretia Mott*, 29.

31 Ibid., 27.

32 Ibid., 31–32.

33 Ibid., 35.

34 Ibid., 36.

35 Ibid., 37.

36 Ibid., 54.

37 Ibid., 37.

38 Ibid., 40.

39 Cima, *Performing Anti-slavery*, 163. Mott's self-deprecation has also been characterized as a rhetorical technique by which female speakers "appear to accept the dominance of male leaders" as they "also activate in their listeners a desire to identify with them, to temporarily transcend their differences in status." Although Mott "defers to the influence of the social hierarchy of gender, she [suggests] that she can create an authority that both acknowledges her 'inferiority' and transcends it." See Bacon, *The Humblest May Stand Forth*, 137–138. My detailed analysis of the substantive, theoretical claims in Mott's speeches shows that she systematically challenges traditional hierarchies and offers egalitarian conceptions of political power and human agency.

40 Greene, *Lucretia Mott*, 111.

41 Ibid., 112.

42 Cima, *Performing Anti-slavery*, 163.

43 Greene, *Lucretia Mott*, 111.

44 Ibid., 217.

45 Ibid., 224.

46 Cima, *Performing Anti-slavery*, 149, 145, 144.

47 Greene, *Lucretia Mott*, 302, cited in Palmer, *Selected Letters of Lucretia Coffin Mott*, xxi. Although I agree that Mott "saw truth as an unfolding and embodied process tied to specific historical circumstances rather than an abstract principle, a creed, or a doctrine," I do not go so far as to conclude that "individuals speaking from an inner light provided the means of worship, and *works rather than faith anchored Hicksite practice.*" See Cima, *Performing Anti-slavery*, 150; emphasis added. To be sure, Mott's progressive Quakerism was largely non-doctrinal and, as such, held considerable appeal to broader audiences. However, Mott's own faith—by her own admission—is still fundamentally rooted in belief in a God who speaks through an inner light. For a discussion of the potential limits of progressive Quaker discourse in diverse, secular communities, see Lyon, *Deliberative Acts*, 22–24.

48 Greene, *Lucretia Mott*, 85; see also 26, 67.

49 Ibid., 101.

50 Ibid., 43.

51 Cima, *Performing Anti-slavery*, 139.

52 Ibid., 149.

53 Ibid., 148.

54 Kraditor, *Means and Ends*, 59 and note 69; DuBois, *Feminism and Suffrage*, 38.

55 For example, a large majority of the Boston Female Anti-Slavery Society voted to separate from its Garrisonian affiliate and formed a new organization "because of their dismay over the old organization's 'no-government friends.'" See Laurie, "Putting Politics Back In," 82. An equally important reason for the schism is the accession of women into leadership positions in the society and its support for women's rights generally.

56 Lewis Perry, "Versions of Anarchism," 770.

57 Greene, *Lucretia Mott*, 42.

58 Ibid., 118.

59 Ibid., 50.

60 Ibid., 184.

61 Ibid., 140.

62 Ibid., 154.

63 Ibid., 156.

64 Ibid., 156–157.

65 Palmer, *Selected Letters of Lucretia Coffin Mott*, 122.

66 Ibid., 399.

67 The same ambivalence about formal associations prevented Mott from demanding sex-integrated reform societies as other activists did.

68 Palmer, *Selected Letters of Lucretia Coffin Mott*, 211.

69 Mott's views on the Civil War also reflect a qualified anarchism that requires state action only when absolutely necessary. Although Mott declared the conflict a "calamity," she also believed that the struggle should not be unduly prolonged or "stayed by any compromises which shall continue the unequal, cruel war . . . waged from generation to generation, with all the physical force of our government." See ibid., 312; emphasis in original.

70 Greene, *Lucretia Mott*, 132.

CHAPTER 6. ELIZABETH CADY STANTON'S RHETORIC OF RIDICULE AND REFORM

1 DuBois and Smith, *Elizabeth Cady Stanton*, 1–2, 4.

2 Kern, *Mrs. Stanton's Bible.*

3 Thomas, "Elizabeth Cady Stanton," 150. Another legal characterization of Stanton describes her as a product of the codification movement, which attacked common law because it relied on the principle of equity as determined by male authorities and perpetuated cultural and political inequalities. As an alternative, according to Sullivan, codifiers like Stanton asserted a radical concept of the individual that is abstracted from particular social and cultural contexts and thereby ruled out the possibility of gradual and more tenable reform through traditional com-

mon law. See Sullivan, *Constitutional Context*. In their reviews of Sullivan's book, Nancy Isenberg and Nancy Cott argue that Sullivan's case against Stanton is thinly supported by evidence and mischaracterizes the early women's rights movement generally. See Isenberg, "Kathleen S. Sullivan, *Constitutional Context*"; and Cott, "Kathleen S. Sullivan, *Constitutional Context*."

4  The influence of Mary Wollstonecraft's work on Stanton's ideas has been examined as well. See Botting and Carey, "Wollstonecraft's Philosophical Impact."

5  Ginzberg, *Elizabeth Cady Stanton*.

6  Mitchell, "Lower Orders"; Stansell, "Missed Connections"; Caraway, *Segregated Sisterhood*; Newman, *White Women's Rights*; and McDaneld, "Harper, Historiography."

7  Stanton would later claim that she agreed to work with Train out of "desperation" and compared him with the "Devil." See Ginzberg, *Elizabeth Cady Stanton*, 216n53.

8  Skinnell, "Elizabeth Cady Stanton's 1854 'Address to the Legislature of New York,'" 131, 138, 141. See also Stillion Southard, "Rhetoric of Epistemic Privilege."

9  Gordon, "Stanton and the Right to Vote," 112.

10  Ibid., 113.

11  Ibid., 124. Others note the dogged determination of Stanton and Anthony to enfranchise women at whatever cost. See Dudden, *Fighting Chance*; and Tetrault, *Myth of Seneca Falls*.

12  Engbers, "With Great Sympathy."

13  Engbers observes that, in her well-known speech, "Solitude of Self," Stanton deploys a similar version of indirect description as the audience is "allowed to listen in on a private conversation of sorts between Stanton and a hypothetical intimate friend, or at Stanton's own private musings to herself." See ibid., 327. Stanton thereby "demonstrates a sympathetic relationship" by establishing a "triad" between the audience, herself, and the hypothetical friend, "effectively 'flattening' her emotions by washing them through this implied intimate." As a result, observers "become more comfortable because they are not bludgeoned with ideas and emotions inconsonant with their own." See ibid., 329. Engbers's analysis expands on the "feminine style" of rhetoric analyzed in Stanton's work by Karlyn Kohrs Campbell, an inferential rhetorical approach that relies on inductive examples to "make audiences feel as though they were reaching their own conclusions." See ibid., 313. For an expansion of Engbers's study that explores the performative aspects of Stanton's rhetoric, see Tell, "Stanton's 'Solitude of Self.'" Skinnell refers to Stanton's use of enthymeme generally; see Skinnell, "Elizabeth Cady Stanton's 1854 'Address to the Legislature of New York.'"

14  Stanton and Anthony, *Selected Papers*, 1:94–95. In spite of the title, there is no evidence that Stanton actually delivered this speech at the Seneca Falls or Rochester conventions.

15  By emphasizing Stanton's use of ridicule, my analysis also expands on Graban's study of irony in the rhetoric of Helen Gougar, a relatively unknown suffragist and

contemporary of Stanton. Gougar's rhetorical skill in "undermining arguments against suffrage by condescending to stereotypes of regional suffragists in order to overturn them" mirrors Stanton's devastating use of ridicule. By "claiming a shared set of assumptions and then making an ironic turn" and "shifting the emphasis from herself (and other Midwestern suffragists) onto male targets," Gougar uses irony "in order to demonstrate the fallibility of their assumptions" in similar fashion to Stanton. See Graban, "Towards a 'Second-Generation' Suffragism," 38, 47.

16 Stanton and Anthony, *Selected Papers*, 1:96. Stanton repeats this passage almost verbatim in her 1854 "Appeal to the Women of the State of New York." See ibid., 1:285–286.

17 Ibid., 1:244; emphasis added.

18 Ibid., 1:244–245.

19 Ibid., 1:96.

20 The idea that men cannot represent women because of their flawed education reappears in Stanton's 1850 "Address to the Ohio Women's Convention." See ibid., 1:164–166.

21 Ibid., 1:100.

22 Ibid., 1:101.

23 Stanton's description of the drunkard reflects her abiding interest in temperance reform, which was evident as early as 1841, when she addressed a temperance society. See Ginzberg, *Elizabeth Cady Stanton*, 53.

24 For a more detailed discussion of Smith's account of worker alienation, see chapter 1.

25 Stanton and Anthony, *Selected Papers*, 1:98–99. As we have seen, Frances Wright describes the plight of women in similar terms.

26 Ibid., 1:100.

27 Ibid., 1:98.

28 Ibid., 1:100.

29 Ibid., 1:98.

30 Ibid.

31 Ibid., 1:96.

32 Ginzberg, *Elizabeth Cady Stanton*, 69–71.

33 Swift's plain style has led people to underestimate the seriousness of his writings in the belief that he is "nothing out of the common road" and that "each of us . . . could have wrote as well" (*LRBL*, i.104). Swift ultimately passes the "propriety" test because "he never uses that sort of ridicule which may be thrown on any subject by the choice of words, his Language is always correct and Proper and no ornaments are ever introduced nor does he ever write but in a manner most suitable to the Nature of the Subject" (*LRBL*, i.119).

34 Swift's skeptical view of religion mirrors Smith's own critique of established religion and especially the Catholic Church and the Church of England (*WN*, V.i.g).

35 Swift's use of ridicule is consistent with his own character, as his "natural moroseness joined to the constant dissapointments and crosses he met with in life would

make contempt natural to his character; and those follies would most provoke him that partake most of gayety and levity" (*LRBL*, i.118). Those who fancy themselves superior are brought low by Swift's merciless exposure.

36 For Smith, the plain man, like Swift, "never gives any reason for his opinions but affirms them boldly without the least hesitation; and when one expect(s) a reason he meets with nothing but such expressions as, I have always been of opinion that, etc. because etc." (*LRBL*, i.91). It is remarkable how much Stanton reflects this characteristic. "If he mentions any sort of a reason it is only to shew how evident and plain a matter it was and expose the stupidity of the others in not perceiving it as well as he. {He is not <at> all ruffled by contradiction or any irritation whatever but is at pains to shew that this proceeds from his confidence in his superior sense and judgment" (*LRBL*, i.86). We might think that such a harsh orator would be angry or emotional, but for Smith, Swift "never expresses any passion but affirms with a dictatorial gravity" (*LRBL*, i.93). There is no "joy," "grief," "compassion," or "admiration" in the plain man's speech. He does not aim to please, instead reflecting "contempt" and disdain for common trifles (*LRBL*, i.86).

37 Smith devotes book 7 of the *Moral Sentiments* to a systematic critique of the major systems of moral philosophy. Among them is the notion that morality derives from intellectual activity alone. Although "it is by reason that we discover those general rules of justice by which we ought to regulate our actions . . . it is altogether absurd and unintelligible to suppose that the first perceptions of right and wrong can be derived from reason" (*TMS*, VII.iii.2.6–7). Smith's pragmatism and his preference for concrete particulars over abstractions align him more closely with Aristotle than with other moral theorists. See Hanley, *Adam Smith*, 88–90. As Hanley notes, for Smith, Swift's "sentiments are admirable because they are geared towards practical reform, and his style is admirable because, unlike the methods of the moderns, they are well suited to such a project. . . . As moralists, both Smith and Swift thus reject the 'general and abstract speculations' of the moderns and rather hark back to the type of moralizing characteristic of the classical tradition." See Hanley, "Style and Sentiment," 92.

38 In a well-known account that is at least partly apocryphal, Stanton related her early experience upon encountering a religious revival led by Charles Finney. Initially falling under the sway of Finney's fiery preaching, Stanton was "cured" by several weeks of reading philosophy under the care of relatives. See Ginzberg, *Elizabeth Cady Stanton*, 24–25. In an 1842 letter Sarah Grimké laments Stanton's lack of religious faith, which Grimké believes compromised her intellectual gifts. See Stanton and Anthony, *Selected Papers*, 1:39.

39 McKenna, *Adam Smith*, 91.

40 "With regard to justice understood as an individual virtue," both Smith and Swift "argue that the savage passion of indignation is capable of being transformed into an other-directed sentiment distinguished both by its commitment to justice and by its moderation. And with regard to justice understood as a political virtue, both suggest that just practical political action can be motivated by the feelings of

indignation experienced by witnesses to injustice." See Hanley, "Style and Sentiment," 98.

41 Others have noted the emergence of ridicule as an important tool for reform on all sides of the suffrage debate. Even "the response to suffrage in many ridiculing and denouncing publications . . . had political uses in constituting deliberative engagement. . . . The tension between ridicule and support created a national public discourse on suffrage. If some chose to narrate women as ridiculous, dependent, or gentle, narrations lacking in recognition, reciprocity, and respect, those narrations served the purpose of eliciting a response." Stanton would also characterize her provocative "acts as outwardly aimed at engaging interlocutors in the consideration of reform (although it is unclear that that was her earliest or only purpose). . . . The short-term goal of creating dispute exceeded an elusive goal of persuasion." See Lyon, *Deliberative Acts*, 170–171.

42 Stanton and Anthony, *Selected Papers*, 1:104–105.

43 In the same passage Stanton explains that "we have no objection to discuss the question of equality, for we feel that the weight of argument lies wholly with us, but we wish the question of equality kept distinct from the question of rights, for the proof of the one does not determine the truth of the other. The right is ours. The question now is, how should we get possession of what rightfully belongs to us." See ibid.

44 Ibid., 1:96.

45 Ibid., 1:241. Stanton brings in "the alien and the ditch digger" who are granted more rights than "educated and refined" women. See ibid., 1:242. Her reasoning is that "the lowest classes of men are invariably the most hostile to the elevation of woman as they have known her only in ignorance and degradation and ever regarded her in the light of a slave." See ibid., 2:195; see also 2:212, 237; and DuBois and Smith, *Elizabeth Cady Stanton*, 191. In so doing Stanton sets her own dubious precedent for including immigrants of various races and ethnicities among the uneducated men who are allowed to make decisions for all women without their consent. And she laments the fact that chauvinistic young lawyers will be the future legal representatives of women and serve as "Presidents, Judges, Husbands and fathers." See Stanton and Anthony, *Selected Papers*, 1:253. Stanton would return to the theme of tyrannical rule by men who make laws for women without their consent throughout her career.

46 "The Anniversaries," *New York Times*, May 10, 1865.

47 Stanton and Anthony, *Selected Papers*, 1:564. Stanton was not alone in her astonishment at Phillips's sudden reversal after supporting women's rights for over twenty years. Frances Dana Gage, Lucy Stone, and others expressed their dismay as well. The African American reformer Frances Ellen Watkins Harper went a step further by arguing that black women had more immediate need of the vote than black men or even white women because of the unique nature of their oppression, which drew from multiple sources. See Ginzberg, *Elizabeth Cady Stanton*, 119.

48 Gordon, "Stanton and the Right to Vote," 112–113.

49  Stanton and Anthony, *Selected Papers*, 1:564–565. Stanton repeats her support for universal suffrage in various writings and speeches during this time. See ibid., 1:550–551, 580–582, 587–588, 601, and 2:28–32, 63, 147–149.

50  DuBois and Smith, *Elizabeth Cady Stanton*, 173.

51  Engbers refers to this passage and others to explain Stanton's use of indirect description. I am expanding on her findings by emphasizing the elements of ridicule in these passages as well. See Engbers, "With Great Sympathy," 322–323.

52  Stanton and Anthony, *Selected Papers*, 1:103.

53  Ibid., 1:104. Stanton offers an extended version of the hypocrisy regarding the denial of the fundamental principles outlined in the Declaration to women in her 1854 "Address to the New York Legislature."

54  Ibid., 1:106.

55  In this passage, Stanton "closely follows" Sarah Grimké's *Letter on the Equality of the Sexes*. See Stanton and Anthony, *Selected Papers*, 1:119n34.

56  Ibid., 1:108.

57  Ibid.

58  Ibid., 1:99.

59  Ibid.; emphasis in original. The originality of Stanton's interpretation of the Fall is reinforced by the fact that, unlike her explanation of Paul's command to women, it departs from Grimké's influential version. See ibid., 1:118n12.

60  Ibid., 1:105.

61  Ibid., 1:107–108.

62  Stanton, *The Woman's Bible*, 12–13.

63  Buhle and Buhle, *The Concise History of Woman Suffrage*, 254–255.

64  Ibid., 258.

## CHAPTER 7. THE SHADOW AND THE SUBSTANCE OF SOJOURNER TRUTH

1  Painter, *Sojourner Truth*, 187.

2  Gilbert and Truth, *Narrative of Sojourner Truth*, 233.

3  The possible reasons for Truth's illiteracy have been explored in detail. Although Truth had a number of opportunities to learn to read throughout her life, by all accounts she chose not to pursue them. As a slave in New York, Truth did not face the same legal barriers to literacy as slaves in the South, and her owner Dumont did not actively forbid her to learn. By contrast, Frederick Douglass learned to read as soon as he was able and considered literacy to be a key component of freedom and citizenship—not to mention assimilation into white culture. Perhaps as a result, Truth "never became a regular lecturer for antislavery societies, as Douglass did. She never became a member of the decision-making inner councils of the abolitionists, or of the Colored Convention movement, or of the women's suffrage movement, all of which Douglass did. She was also often poor, doubtless in part because of her illiteracy." Truth may have had a learning disability or visual impairment, or perhaps she shrewdly chose to remain illiterate to charm

her white audience and to avoid confrontation with them. See Mabee, "Sojourner Truth, Bold Prophet," 70–73.

4 These accounts and reports of other speeches, taken from various sources, including newspapers as well as Truth's own *Narrative*, were published together in Fitch and Mandziuk, *Sojourner Truth as Orator*.

5 Bennett, *Democratic Discourses*, 78. See also Sernett, *Harriet Tubman*, 15. Truth is an "overdetermined historical figure" because she "comes to us as always already interpreted by others from their own situated and partial perspectives." See Carla Peterson, *"Doers of the Word*," 24.

6 McDaneld, "Harper, Historiography," 393.

7 Truth's experience is uniquely "African American" because it constitutes "a set of performative strategies for resituating and rereading white representation, negotiating the terms not simply of blackness but also of subjectivity and authority, with blackness understood as the historically constituted and contending frameworks within which those negotiations are moderated." See Ernest, "Floating Icon," 461.

8 Painter, *Sojourner Truth*, 9.

9 Painter claims that Truth was emotionally and sexually abused by Joseph and Sally Dumont, based on allusions contained within the *Narrative*. See ibid., 14–15.

10 Quoted in ibid., 180.

11 Carla Peterson, *"Doers of the Word*," 40–41.

12 Another variation, "a'r'n't," appears in Gage's account that was published in the *Anti-Slavery Standard* the same year. See Fitch and Mandziuk, *Sojourner Truth as Orator*, 103–104. By comparison, other references to the speech simply state that Truth identified herself as a woman. See Washington, *Sojourner Truth's America*, 129.

13 Painter, *Sojourner Truth*, 7.

14 Quoted in ibid., 158. Gage's portrayal of Truth, like Stowe's, reinforces another white supremacist stereotype, the "African exotic." This depiction "paradoxically conveyed her oppositional voice yet diminished her presence." Supporters and opponents "alike reverted to this imagery of the pastoral exotic in their struggle to respond to the challenge Truth posed to dominant conceptions of race and gender roles." See Mandziuk, "Grotesque and Ludicrous, but yet Inspiring," 472.

15 Margaret Washington, *Narrative of Sojourner Truth*, xxxii.

16 Bennett, *Democratic Discourses*, 83.

17 Douglass, "What I Found at the Northampton Association," 131–132.

18 Another well-known encounter between Truth and Douglass occurred in 1852. According to several newspaper accounts written right afterward, upon hearing Douglass concede that slavery could only be abolished through force, Truth rose and asked, "Is God gone?" The popular account, which was created by Stowe several years later, rewords Truth's question, "Frederick, is God dead?" As with Truth's Akron speech, the popular account took hold in the minds of Americans, even appearing on her tombstone. "Is God dead?" became shorthand for Truth's abiding faith in God and divine providence. However, the earlier newspaper accounts depicted a dramatic clash of ideas between Douglass, who supported

federal military intervention to end slavery, and Truth, who continued to preach non-violence. Truth's question alludes to what many would consider Douglass's betrayal of his own principles, his turn to violence symbolizing his degradation to a mere "politician" who had also lost his faith in a benevolent God, using his rhetorical gifts not to uplift his audience but rather to provoke them. In his later recollection of the event, Douglass admitted that Truth, his "quaint old sister," was "shocked at my sanguinary doctrine" and observed that, after she spoke, "we were all for a moment brought to a stand-still, just as we should have been if someone had thrown a brick through the window." Other accounts would corroborate Truth's ability to attack her opponents, especially politicians, with a single word or phrase, like a "bullet," "arrow," or "dart." See Mabee, *Sojourner Truth: Slave, Prophet, Legend*, 83–88.

19  Mandziuk, "Grotesque and Ludicrous, but yet Inspiring," 469–470. A description of Truth that conveys similar mixed messages appears in a Rochester, New York, newspaper: "The lecturer is a child of nature, gifted beyond the common measure, witty, shrewd, sarcastic, with an open, broad honesty of heart, and unbounded kindness. Wholly untaught in the schools, she is herself a study for the philosophers, and a wonder to all. Her natural powers of observation, discrimination, comparison, and intuition are rare indeed, and only equaled by her straightforward common sense and earnest practical benevolence. She is always sensible, always suggestive, always original, earnest, and practical, often eloquent and profound." Those who attend will be "edified, entertained, and even amused, without frivolity." See Gilbert and Truth, *Narrative of Sojourner Truth*, 227–228.

20  Mandziuk, "Grotesque and Ludicrous, but yet Inspiring," 480.

21  Ibid., 470.

22  In the same volume that contains Douglass's "What I Found at the Northampton Association," Truth is revealed to be the "chief laundress of week days." See Sheffeld, *History of Florence*, 96.

23  Mabee, "Sojourner Truth, Bold Prophet," 70–71.

24  Ibid.

25  Ibid. A possible indication that Truth envisioned herself among equals appears in the description of her decision to live with the Northampton Association of Education and Industry, a utopian community in Massachusetts composed of white abolitionists and freed blacks that was based on cooperative ownership. "As soon as she saw that accomplished, literary and refined persons were living in that plain and simple manner, and submitting to the labors and privations incident to such an infant institution . . . she gradually became pleased with, and attached to, the place and the people." See Gilbert and Truth, *Narrative of Sojourner Truth*, 120.

26  Gilbert and Truth, *Narrative of Sojourner Truth*, 108.

27  Ibid., 111–112. Truth views another important Christian doctrine, the Trinity, with equal skepticism. Given Truth's involvement with Quakers during her lawsuit, it would not be surprising to see elements of their religious beliefs in her own as well.

28 Ibid., 108–109.

29 Ibid., 109.

30 Mandziuk, "Grotesque and Ludicrous, but yet Inspiring," 478–479. Gage herself should be counted among those who were wary of allowing black women to attend or speak at the meeting because they were influenced by Jane Swisshelm, a novelist and newspaper editor who supported women's rights only if they were considered separately from abolitionism.

31 Buhle and Buhle, *The Concise History of Woman Suffrage*, 104.

32 Given that Truth would later criticize women's rights advocates for their frippery and fashionable dress, it is possible that she is mocking their apparent embrace of feminine weakness here as well. See Mabee, *Sojourner Truth: Slave, Prophet, Legend*, 190–191.

33 Washington, *Narrative of Sojourner Truth*, 117–118.

34 Ibid.

35 Ibid.

36 Buhle and Buhle, *The Concise History of Woman Suffrage*, 235–236.

37 Ibid.

38 Stanton and Anthony, *Selected Papers*, 1:564–565; see also 1:581–582, and 2:65–66, 194–198, 215–219, 261.

39 Buhle and Buhle, *The Concise History of Woman Suffrage*, 235.

40 Benhabib, "The Generalized and the Concrete Other."

CONCLUSION

1 Adewunmi, "Kimberlé Crenshaw."

2 Jason Frank, *Constituent Moments*; and Holland, "After Antigone," 1129.

3 Beaumont, *Civic Constitution*, 2.

# BIBLIOGRAPHY

Abruzzo, Margaret Nicola. *Polemical Pain: Slavery, Cruelty, and the Rise of Humanitarianism*. Baltimore: Johns Hopkins University Press, 2011.

Adewunmi, Bim. "Kimberlé Crenshaw on Intersectionality: 'I Wanted to Come up with an Everyday Metaphor That Anyone Could Use.'" *New Statesman*, April 2, 2014.

Allen, Barbara. *Tocqueville, Covenant, and the Democratic Revolution: Harmonizing Earth with Heaven*. Lanham, MD: Lexington Books, 2005.

Anderson, Bonnie S. *Joyous Greetings: The First International Women's Movement, 1830–1860*. New York: Oxford University Press, 2000.

Bacon, Jacqueline. *The Humblest May Stand Forth: Rhetoric, Empowerment, and Abolition*. Columbia: University of South Carolina Press, 2002.

Bacon, Jacqueline, and Glen McClish. "Reinventing the Master's Tools: Nineteenth-Century African-American Literary Societies of Philadelphia and Rhetorical Education." *Rhetoric Society Quarterly* 30, no. 4 (2000): 19–47.

Bartlett, Elizabeth Ann. *Liberty, Equality, Sorority: The Origins and Interpretation of American Feminist Thought: Frances Wright, Sarah Grimke, and Margaret Fuller*. Brooklyn, NY: Carlson Publishers, 1994.

Beaumont, Elizabeth. *The Civic Constitution: Civic Visions and Struggles in the Path toward Constitutional Democracy*. New York: Oxford University Press, 2014.

Bederman, Gail. "Revisiting Nashoba: Slavery, Utopia, and Frances Wright in America, 1818–1826." *American Literary History* 17, no. 3 (Fall 2005): 438–459.

Beecher, Catharine E. *An Essay on Slavery and Abolitionism: With Reference to the Duty of American Females*. 2nd ed. Philadelphia: Henry Perkins, 1837.

———. "The Peculiar Responsibilities of American Women." Chap. 1 in *A Treatise on Domestic Economy*, 3–38. New York: Source Book Press, 1970.

———. *A Treatise on Domestic Economy*. Boston: Marsh, Capen, Lyon, & Webb, 1841.

Benhabib, Seyla. "The Generalized and the Concrete Other: The Kohlberg-Gilligan Controversy and Feminist Theory." *Praxis International* 5, no. 23 (1986): 402–424.

Bennett, Michael. *Democratic Discourses: The Radical Abolition Movement and Antebellum American Literature*. New Brunswick, NJ: Rutgers University Press, 2005.

Bentham, Jeremy. *The Works of Jeremy Bentham*. Edited by John Bowring. Edinburgh: Tait, 1843.

Berlant, Lauren Gail. *The Female Complaint: The Unfinished Business of Sentimentality in American Culture*. Durham, NC: Duke University Press, 2008.

———. *The Queen of America Goes to Washington City: Essays on Sex and Citizenship.* Durham, NC: Duke University Press, 1997.

Bevilacqua, Vincent M. "Adam Smith and Some Philosophical Origins of Eighteenth-Century Rhetorical Theory." *Modern Language Review* 63, no. 3 (1968): 559–568.

Botting, Eileen Hunt. *Family Feuds: Wollstonecraft, Burke, and Rousseau on the Transformation of the Family.* Albany: State University of New York Press, 2006.

———. "Wollstonecraft in Europe, 1792–1904: A Revisionist Reception History." *History of European Ideas* 39, no. 4 (2013): 503–527.

Botting, Eileen Hunt, and Christine Carey. "Wollstonecraft's Philosophical Impact on Nineteenth-Century American Women's Rights Advocates." *American Journal of Political Science* 48, no. 4 (2004): 707–722.

Botting, Eileen Hunt, and Sarah L. Houser. "'Drawing the Line of Equality': Hannah Mather Crocker on Women's Rights." *American Political Science Review* 100, no. 2 (2006): 265–278.

Botting, Eileen Hunt, and Charlotte Hammond Matthews. "Overthrowing the Floresta-Wollstonecraft Myth for Latin American Feminism." *Gender and History* 26, no. 1 (2014): 64–83.

Boyd, Richard, and Ewa Atanassow, eds. *Tocqueville and the Frontiers of Democracy.* Cambridge: Cambridge University Press, 2013.

Branson, Roy. "James Madison and the Scottish Enlightenment." *Journal of the History of Ideas* 40, no. 2 (1979): 235–250.

Broadie, Alexander. "Sympathy and the Impartial Spectator." In *The Cambridge Companion to Adam Smith*, edited by Knud Haakonssen, 158–188. New York: Cambridge University Press, 2006.

Brodie, Janet Farrell. *Contraception and Abortion in Nineteenth-Century America.* Ithaca, NY: Cornell University Press, 1994.

Brown, Amy Benson. "'A System of Complicated Crimes': Confusion of Subjects in Angelina Grimke's Public Speeches." *Women's Studies* 27, no. 1 (1998): 31–52.

Browne, Stephen H. *Angelina Grimké: Rhetoric, Identity, and the Radical Imagination.* East Lansing: Michigan State University Press, 1999.

———. "Encountering Angelina Grimke: Violence, Identity, and the Creation of Radical Community." *Quarterly Journal of Speech* 82, no. 1 (1996): 55–73.

Buccola, Nicholas. *The Political Thought of Frederick Douglass: In Pursuit of American Liberty.* New York: New York University Press, 2012.

Buhle, Mari Jo, and Paul Buhle, eds. *The Concise History of Woman Suffrage: Selections from History of Woman Suffrage, Edited by Elizabeth Cady Stanton, Susan B. Anthony, Matilda Joslyn Gage, and the National American Woman Suffrage Association.* Urbana: University of Illinois Press, 2005.

Caine, Barbara. *English Feminism, 1780–1980.* New York: Oxford University Press, 1997.

Callanan, Laura. "Race and the Politics of Interpretative Disruption in Harriet Martineau's 'The Hour and the Man' (1841)." *Women's Writing* 9, no. 3 (2002): 413–432.

Calvert, Jane E. *Quaker Constitutionalism and the Political Thought of John Dickinson.* Cambridge: Cambridge University Press, 2009.

———. "The Quaker Theory of a Civil Constitution." *History of Political Thought* 27, no. 4 (2006): 586–619.

Camfield, Gregg. "The Moral Aesthetics of Sentimentality: A Missing Key to 'Uncle Tom's Cabin.'" *Nineteenth-Century Literature* 43, no. 3 (1988): 319–345.

Campbell, Karlyn Kohrs. "Femininity and Feminism: To Be or Not to Be a Woman." *Communication Quarterly* 31, no. 2 (1983): 101–108.

Caraway, Nancie. *Segregated Sisterhood: Racism and the Politics of American Feminism.* 1st ed. Knoxville: University of Tennessee Press, 1991.

Carlacio, Jami. "'Ye Knew Your Duty, but Ye Did It Not': The Epistolary Rhetoric of Sarah Grimké." *Rhetoric Review* 21, no. 3 (2002): 247–263.

Ceniza, Sherry. *Walt Whitman and 19th-Century Women Reformers.* Tuscaloosa: University of Alabama Press, 1998.

Ceplair, Larry, ed. *The Public Years of Sarah and Angelina Grimke: Selected Writings, 1835–1839.* New York: Columbia University Press, 1989.

Cima, Gay Gibson. *Performing Anti-slavery: Activist Women on Antebellum Stages.* Cambridge: Cambridge University Press, 2014.

Claeys, Gregory. *Citizens and Saints: Politics and Anti-politics in Early British Socialism.* Cambridge: Cambridge University Press, 1989.

———. "Utopianism, Property, and the French Revolution Debate in Britain." In *Utopias and the Millennium,* edited by Krishan Kumar and Stephen Bann, 46–62. London: Reaktion, 1993.

Cooke, Jacob E., ed. *The Federalist.* Middletown, CT: Wesleyan University Press, 1961.

Corrigan, John. "'Habits from the Heart': The American Enlightenment and Religious Ideas about Emotion and Habit." *Journal of Religion* 73, no. 2 (1993): 183–199.

Cott, Nancy F. *The Bonds of Womanhood: "Woman's Sphere" in New England, 1780–1835.* 2nd ed. New Haven, CT: Yale University Press, 1977.

———. "Kathleen S. Sullivan, *Constitutional Context: Women and Rights Discourse in Nineteenth-Century America*" (review). *American Historical Review* 113, no. 5 (2008): 1534.

Craiutu, Aurelian, and Jeffrey C. Isaac, eds. *America through European Eyes: British and French Reflections on the New World from the Eighteenth Century to the Present.* University Park: Pennsylvania State University Press, 2009.

Crook, D. P. "The United States in Bentham's Thought." In *Jeremy Bentham: Critical Assessments,* edited by Bhikhu C. Parekh, 276–286. New York: Routledge, 1993.

Darwall, Stephen. "Sympathetic Liberalism: Recent Work on Adam Smith." *Philosophy and Public Affairs* 28, no. 2 (1999): 139–164.

David, Deirdre. *Intellectual Women and Victorian Patriarchy: Harriet Martineau, Elizabeth Barrett Browning, George Eliot.* Ithaca, NY: Cornell University Press, 1987.

Davis, Sue. *The Political Thought of Elizabeth Cady Stanton: Women's Rights and the American Political Tradition.* New York: NYU Press, 2008.

Debes, Remy. "Adam Smith on Dignity and Equality." *British Journal for the History of Philosophy* 20, no. 1 (2012): 109–140.

Deneen, Patrick J., and Joseph Romance, eds. *Democracy's Literature: Politics and Fiction in America.* Lanham, MD: Rowman & Littlefield, 2005.

Donovan, Josephine. *Feminist Theory: The Intellectual Traditions.* 4th ed. New York: Continuum, 2012.

Douglas, Ann. *The Feminization of American Culture.* 1st ed. New York: Knopf, 1977.

Douglass, Frederick. "What I Found at the Northampton Association." In *The History of Florence, Massachusetts,* edited by Charles Arthur Sheffeld. Florence, MA: Charles Arthur Sheffeld, 1895.

DuBois, Ellen Carol. *Feminism and Suffrage: The Emergence of an Independent Women's Movement in America, 1848–1869.* Ithaca, NY: Cornell University Press, 1999.

———. "Outgrowing the Compact of the Fathers: Equal Rights, Woman Suffrage, and the United States Constitution, 1820–1878." *Journal of American History* 74, no. 3 (1987): 836–862.

DuBois, Ellen Carol, and Richard Cándida Smith, eds. *Elizabeth Cady Stanton, Feminist as Thinker: A Reader in Documents and Essays.* New York: New York University Press, 2007.

Dudden, Faye E. *Fighting Chance: The Struggle over Woman Suffrage and Black Suffrage in Reconstruction America.* New York: Oxford University Press, 2011.

Durso, Pamela R. *The Power of Woman: The Life and Writings of Sarah Moore Grimke.* 1st ed. Macon, GA: Mercer University Press, 2003.

Easley, Alexis. "Gendered Observations: Harriet Martineau and the Woman Question." In *Victorian Women Writers and the Woman Question,* edited by Nicola Diane Thompson, 80–98. New York: Cambridge University Press, 1999.

Eastman, Carolyn. *A Nation of Speechifiers: Making an American Public after the Revolution.* Chicago: University of Chicago Press, 2010.

Elbert, Monika M. *Separate Spheres No More: Gender Convergence in American Literature, 1830–1930.* Tuscaloosa: University of Alabama Press, 2000.

Engbers, Susanna Kelly. "With Great Sympathy: Elizabeth Cady Stanton's Innovative Appeals to Emotion." *Rhetoric Society Quarterly* 37, no. 3 (2007): 307–332.

Ernest, John. "The Floating Icon and the Fluid Text: Rereading the Narrative of Sojourner Truth." *American Literature* 78, no. 3 (2006): 459–486.

Fanuzzi, Robert. *Abolition's Public Sphere.* Minneapolis: University of Minnesota Press, 2003.

Faulkner, Carol. *Lucretia Mott's Heresy: Abolition and Women's Rights in Nineteenth-Century America.* Philadelphia: University of Pennsylvania Press, 2011.

Faulkner, Carol, and Alison M. Parker, eds. *Interconnections: Gender and Race in American History.* Rochester, NY: University of Rochester Press, 2012.

Fitch, Suzanne Pullon, and Roseann M. Mandziuk, eds. *Sojourner Truth as Orator: Wit, Story, and Song.* Westport, CT: Greenwood Press, 1997.

Fleischacker, Samuel. "Adam Smith and Cultural Relativism." *Erasmus Journal for Philosophy and Economics* 4, no. 2 (2011): 20–41.

———. "Adam Smith's Reception among the American Founders, 1776–1790." *William and Mary Quarterly* 59, no. 4 (2002): 897–915.

Flexner, Eleanor, and Ellen F. Fitzpatrick, eds. *Century of Struggle: The Woman's Rights Movement in the United States.* Cambridge, MA: Belknap Press of Harvard University Press, 1996.

Fong, Edmund. *American Exceptionalism and the Remains of Race: Multicultural Exorcisms.* New York: Routledge, 2015.

Fornieri, Joseph R. *Abraham Lincoln: Philosopher Statesman.* Carbondale: Southern Illinois University Press, 2014.

———. *Abraham Lincoln's Political Faith.* DeKalb: Northern Illinois University Press, 2005.

Frank, David A., and Mark Lawrence McPhail. "Barack Obama's Address to the 2004 Democratic National Convention: Trauma, Compromise, Consilience, and the (Im)Possibility of Racial Reconciliation." *Rhetoric and Public Affairs* 8, no. 4 (2006): 571–593.

Frank, Jason. "'Besides Our Selves': An Essay on Enthusiastic Politics and Civil Subjectivity." *Public Culture* 17, no. 3 (2005): 371–392.

———. *Constituent Moments: Enacting the People in Postrevolutionary America.* Durham, NC: Duke University Press, 2010.

———, ed. *Political Companion to Herman Melville.* Lexington: University Press of Kentucky, 2014.

———. "Promiscuous Citizenship." In *A Political Companion to Walt Whitman*, edited by John Evan Seery, 155–184. Lexington: University Press of Kentucky, 2011.

———. "Publius and Political Imagination." *Political Theory* 37, no. 1 (2009): 69–98.

Fraser, Nancy. "Rethinking the Public Sphere: A Contribution to the Critique of Actually Existing Democracy." In *Habermas and the Public Sphere*, edited by Craig Calhoun, 109–142. Cambridge, MA: MIT Press, 1992.

Freedgood, Elaine. "Banishing Panic: Harriet Martineau and the Popularization of Political Economy." *Victorian Studies* 39, no. 1 (1995): 33–52.

Fruchtman, Jack. *The Political Philosophy of Thomas Paine.* Baltimore: Johns Hopkins University Press, 2009.

Gardner, Catherine Villanueva. *Empowerment and Interconnectivity: Toward a Feminist History of Utilitarian Philosophy.* University Park: Pennsylvania State University Press, 2013.

Gilbert, Olive, and Sojourner Truth. *Narrative of Sojourner Truth, a Bondswoman of Olden Time: With a History of Her Labors and Correspondence Drawn from Her "Book of Life."* Schomburg Library of Nineteenth-Century Black Women Writers. New York: Oxford University Press, 1991.

Ginzberg, Lori D. *Elizabeth Cady Stanton: An American Life.* 1st ed. New York: Hill & Wang, 2009.

———. *Untidy Origins: A Story of Woman's Rights in Antebellum New York.* Chapel Hill: University of North Carolina Press, 2005.

———. *Women and the Work of Benevolence: Morality, Politics, and Class in the Nineteenth-Century United States.* New Haven, CT: Yale University Press, 1990.

Goldstein, Leslie Friedman. "Europe Looks at American Women, 1820–1840." *Social Research* 54, no. 3 (1987): 419–542.

Gordon, Ann D. "Stanton and the Right to Vote: On Account of Race and Sex." In *Elizabeth Cady Stanton, Feminist as Thinker: A Reader in Documents and Essays*, edited by Ellen Carol DuBois and Richard Cándida Smith, 111–127. New York: New York University Press, 2007.

Graban, Tarez Samra. "Towards a 'Second-Generation' Suffragism: Language Politics in the Ironic Discourse of an American Suffragist." *Gender and Language* 5, no. 1 (2011): 31–59.

Greene, Dana, ed. *Lucretia Mott: Her Complete Speeches and Sermons*, vol. 4. Lewiston, ME: Edwin Mellen Press, 1980.

Greiner, Rae. *Sympathetic Realism in Nineteenth-Century British Fiction*. Baltimore: Johns Hopkins University Press, 2012.

Griswold, Charles L. *Adam Smith and the Virtues of Enlightenment*. New York: Cambridge University Press, 1999.

Gunther-Canada, Wendy. *Rebel Writer: Mary Wollstonecraft and Enlightenment Politics*. DeKalb: Northern Illinois University Press, 2001.

Haakonssen, Knud, ed. *Adam Smith: The Theory of Moral Sentiments*. New York: Cambridge University Press, 2002.

Habermas, Jürgen, Sara Lennox, and Frank Lennox. "The Public Sphere: An Encyclopedia Article (1964)." *New German Critique*, no. 3 (Autumn 1974): 49–55.

Hall, Mark David. "Beyond Self-Interest: The Political Theory and Practice of Evangelical Women in Antebellum America." *Journal of Church and State* 44, no. 3 (2002): 477–499.

Hanley, Ryan Patrick. *Adam Smith and the Character of Virtue*. New York: Cambridge University Press, 2009.

———. "Style and Sentiment: Smith and Swift." In "Symposium: Adam Smith and His Sources," guest editor, Douglas J. Den Uyl. *The Adam Smith Review*, vol. 4, edited by Vivienne Brown, 88–105. London: Routledge, in association with the Adam Smith Society, 2008.

Hardesty, Nancy. *Women Called to Witness: Evangelical Feminism in the Nineteenth Century*. 2nd ed. Knoxville: University of Tennessee Press, 1999.

Henderson, Christine Dunn, ed. *Seers and Judges: American Literature as Political Philosophy*. Lanham, MD: Lexington Books, 2002.

Hendler, Glenn. *Public Sentiments: Structures of Feeling in Nineteenth-Century American Literature*. Chapel Hill: University of North Carolina Press, 2001.

Henry, Katherine. *Liberalism and the Culture of Security: The Nineteenth-Century Rhetoric of Reform*. Tuscaloosa: University of Alabama Press, 2011.

Hersh, Blanche Glassman. *The Slavery of Sex: Feminist-Abolitionists in America*. Urbana: University of Illinois Press, 1978.

Hewitt, Nancy A. "From Seneca Falls to Suffrage? Reimagining a 'Master' Narrative in U.S. Women's History." In *No Permanent Waves: Recasting Histories of U.S. Feminism*, 15–38. New Brunswick, NJ: Rutgers University Press, 2010.

———. "'Seeking a Larger Liberty': Remapping First Wave Feminism." In *Women's Rights and Transatlantic Antislavery in the Era of Emancipation*, edited by Kathryn

Kish and James Brewer Stewart Sklar, 266–278. New Haven, CT: Yale University Press, 2007.

———. *Women's Activism and Social Change: Rochester, New York, 1822–1872.* Ithaca, NY: Cornell University Press, 1984.

Hill, Michael R., and Susan Hoecker-Drysdale. "Taking Harriet Martineau Seriously in the Classroom and Beyond." In *Harriet Martineau: Theoretical and Methodological Perspectives,* edited by Michael R. Hill and Susan Hoecker-Drysdale. New York: Routledge, 2001.

Hoecker-Drysdale, Susan. *Harriet Martineau: First Woman Sociologist.* New York: St. Martin's Press, 1992.

Hoffert, Sylvia D. *When Hens Crow: The Woman's Rights Movement in Antebellum America.* Bloomington: Indiana University Press, 1995; reprint, 2002.

Holland, Catherine A. "After Antigone: Women, the Past, and the Future of Feminist Political Thought." *American Journal of Political Science* 42, no. 4 (1998): 1108–1132.

Hovet, Ted. "Harriet Martineau's Exceptional American Narratives: Harriet Beecher Stowe, John Brown, and the 'Redemption of Your National Soul.'" *American Studies* 48, no. 1 (2007): 63–76.

Howard, June. "What Is Sentimentality?" *American Literary History* 11, no. 1 (1999): 63–81.

Hunter, Shelagh. *Harriet Martineau: The Poetics of Moralism.* Brookfield, VT: Scolar Press, 1995.

Huzel, James P. *The Popularization of Malthus in Early Nineteenth-Century England: Martineau, Cobbett and the Pauper Press.* Burlington, VT: Ashgate, 2006.

Isaac, Jeffrey C. "Republicanism v. Liberalism? A Reconsideration." *History of Political Thought* 9 (Summer 1988): 349–377.

Isenberg, Nancy. "Kathleen S. Sullivan, *Constitutional Context: Women and Rights Discourse in Nineteenth-Century America*" (review). *Law and History Review* 26, no. 2 (2008): 446–448.

———. *Sex and Citizenship in Antebellum America.* Chapel Hill: University of North Carolina Press, 1998.

Jaffa, Harry V. *Crisis of the House Divided: An Interpretation of the Issues in the Lincoln-Douglas Debates.* Chicago: University of Chicago Press, 1982.

Janara, Laura. *Democracy Growing Up: Authority, Autonomy, and Passion in Tocqueville's Democracy in America.* Albany: State University of New York Press, 2002.

Johnson, Nan. *Nineteenth-Century Rhetoric in North America.* Carbondale: Southern Illinois University Press, 1991.

Jose, Jim. "No More like Pallas Athena: Displacing Patrilineal Accounts of Modern Feminist Political Theory." *Hypatia* 19, no. 4 (2004): 1–22.

Kapust, Daniel J., and Michelle A. Schwarze. "The Rhetoric of Sincerity: Cicero and Smith on Propriety and Political Context." *American Political Science Review* 110, no. 1 (2016): 100–111.

Karcher, Carolyn. "Frances Wright of the *Free Enquirer*: Woman Editor in a Man's World." In *Blue Pencils and Hidden Hands: Women Editing Periodicals, 1830–1910,* edited by Sharon M. Harris and Ellen Gruber Garvey, 80–95. Boston: Northeastern University Press, 2004.

Kateb, George. *Lincoln's Political Thought*. Cambridge, MA: Harvard University Press, 2015.

Kelly, Duncan. *The Propriety of Liberty: Persons, Passions and Judgment in Modern Political Thought*. Princeton, NJ: Princeton University Press, 2011.

Kerber, Linda K. "Separate Spheres, Female Worlds, Woman's Place: The Rhetoric of Women's History." *Journal of American History* 75, no. 1 (1988): 9–39.

Kern, Kathi. *Mrs. Stanton's Bible*. Ithaca, NY: Cornell University Press, 2001.

Kissel, Susan S. *In Common Cause: The "Conservative" Frances Trollope and the "Radical" Frances Wright*. Bowling Green, OH: Bowling Green State University Popular Press, 1993.

Klaver, Claudia C. *A/Moral Economics: Classical Political Economy and Cultural Authority in Nineteenth-Century England*. Columbus: Ohio State University Press, 2003.

Kloppenberg, James T. *Reading Obama: Dreams, Hope, and the American Political Tradition*. Princeton, NJ: Princeton University Press, 2011.

———. "The Virtues of Liberalism: Christianity, Republicanism, and Ethics in Early American Political Discourse." *Journal of American History* 74, no. 1 (1987): 9–33.

Kornfeld, Eve. "From Republicanism to Liberalism: The Intellectual Journey of David Ramsay." *Journal of the Early Republic* 9, no. 3 (1989): 289–313.

Kotef, Hagar. "On Abstractness: First Wave Liberal Feminism and the Construction of the Abstract Woman." *Feminist Studies* 35, no. 3 (2009): 495–522.

Kraditor, Aileen. *Means and Ends in American Abolitionism*. New York: Pantheon, 1969.

Laurie, Bruce. "Putting Politics Back In: Rethinking the Problem of Political Abolitionism." In *William Lloyd Garrison at 200: History, Legacy, and Memory*, edited by James Brewer Stewart. New Haven, CT: Yale University Press, 2008.

Lawler, Peter Augustine. "Walt Whitman as Political Thinker." In *A Political Companion to Walt Whitman*, edited by John Evan Seery. Lexington: University Press of Kentucky, 2011.

Lee, Maurice S. *Slavery, Philosophy, and American Literature, 1830–1860*. New York: Cambridge University Press, 2005.

Leeman, Richard W. *The Teleological Discourse of Barack Obama*. Lanham, MD: Lexington Books, 2012.

Lerner, Gerda. "Comment on Lerner's 'Sarah M. Grimké's "Sisters of Charity."'" *Signs: Journal of Women in Culture and Society* 10, no. 4 (1985): 811–815.

———. *The Creation of Feminist Consciousness: From the Middle Ages to Eighteen-Seventy*. New York: Oxford University Press, 1993.

———. *The Feminist Thought of Sarah Grimké*. New York: Oxford University Press, 1998.

———. *The Grimké Sisters from South Carolina: Rebels against Slavery*. Boston: Houghton Mifflin, 1967. Reprinted and retitled as *The Grimké Sisters from South Carolina:*

*Pioneers for Woman's Rights and Abolition.* New York: Oxford University Press, 1998; reprint, Chapel Hill: University of North Carolina Press, 2004.

———. "Sarah M. Grimke's 'Sisters of Charity.'" *Signs: Journal of Women in Culture and Society* 1, no. 1 (1975): 246–256.

Lipset, Seymour Martin, ed. *Harriet Martineau: Society in America.* 1962; reprint, New Brunswick, NJ: Transaction Books, 1981.

Logan, Deborah Anna, ed. *Harriet Martineau: Illustrations of Political Economy, Selected Tales.* Peterborough, Ontario: Broadview Press, 2004.

———. *The Hour and the Woman: Harriet Martineau's "Somewhat Remarkable" Life.* DeKalb: Northern Illinois University Press, 2002.

Lyon, Arabella. *Deliberative Acts: Democracy, Rhetoric, and Rights.* University Park: Pennsylvania State University Press, 2013.

Mabee, Carleton. "Sojourner Truth, Bold Prophet: Why Did She Never Learn to Read?" *New York History* 69, no. 1 (1988): 55–77.

———. *Sojourner Truth: Slave, Prophet, Legend.* With Susan Mabee Newhouse. New York: New York University Press, 1993.

Mandziuk, R. M. "'Grotesque and Ludicrous, but yet Inspiring': Depictions of Sojourner Truth and Rhetorics of Domination." *Quarterly Journal of Speech* 100, no. 4 (2014): 467–487.

Marilley, Suzanne M. *Woman Suffrage and the Origins of Liberal Feminism in the United States, 1820–1920.* Cambridge, MA: Harvard University Press, 1996.

Martineau, Harriet. *Harriet Martineau's Autobiography.* Edited by Linda Peterson. Peterborough, ON: Broadview Press, 2007.

———. *How to Observe: Morals and Manners.* London: Charles Knight & Co., 1838; reprint, Brunswick, NJ: Transaction Publishers, 1989.

———. *Miscellanies.* Boston: Hilliard, Gray, 1836; reprint, New York: AMS Press, 1975.

———. *Retrospect of Western Travel.* 3 vols. London: Saunders & Otley, 1838.

———. *Society in America.* 3 vols. New York: Saunders & Otley, 1837; reprint, New York: AMS Press, 1966.

———. *Writings on Slavery and the American Civil War.* Edited by Deborah Anna Logan. DeKalb: Northern Illinois University Press, 2002.

Matthews, Jean. "Race, Sex, and the Dimensions of Liberty in Antebellum America." *Journal of the Early Republic* 6, no. 3 (1986): 275–291.

McCoy, Drew R. *The Last of the Fathers: James Madison and the Republican Legacy.* New York: Cambridge University Press, 1989.

McDaneld, Jen. "Harper, Historiography, and the Race/Gender Opposition in Feminism." *Signs: Journal of Women in Culture and Society* 40, no. 2 (Winter 2015): 393–415.

McKenna, Stephen J. *Adam Smith: The Rhetoric of Propriety.* Albany: State University of New York Press, 2006.

Melder, Keith E. *Beginnings of Sisterhood: The American Woman's Rights Movement, 1800–1850.* New York: Schocken Books, 1977.

Michaelson, Patricia Howell. *Speaking Volumes: Women, Reading, and Speech in the Age of Austen.* Stanford, CA: Stanford University Press, 2002.

Mitchell, Michele. "'Lower Orders,' Racial Hierarchies, and Rights Rhetoric: Evolutionary Echoes in Elizabeth Cady Stanton's Thought during the Late 1860s." In *Elizabeth Cady Stanton, Feminist as Thinker: A Reader in Documents and Essays*, edited by Ellen Carol DuBois and Richard Cándida Smith, 128–154. New York: New York University Press, 2007.

Morel, Lucas E. *Lincoln's Sacred Effort: Defining Religion's Role in American Self-Government*. Lanham, MD: Lexington Books, 2000.

Morris, Celia. *Fanny Wright: Rebel in America*. Urbana: University of Illinois Press / Illini Books, 1992.

Murphy, Andrew R. *Conscience and Community: Revisiting Toleration and Religious Dissent in Early Modern England and America*. University Park: Pennsylvania State University Press, 2001.

———. "The Limits and Promise of Political Theorizing: William Penn and the Founding of Pennsylvania." *History of Political Thought* 34, no. 4 (2013): 639–688.

———. "Trial Transcript as Political Theory: Principles and Performance in the Penn-Mead Case." *Political Theory* 41, no. 6 (2013): 775–808.

Newman, Louise Michele. *White Women's Rights: The Racial Origins of Feminism in the United States*. New York: Oxford University Press, 1999.

Obama, Barack. "Inaugural Address." In *Compilation of Presidential Documents*. Washington, DC: Office of the Federal Register, National Archives and Records Administration, 2013.

———. "Remarks Commemorating the 50th Anniversary of the Selma to Montgomery Marches for Voting Rights." In *Compilation of Presidential Documents*. Washington, DC: Office of the Federal Register, National Archives and Records Administration, 2015.

O'Neill, Daniel I. "John Adams versus Mary Wollstonecraft on the French Revolution and Democracy." *Journal of the History of Ideas* 68, no. 3 (2007): 451–476.

Owen, Robert. *Observations on the Effect of the Manufacturing System with Hints for the Improvement of Those Parts of Which Are Most Injurious to Health and Morals*. London, Edinborough, and Glasgow: Longman, Hurst, Rees, Orme, & Brown [etc.], 1817.

Pagliaro, Penny. "The Uncommon Education of Lucretia Mott." *Educational Perspectives* 16, no. 1 (1977): 16–22.

Painter, Nell Irvin. *Sojourner Truth: A Life, a Symbol*. 1st ed. New York: W. W. Norton, 1996.

Palmer, Beverly Wilson, ed. *Selected Letters of Lucretia Coffin Mott*. Urbana: University of Illinois Press, 2002.

Pangle, Lorraine Smith. *The Political Philosophy of Benjamin Franklin*. Baltimore: Johns Hopkins University Press, 2007.

Parker, Alison M. *Articulating Rights: Nineteenth-Century American Women on Race, Reform, and the State*. DeKalb: Northern Illinois University Press, 2010.

Perry, Lewis. "Versions of Anarchism in the Antislavery Movement." *American Quarterly* 20, no. 4 (1968): 768–782.

Peterson, Carla L. *"Doers of the Word": African-American Women Speakers and Writers in the North (1830–1880)*. New York: Oxford University Press, 1995.

Peterson, Linda H. *Becoming a Woman of Letters: Myths of Authorship and Facts of the Victorian Market*. Princeton, NJ: Princeton University Press, 2009.

———. "From French Revolution to English Reform: Hannah More, Harriet Martineau, and the 'Little Book.'" *Nineteenth-Century Literature* 60, no. 4 (2006): 409–450.

Pichanick, Valerie Kossew. *Harriet Martineau, the Woman and Her Work, 1802–76*. Ann Arbor: University of Michigan Press, 1980.

Pierson, George Wilson. *Tocqueville and Beaumont in America*. New York: Oxford University Press, 1938.

Pitts, Jennifer. *A Turn to Empire: The Rise of Imperial Liberalism in Britain and France*. Princeton, NJ: Princeton University Press, 2005.

Poston, Carol, ed. *Mary Wollstonecraft: A Vindication of the Rights of Woman*. 2nd ed. New York: W. W. Norton, 1988.

Prochaska, F. K. *Eminent Victorians on American Democracy: The View from Albion*. New York: Oxford University Press, 2012.

Quanquin, Helene. "'There Are Two Great Oceans': The Slavery Metaphor in the Antebellum Women's Rights Discourse as Redescription of Race and Gender." In *Interconnections: Gender and Race in American History*, edited by Carol Faulkner and Alison M. Parker, 75–104. Rochester, NY: University of Rochester Press, 2012.

Reinhardt, Mark. *The Art of Being Free: Taking Liberties with Tocqueville, Marx, and Arendt*. Ithaca, NY: Cornell University Press, 1997.

Rendall, Jane. "Prospects of the American Republic, 1795–1821: The Radical and Utopian Politics of Robina Millar and Frances Wright." In *Enlightenment and Emancipation*, edited by Susan and Peter France Manning. Lewisburg, PA: Bucknell University Press, 2006.

Rhode, Deborah L. "Feminist Critical Theories." *Stanford Law Review* 42, no. 3 (1990): 617–638.

Roberts, Caroline. *The Woman and the Hour: Harriet Martineau and Victorian Ideologies*. Toronto: University of Toronto Press, 2002.

Rosen, F. Introduction. In *The Collected Works of Jeremy Bentham: An Introduction to the Principles of Morals and Legislation*, edited by J. H. Burns and H. L. A. Hart, xxxi–lxix. New York: Oxford University Press, 1996.

Ryan, Mary P. *Women in Public: Between Banners and Ballots, 1825–1880*. Baltimore: Johns Hopkins University Press, 1992.

Sanchez-Eppler, Karen. "Bodily Bonds: The Intersecting Rhetorics of Feminism and Abolition." In *The Culture of Sentiment: Race, Gender, and Sentimentality in Nineteenth-Century America*, edited by Shirley Samuels. New York: Oxford University Press, 1992.

Sanders, Valerie, and Gaby Weiner. "Introduction: The Disciplines and Harriet Martineau." In *Harriet Martineau and the Birth of Disciplines: Nineteenth Century Intellectual Powerhouse*, edited by Valerie Sanders and Gaby Weiner. New York: Routledge, 2017.

Sapiro, Virginia. *A Vindication of Political Virtue: The Political Theory of Mary Woll-stonecraft*. Chicago: University of Chicago Press, 1992.

Scholl, Lesa. "Mediation and Expansion: Harriet Martineau's Travels in America." *Women's History Review* 18, no. 5 (2009): 819–833.

———. *Translation, Authorship and the Victorian Professional Woman: Charlotte Brontë, Harriet Martineau and George Eliot*. Burlington, VT: Ashgate, 2011.

Schultz, Bart. "Obama's Political Philosophy: Pragmatism, Politics, and the University of Chicago." In *Barack Obama: Political Frontiers and Racial Agency*, edited by Ama Mazama and Molefi Kete Asante, 87–130. Thousand Oaks, CA: CQ Press/SAGE, 2012.

Seery, John Evan, ed. *A Political Companion to Walt Whitman*. Lexington: University Press of Kentucky, 2011.

Segrest, Scott Philip. *America and the Political Philosophy of Common Sense*. Columbia: University of Missouri Press, 2010.

Selvidge, Marla. *Notorious Voices: Feminist Biblical Interpretation, 1500–1920*. New York: Continuum Publishing, 1996.

Sernett, Milton C. *Harriet Tubman: Myth, Memory, and History*. Durham, NC: Duke University Press, 2007.

Sheffeld, Charles A. *The History of Florence, Massachusetts*. Florence, MA: Charles A. Sheffeld, 1895.

Sheldon, Garrett Ward. *The Political Philosophy of James Madison*. Baltimore: Johns Hopkins University Press, 2001.

———. *The Political Philosophy of Thomas Jefferson*. Baltimore: Johns Hopkins University Press, 1991.

Skinnell, Ryan. "Elizabeth Cady Stanton's 1854 'Address to the Legislature of New York' and the Paradox of Social Reform Rhetoric." *Rhetoric Review* 29, no. 2 (2010): 129–144.

Sklar, Kathryn Kish. "Women as Good Citizens, 1830–1920." *Communication Review* 4, no. 1 (2000): 55–65.

Sklar, Kathryn Kish, Anja Schüler, and Susan Strasser, eds. *Social Justice Feminists in the United States and Germany: A Dialogue in Documents, 1885–1933*. Ithaca, NY: Cornell University Press, 1998.

Sklar, Kathryn Kish, and James Brewer Stewart, eds. *Women's Rights and Transatlantic Antislavery in the Era of Emancipation*. New Haven, CT: Yale University Press, 2007.

Smith, Adam. *An Inquiry into the Nature and Causes of the Wealth of Nations*. Edited by R. H. Campbell, A. S. Skinner, and W. B. Todd. Indianapolis: Liberty Fund, 1981.

———. *Lectures on Rhetoric and Belles Lettres*. Edited by J. C. Bryce. Indianapolis: Liberty Fund, 1985.

———. *The Theory of Moral Sentiments*. Edited by D. D. Raphael and A. L. Macfie. Indianapolis: Liberty Fund, 1982.

Smith, Kimberly K. *The Dominion of Voice: Riot, Reason, and Romance in Antebellum Politics*. Lawrence: University Press of Kansas, 1999.

———. "Storytelling, Sympathy and Moral Judgment in American Abolitionism." *Journal of Political Philosophy* 6, no. 4 (1998): 356–377.

Smith, Rogers M. "Beyond Tocqueville, Myrdal, and Hartz: The Multiple Traditions in America." *American Political Science Review* 87, no. 3 (1993): 549–566.

Smith, Steven B., Danilo Petranovic, Ralph Lerner, and Benjamin A. Kleinerman, eds. *The Writings of Abraham Lincoln.* New Haven, CT: Yale University Press, 2012.

Speicher, Anna M. *The Religious World of Antislavery Women: Spirituality in the Lives of Five Abolitionist Lecturers.* 1st ed. Syracuse, NY: Syracuse University Press, 2000.

Stansell, Christine. "Missed Connections: Abolitionist Feminism in the Nineteenth Century." In *Elizabeth Cady Stanton, Feminist as Thinker: A Reader in Documents and Essays,* edited by Ellen Carol DuBois and Richard Cándida Smith, 32–49. New York: New York University Press, 2007.

Stanton, Elizabeth Cady. *The Woman's Bible: A Classic Feminist Perspective.* Mineola, NY: Dover Publications, 2002.

Stanton, Elizabeth Cady, and Susan B. Anthony. *The Selected Papers of Elizabeth Cady Stanton and Susan B. Anthony.* Vol. 1, *In the School of Anti-Slavery, 1840–1866.* Edited by Ann D. Gordon. New Brunswick, NJ: Rutgers University Press, 1997.

———. *The Selected Papers of Elizabeth Cady Stanton and Susan B. Anthony.* Vol. 2, *Against an Aristocracy of Sex, 1866 to 1873.* Edited by Ann D. Gordon. New Brunswick, NJ: Rutgers University Press, 2000.

Stanton, Elizabeth Cady, Susan B. Anthony, Matilda Joslyn Gage, and Ida Harper, eds. *History of Woman Suffrage.* 6 vols. Rochester, NY: Charles Mann Press, 1881–1922.

Stevens, Jacqueline. "Beyond Tocqueville, Please!" *American Political Science Review* 89, no. 4 (1995): 987–990.

Stillion Southard, Belinda A. "A Rhetoric of Epistemic Privilege: Elizabeth Cady Stanton, Harriot Stanton Blatch, and the Educated Vote." *Advances in the History of Rhetoric* 17, no. 2 (2014): 157–178.

Strong, Douglas M. *Perfectionist Politics: Abolitionism and the Religious Tensions of American Democracy.* 1st ed. Syracuse, NY: Syracuse University Press, 1999.

Sullivan, Kathleen S. *Constitutional Context: Women and Rights Discourse in Nineteenth-Century America.* Baltimore: Johns Hopkins University Press, 2007.

Sutton, Jane S. *The House of My Sojourn: Rhetoric, Women, and the Question of Authority.* Tuscaloosa: University of Alabama Press, 2010.

Taylor, Natalie Fuehrer. *The Rights of Woman as Chimera: The Political Philosophy of Mary Wollstonecraft.* New York: Routledge, 2006.

Tell, Dave. "Stanton's 'Solitude of Self' as Public Confession." *Communication Studies* 61, no. 2 (2010): 172–183.

Tetrault, Lisa. *The Myth of Seneca Falls: Memory and the Women's Suffrage Movement, 1848–1898.* Chapel Hill: University of North Carolina Press, 2014.

Thomas, Tracy A. "Elizabeth Cady Stanton and the Notion of a Legal Class of Gender." In *Feminist Legal History: Essays on Women and Law,* edited by Tracy A. Thomas and Tracey Jean Boisseau, 139–155. New York: New York University Press, 2011.

Thomson, Dorothy Lampen. *Adam Smith's Daughters*. New York: Exposition Press, 1973.

Tillery, Alvin B., Jr. "Tocqueville as Critical Race Theorist: Whiteness as Property, Interest Convergence, and the Limits of Jacksonian Democracy." *Political Research Quarterly* 62, no. 4 (2009): 639–652.

Tocqueville, Alexis de. *Democracy in America*. Translated by George Lawrence and edited by J. P. Mayer. New York: Perennial/Harper Collins Publishers, 2000.

Tompkins, Jane P. *Sensational Designs: The Cultural Work of American Fiction, 1790–1860*. New York: Oxford University Press, 1985.

Traubel, Horace. *With Walt Whitman in Camden*. Vol. 1. Boston: Small, Maynard, 1906.

———. *With Walt Whitman in Camden*. Vol. 2. New York: Mitchell Kennerley, 1915.

Travis, Molly Abel. "Frances Wright: The Other Woman of Early American Feminism." *Women's Studies* 22, no. 3 (1993): 389–397.

Turner, Jack, ed. *A Political Companion to Henry David Thoreau*. Lexington: University Press of Kentucky, 2009.

Tyler, Alice Felt. *Freedom's Ferment: Phases of American Social History to 1860*. New York: Harper & Row, 1962.

Vargo, Gregory. "Contested Authority: Reform and Local Pressure in Harriet Martineau's Poor Law Stories." *Nineteenth-Century Gender Studies* 3, no. 2 (2007). www.ncgsjournal.com/issue32/vargo.htm.

Vetter, Lisa Pace. "Sympathy, Equality, and Consent: Tocqueville and Harriet Martineau on Women and Democracy in America." In *Feminist Interpretations of Alexis De Tocqueville*, edited by Jill Locke and Eileen Hunt Botting. University Park: Pennsylvania State University Press, 2009.

Warner, Laceye C. *Saving Women: Retrieving Evangelistic Theology and Practice*. Waco, TX: Baylor University Press, 2007.

Washington, Margaret. *The Narrative of Sojourner Truth*. Vintage Classics. 1st ed. New York: Vintage Books, 1993.

———. *Sojourner Truth's America*. Urbana: University of Illinois Press, 2009.

Webb, R. K. *Harriet Martineau: A Radical Victorian*. New York: Columbia University Press, 1960.

Weiss, Penny A. *Canon Fodder: Historical Women Political Thinkers*. University Park: Pennsylvania State University Press, 2009.

Welch, Cheryl B. *De Tocqueville*. New York: Oxford University Press, 2001.

———. "Tocqueville on Democracy after Abolition: Slaves, Souls, Subjects, Citizens." *Tocqueville Review* 27, no. 2 (2006): 227–254.

Wellman, Judith. *The Road to Seneca Falls: Elizabeth Cady Stanton and the First Woman's Rights Convention*. Urbana: University of Illinois Press, 2004.

———. "The Seneca Falls Women's Rights Convention: A Study of Social Networks." *Journal of Women's History* 3, no. 1 (1991): 9–37.

Welter, Barbara. "The Cult of True Womanhood: 1820–1860." *American Quarterly* 18, no. 2 (1966): 151–174.

Williamson, C. "Bentham Looks at America." In *Jeremy Bentham: Critical Assessments*, edited by Bhikhu C. Parekh. New York: Routledge, 1993.

Wollstonecraft, Mary. *A Vindication of the Rights of Men; with, a Vindication of the Rights of Woman, and Hints.* Edited by Sylvia Tomaselli. New York: Cambridge University Press, 1995.

Wright, Frances. *Reason, Religion, and Morals.* Foreword by Susan S. Adams. Amherst, NY: Humanity Books, 2004. First published as *Course of Popular Lectures.* London: James Watson, 1834.

———. *Views of Society and Manners in America.* Edited by Paul R. Baker. Cambridge, MA: Belknap Press of Harvard University Press, 1963.

Zaeske, Susan. *Signatures of Citizenship: Petitioning, Antislavery, and Women's Political Identity.* Chapel Hill: University of North Carolina Press, 2003.

Zagarri, Rosemarie. "Morals, Manners, and the Republican Mother." *American Quarterly* 44 (1992): 192–216.

Zerilli, Linda M. G. "Feminist Theory and the Canon of Political Thought." In *The Oxford Handbook of Political Theory*, edited by John S. Dryzek, Bonnie Honig, and Anne Phillips, 106–124. New York: Oxford University Press, 2008.

———. "Machiavelli's Sisters: Women and 'the Conversation' of Political Theory." *Political Theory* 19, no. 2 (1991): 252–276.

Zink-Sawyer, Beverly A. "From Preachers to Suffragists: Enlisting the Pulpit in the Early Movement for Woman's Rights." *American Transcendental Quarterly* 14, no. 3 (2000): 193–209.

Zuckert, Catherine H. *Natural Right and the American Imagination: Political Philosophy in Novel Form.* Savage, MD: Rowman & Littlefield, 1990.

# INDEX

abolitionism: American political thought, central to, 3, 5, 7; American political thought, unexamined in, 6; anarchist, 150, 158; collective action, citizenship and, 6, 15–18, 22–23; Grimké, S., and, 129; immediate, 108; institutionalist, 9; Liberty Party, 9, 149, 158; racism in, 21, 103, 141; reformist, 149–150; Scripture, parallels with, 118; sympathy and sentimentality, 10–12; Tocqueville and, 90, 218n17; women's rights and, 3, 8, 104, 205, 217n8. *See also* Beecher, Catherine; Douglass, Frederick; Garrisonian abolitionists; Grimké, Angelina; Martineau, Harriet; Mott, Lucretia; Truth, Sojourner; Wright, Frances

African Americans, 1, 20, 25; Grimké, A., and, 1033; Mott and, 146; Stanton and, 197; Truth as freed, 21, 31, 199, 202, 215, 258n7

amalgamation, 122. *See also* miscegenation

American Anti-Slavery Society, 185; 1840 schism, 8, 158

American Constitution, 46, 86, 128, 131, 143, 186–187; amendments to, 126; civic constitution and, 23, 143; as pro-slavery, 149, 158; and Quaker constitutionalism, 28, 128–129, 131, 214, 245n19

American Equal Rights Association, 209

American Revolution, 39, 140, 188

*American Slavery as It Is* (Weld, Grimké, A., and Grimké S.), 126

Anthony, Susan B.: contributions of, 2, 4, 16, 147, 223n114, 249n7, 253n11. *See also The History of Woman Suffrage*

antidogmatism: progressive Quaker, 10, 133, 152, 153, 250n29; Wright's, 65, 70. *See also* Mott, Lucretia

*Appeal to the Christian Women of the South* (Grimké, A.). *See* Grimké, Angelina

ascriptivism, 166, 169; ascriptive inegalitarianism, 29. *See also* Smith, Rogers

assimilation: of Douglass and Truth, 257n3; through education, 51–52; as racism, 117, 219n71

Beecher, Catherine, 4, 242n18; and abolitionism, 108; criticizes Garrisonians, 106, 107–109; criticizes Grimké, A., 27, 101, 102, 104, 107–109, 113–114; criticizes Martineau, 64, 97, 240n108; criticizes Wright, 63–64; emancipation, "expediency" over "immediacy," 108; *Essay on Slavery and Abolitionism*, 105; and feminine domesticity, 64, 97; as head of Hartford Female Seminary, 106; and private realm of women, 114; rhetoric and sympathy, views of, 102–103, 109–111; and separate spheres for women, 130, 244n16; *A Treatise on Domestic Economy*, 64, 97; and utilitarianism, 226n19. See also *Letters to Catherine E. Beecher*

## ABOUT THE AUTHOR

Lisa Pace Vetter is Assistant Professor of Political Science and Affiliate Faculty Member of the Gender and Women's Studies Department at the University of Maryland, Baltimore County. She is the author of *"Women's Work" as Political Art: Weaving and Dialectical Politics in Homer, Aristophanes, and Plato.*